2.50

MADNESS IN LITERATURE

Madness in Literature

LILLIAN FEDER

Princeton University Press

PRINCETON, N.J.

to my brother, Irving Leonard Feder

Acknowledgments

I am grateful to the National Endowment for the Humanities for granting me a Senior Fellowship in 1974-75 which provided free time for early work on this book. For their thoughtful assistance I wish to thank the librarians at Queens College and the Graduate Center of the City University of New York, Columbia University, the New York Public Library, Yale University, and the Library of Congress. Miss Miriam Brokaw, Associate Director and Editor, and Mrs. Arthur Sherwood, Literature Editor, at Princeton University Press, were interested in this book from its very inception. Their encouragement and counsel were invaluable during the years I worked on it. No author could be more fortunate in her editors. Dr. Rudolph Wittenberg offered expert guidance on psychoanalytic readings and theory. He read the entire manuscript and made many valuable suggestions. In writing this book, as with earlier ones, I relied on his wisdom and kindness. Conversations with Seymour Bernstein, as well as his brilliant recording of Beethoven's Opus 111, helped me to formulate its role in Thomas Mann's *Dr. Faustus*. Other friends and colleagues at Queens College and the Graduate School of the City University of New York who provided generous assistance in various fields are: Yvette Louria, Professor of French and Comparative Literature; Burton Pike, Professor of Comparative Literature and German; Mariam Slater, Professor of Anthropology; and Robert Miller and Michael Timko, Professors of English. Betty Rizzo, my former student and now Associate Professor of English at the City College of New York, was also most helpful. I hope that my work reflects the perspective I gained from the concern, sense of humor, and good judgment of my brother Irving Leonard Feder, and it is to him and our long friendship that I dedicate this book.

In somewhat different form sections of chapter v appeared in the *Psychocultural Review* 1, 2 (Spring 1977) and in *Classical*

Mythology in Twentieth-Century Thought and Literature, Proceedings of the Comparative Literature Symposium, January 1978, ed. Wendell Aycock and Theodore Klein (Lubbock: Texas Tech University Press, 1980). I thank these publications for permission to reprint.

I am also grateful to the Beinecke Rare Book and Manuscript Library of Yale University for permission to quote from James Carkesse, *Lucida Intervalla* (London, 1679) and to the following for permission to quote from copyrighted materials:

Alfred A. Knopf, Inc. for excerpts from Thomas Mann, *Death in Venice and Seven Other Stories*, Copyright 1930, 1931, 1936 by Alfred A. Knopf, Inc. and Thomas Mann, *Doctor Faustus*, Copyright 1948 by Alfred A. Knopf, Inc., both books translated by H. T. Lowe-Porter. Excerpts from Doris Lessing, *Briefing for a Descent into Hell*, Copyright © 1971 by Doris Lessing also reprinted by permission of Alfred A. Knopf.

Excerpts from Allen Ginsberg, *Howl and Other Poems*, Copyright © 1956, 1959 by Allen Ginsberg, reprinted by permission of City Lights Books. Excerpts from Allen Ginsberg, *Kaddish and Other Poems*, Copyright © 1961 by Allen Ginsberg, reprinted by permission of City Lights Books. Excerpts from Allen Ginsberg, *Reality Sandwiches*, Copyright © 1963 by Allen Ginsberg, reprinted by permission of City Lights Books. Excerpts from Allen Ginsberg, *Indian Journals*, Copyright © 1970 by Allen Ginsberg, reprinted by permission of City Lights Books. Excerpts from Allen Ginsberg, *Mind Breaths*, Copyright © 1978 by Allen Ginsberg, reprinted by permission of City Lights Books. Excerpts from Allen Ginsberg, *Journals Early Fifties Early Sixties*, Copyright © by Allen Ginsberg, reprinted by permission of Grove Press, Inc.

Excerpts from Wole Soyinka, *The Bacchae of Euripides, Collected Plays 1*, © Wole Soyinka, and by permission of Oxford University Press.

Passim lines of poetry from "They Sing, They Sing," Copyright © 1956 by Theodore Roethke, "The Pure Fury," Copyright © 1958 by Theodore Roethke, "The Abyss," Copyright © 1963 by Beatrice Roethke, Administratrix of the

Estate of Theodore Roethke, "The Exorcism," all appear in the book *The Collected Poems of Theodore Roethke*. Reprinted by permission of Doubleday and Company, Inc. and Faber and Faber, Ltd.

Selections from *The Dream Songs* by John Berryman. Copyright © 1959, 1962, 1963, 1964, 1965, 1966, 1967, 1968, 1969 by John Berryman. Reprinted with the permission of Farrar, Straus & Giroux, Inc. From *Delusions, etc.* by John Berryman. Copyright © 1969, 1971 by John Berryman. Copyright © 1972 by the Estate of John Berryman. From *Love and Fame* by John Berryman. Copyright © 1970 by John Berryman. Reprinted with the permission of Farrar, Straus & Giroux and Faber and Faber, Ltd.

Selections from Antonin Artaud, *Selected Writings*. Translated from the French by Helen Weaver. Translation Copyright © 1976 by Farrar, Straus & Giroux, Inc. Translated from the French *Œuvres Complètes* © Editions Gallimard 1956, 1961, 1964, 1966, 1967, 1969, 1970, 1971, 1974. Reprinted with the permission of Farrar, Straus & Giroux, Inc. and with grateful acknowledgment for British rights to quote from *The Collected Works of Antonin Artaud*, published by John Calder (Publishers) Ltd.

Excerpts from Margaret Atwood, *Surfacing* reprinted by permission of Simon and Schuster.

Excerpts from Sylvia Plath, *Ariel*, Copyright © 1965 by Ted Hughes, reprinted by permission of Harper and Row, Publishers, Inc. and Faber and Faber, Ltd. British rights by permission of Olwyn Hughes © 1965 by Ted Hughes.

Preface

"I want to be human and I don't want to kill you. But I am very tired and a little confused. Now you have an inkling of a lunatic's mind at work." In this curious, self-reflective way, William Böse, one of the hijackers of an Air France plane en route to New York from Tel Aviv, addressed the passengers who had become his prisoners as they sat in the plane in Entebbe, Uganda on June 28, 1976. Although Böse may seem remote from the material of this book—the mad protagonists of literature and the writers for whom madness is a vehicle of self-revelation—his comments on his political action as a member of a group that identified itself as "The Popular Front for the Liberation of Palestine" are not irrelevant. Madness as a theme of myth and literature has always dealt with personal responses to environmental influences, which include political, social, and cultural pressures, or perhaps it would be more correct to say which exclude nothing.

In offering an "inkling" of enlightenment regarding the workings of the mind of the lunatic, Böse reflects a popular interest of the time, but it is by no means a new one. Imaginative writers from the fifth century b.c. to the present have always been concerned with madness as a revelation of processes of the human mind, indeed processes not limited to the minds of the insane. Still, Böse's remarks and their context have a particularly contemporary flavor. In his confessional tone, his superficial and somewhat pretentious self-exploration (considering the circumstances), and his apparent assumption that madness is an acceptable revolutionary trait, he seems to be speaking not only for himself but for a trend of his time.

The term madness is currently used to describe a wide variety of contradictory attitudes and almost any conduct that can be either justified or attacked as extreme: politically, madness is used to designate a long-repressed sense of injustice and therefore a legitimate motive for confrontation and as a charge against dissenters that carries the penalty of incarceration in a mental hospital; socially, it is interpreted as an illness of the mind or as an acceptable personal withdrawal from the values of a repressive society; and aesthetically, it is depicted as a consummation, the ultimate self-expression that is inevitably self-destructive. The connection among all these is a concern—however primitive or sophisticated—with mind, with deviation from some norm of thought and feeling, whether as a threat, a challenge, or a field of exploration which must yield revelation.

Literature has always recorded and interpreted such concern, and it continues to do so; at present this is among its major themes. My subject, literary madness as an exploration of mind, is a vast one, and no single book could encompass all the important works in which this theme appears. Indeed, no subject more surely defeats an investigator's desire to be comprehensive, and I am well aware that I have omitted much literature in which madness serves an important function. One obvious basis of my choice of literary works to be discussed is that madness is essential to their theme and structure. Although the works I deal with all in some way reflect contemporary religious, medical, and cultural attitudes toward the human mind, my emphasis is on those that disclose a social or individual awareness that challenges fundamental assumptions. Thus, I include works by minor figures (in one case, hardly a poet at all) who are able to break through the barriers of medical and religious clichés regarding madness that great writers of the period employ.

In combining a thematic with a basically—although not entirely—chronological approach, I have attempted to write not a history of madness in literature but a study of representative literary explorations of the deranged mind. Considering these within their historical context, I emphasize the psychological revelations inherent in the continuity, variation, and changes in the theme of madness. What I hope to reveal are some of the discoveries regarding mental functioning and aberration that imaginative writers have made in their very depictions of madness. Although this is an investigation of literary representations of mental and emotional conflict, my approach is by no means merely a psychological one. I hope, in fact, to show how the mad protagonists and personae of literature convey the intricate connections between psychic requirements and the social and cultural milieux in which these, however obliquely, are expressed.

In treating madness as both a continuous theme and a historical manifestation, I have tried to discover the ways in which individual works reflect the philosophical, medical, social, religious, and political assumptions regarding mental aberration characteristic of the periods in which they were created. At the same time I have employed what I regard as useful and appropriate current views on mental processes and pathology. Although I have drawn on the works of Freud, on theories of ego psychology that grow out of his discoveries, and other works dealing with mental pathology, my aim is not merely to apply a psychological system to literature. In the study of madness in literature, psychoanalytic and psychological theory provides but one discipline that, along with others—especially literary, religious, and social history—helps to elucidate the various symbolic forms into which the human mind transforms experience. I have tried to avoid technical terms as much as possible, but, when I do think it necessary to use them, I treat them as concepts to be interpreted by as well as to assist in interpreting the emotional experience portrayed in literature.

Although the mad characters or personae of literature may be modeled on actual persons or the authors themselves, it is also true that literary constructs of the extreme possibilities of mental experience differ in important respects from actual manifestations of madness. The very distortions of the powerful visionaries or isolated victims of the literature of madness are designed to portray the mind constructing and exposing its own symbolic framework out of fragments that all readers recognize as familiar—customs, attitudes, places, institutions, traits of character, desires, and fears they have encountered in their own lives. The mind of the mad protagonist or persona of literature discloses the transformation of these into the ultimate sources of psychic disintegration or survival.

Contents

MADNESS IN LITERATURE

I

Varieties of Madness:
Approach and Method

Madness has been a continuous theme in Western literature from its beginnings to the present time. Evidence indicates, moreover, that human beings were preoccupied with extreme forms of mental and psychic experience long before they recorded it in literature. Myths and legends appearing in Homer, the Bible, and ancient Greek drama contain primordial symbolizations of delusions, mania, and other bizarre forms of thought and behavior. In some respects, the prototypical mad man or woman is analogous to the wild man, an imaginary being who occurs in various forms throughout Western literature and art, and who also emerges from myth and ritual, the remnants of which can be observed even in the most sophisticated aesthetic representations. In a comprehensive study of wild men in the Middle Ages, Richard Bernheimer suggests that "the notion of the wild man must respond and be due to a persistent psychological urge. We may define this urge as the need to give external expression and symbolically valid form to the impulses of reckless physical self-assertion which are hidden in all of us, but which are normally kept under control."[1] Whereas similar impulses are expressed in many literary and artistic representations of mad figures, these also convey more varied and more complicated psychic and social experience.

The mad protagonist generally inhabits the familiar world of civilized people, although in his madness he may retreat to the savage environment and condition of the traditional wild man. Furthermore, although his aberrant thoughts and behavior may determine his essential role, as savagery does the wild man's, madness is still but one aspect of his nature, and it may emerge only in extreme or extraordinary circumstances. The most crucial difference lies in the extent to which the mad protagonist not only symbolizes but reveals the very psychic processes that account for strange and violent behavior and the inextricable connection of such processes with the most ordinary relationships and conduct of daily life.

My aim in this book is to trace early developments, continuity, and changes in literary depictions of various forms of mental derangement, and to determine the nature of the psychological experience revealed through the bizarre language and action of fictive characters designated as mad and the personae of accounts of madness. I hope to demonstrate that literary interpretations of madness both reflect and question medical, cultural, political, religious, and psychological assumptions of their time, that they explore the very processes of symbolic transformation of these influences and disclose their psychic consequences in the minds of individual characters or personae. The study of the symbolic expression of such complex inner experience will, I hope, elucidate not only particular works of literature and madness as a literary motif, but something of the nature of madness itself as an incorporation of the very values and prohibitions it challenges.

From the earliest extant myths to the most recent confessions, fiction, poetry, and drama, portrayals of madness convey in symbolic form human beings' preoccupation with their own mental functioning, with the enormous range of their psychic experience. The treatment of madness in literature reflects human ambivalence toward the mind itself; madness, comprising its strangest manifestations, is also familiar, a fascinating and repellent exposure of the structures of dream and fantasy, of irrational fears and bizarre desires ordinarily hidden from the world and the conscious self. In literature, as in daily life, madness is the perpetual amorphous threat within and the extreme of the unknown in fellow human beings. In fact, recurrent literary representations of madness constitute a history of explorations of the mind in relation to itself, to other human beings, and to social and political institutions. The madman, like other people, does not exist alone. He both reflects and influences those involved with him. He embodies and symbolically transforms the values and aspirations of his family, his tribe, and his society, even if he renounces them, as well as their delusions, cruelty, and violence, even in his inner flight.

The most obvious and natural question that arises at this point is what is madness: how is one to define a concept charged with centuries of political, social, religious, medical, and personal assumptions? There is, of course, no one description that evokes all the varieties of aberrant or bizarre thought and conduct that have been regarded as insane throughout human existence. Although similar individual and group manifestations of extreme psychic confusion and suffering have appeared throughout history, it is clear that certain symptoms are characteristic of their different times. Inappropriate, pathological guilt, for example, was among the most common symptoms of mental disturbance prevalent in Western civilization so long as the authority of state, church, and patriarchal family was assumed; the pathological absence of guilt that one observes at present in America and much of Europe surely reflects the disintegration of such authorities. Yet pathological guilt persists, manifesting itself in obsession with sin, as do grandiose identifications with Christ and other gods and heroes, traditional symbols strangely adapted to current narcissism and alienation. In attempting to cover persistent and variable characteristics of actual as well as literary madness, I define madness as a state in which unconscious processes predominate over conscious ones to the extent that they control them and determine perceptions of and responses to experience that, judged by prevailing standards of logical thought and relevant emotion, are confused and inappropriate.[2]

Curiously, one finds a basic similarity in the types of responses to insanity from earliest records to the present, which indicate that few, if any, societies have had a consistent attitude toward madness. Franz Alexander and Sheldon

Selesnick group such continuous approaches in three main categories: the organic, the psychological, and the magical.[3] The common assumption that madness in ancient Greek society was regarded as a blessing, an inducement to prophecy and poetry, reflects only one of these approaches, which was taken at the very time that the "Hippocratics inaugurated the first classification of mental illness, and one that was extremely rational. They included in the schema epilepsy, mania (excitement), melancholia, and paranoia."[4] Furthermore, ancient Greek philosophy and drama treat madness as both divine influence and sickness.[5] Such inconsistencies can be traced from earliest recorded history to the present. The establishment of psychiatry in the eighteenth century and psychoanalysis in the twentieth as branches of medicine has not precluded magical approaches either employed or inspired by physicians themselves. Among both traditional and radical therapists, the omniscient seer and the guru appear in practice and print. A well-known recent movement in so-called radical psychoanalysis is the retreat from the hospital to the commune, where cures are undertaken through induced regressive and even anarchic behavior. The descriptions of cure and self-discovery in such places employ the language and concepts of religion and mysticism. Concomitantly, within the various orthodox institutions of psychiatric training and practice much difference of opinion exists on the nature and treatment of the psychoses.

Despite such continuous diversity of approaches to madness, it still seems possible to designate those qualities of thought, speech, and behavior which have been considered aberrant from the norm throughout human history and which have consistently been perceived as the expression by certain individuals that their mental experience is markedly different from that of most other people. The study of literary representations of these mysterious communications, and especially of their symbolic structure, is elucidated by recent psychoanalytic approaches to mental illness as "impairments of symbolization."[6] Imaginative literature, in turn, provides remarkable clues to the mental processes that produce the actual symbolizations of the psychotic, for the poet, dramatist, and novelist explore and illuminate psychic conflict and confusion through the very symbols they employ to depict these states. Intrinsic distortion of experience, as in myth, or personal records replete with clinical details, as in diaries and confessions, or—somewhere in between—imaginative transformations of observations of madness, as in much poetry, fiction, and drama, are consciously ordered versions of delirium, delusion, mania, paranoia, and the many other symptoms now classed under the general term psychoses.

The varieties of madness created in literature are in most respects no different from those to be discovered throughout human society. Since the literary artist employs structures—myth, metaphor, symbol—which continually mediate between unconscious and conscious processes, he is often a gifted explorer of what have been called the *"unlabeled metaphors"*[7] of the schizophrenic, an interpreter of the madman's apparently indecipherable "messages." Schizophrenics' "conspicuous or exaggerated errors and distortions regarding the nature and typing of their own messages (internal and external), and of the messages which they receive from others,"[8] may be transformed in imaginative literature into revelations concerning the nature and processes of hidden layers of psychic reality. Antonin Artaud's declaration that delirium is "as legitimate, as logical, as any other succession of human ideas or acts" is at once a cry of protest against "the official definition" of madness and a plea for understanding of an alternate mode of communication. It is also a protest against "the repression of anti-social reactions." When Artaud asserts that "madmen are, above all, individual victims of social dictatorship,"[9] he implies that madmen's "internalized systems of symbolization"[10] must be regarded in relation and opposition to social and political institutions regulating the human mind, which become internalized as prevailing cultural assumptions.

Although there are several critical and scholarly studies of madness as a literary theme,[11] they are restricted to discussions of single works, figures, or, at most, periods. In under-

taking a study of madness in representative works of imaginative literature from the fifth century B.C. to the present, I
hope to view the subject from a larger perspective than any
one figure or period can offer. Since I have not attempted to
write a chronological survey, I omit many works that deal
with madness and occasionally violate chronology for thematic continuity. Still, my method is essentially a combined
thematic-chronological one. I find this approach most effective in treating madness as a continuous subject of literature
and necessary for the elucidation of developments and
changes in aesthetic approaches to certain mental operations
the symptoms of madness manifest. The memories and associations of fictive madmen and personae of accounts of madness contain not only their personal past but social and
literary history as well.

The works I have chosen to discuss are particularly important as individual explorations and cultural interpretations of
psychic experience consistently regarded as aberrant. The ancient prototypes analyzed in chapter II persist; in some form,
Dionysiac and mantic frenzy and insight, guilt and terror of
divine punishment, and suicidal alienation recur in literature.
These are, moreover, mythical constructs of the internalization of societal demands and pressures. In chapters III, IV,
and V, I discuss works in which madness reveals not only
such persistent psychic manifestations adapted to very different circumstances, but additional ways in which the self is
continually created, assaulted, and redefined in its relation to
society and history. First expressed in the symbolic action of
Dionysiac ritual, reason in madness emerges as tentative
self-exploration in the poetry of Thomas Hoccleve and as the
revelations of the individual psyche shattering its own defenses, its political, social, and psychological internalizations
in *King Lear* (chapter III). Furthermore, *Lear* is a dramatic
enactment of the reconstitution of the self, a concept of great
historical and psychological significance. Shakespeare's play
is a paramount expression of one major field of Renaissance
exploration: the psychological bases of human nature and
conduct. Yet, as is evident in chapter IV, such explorations

had little effect on medical, religious, and legal approaches to the insane during the Enlightenment, when reason and madness were generally regarded as irreconcilable opposites. Poets of the period from the late seventeenth to the mid-eighteenth century in England convey an underside of the Enlightenment, exposing the inherited medical and religious dogma that permeated its concept of reason. No other country of the period produced a body of literature that portrays so effectively the psychic effects of repression and denial of the irrational and aberrant human response. The minor poets considered in chapter IV, questioning or ignoring the prevalent mechanistic treatment of mental aberration, employ the act of creation as a means of preserving and reconstituting the self in dissociation and isolation. This psychological and aesthetic goal is renounced in late and post-Romantic literature. The two sections of chapter V deal with the ironic reversal that confronts contemporary Western civilization: the quest for personal and artistic fulfillment, for social and political freedom, through psychic dissolution.

Throughout this study I analyze literary representations of madness as ordered composites and fusions of the same elements—phylogenetic, ontogenetic, and environmental—that produce the apparently anarchic inner and overt symbolizations of the psychotic. I am, however, continually aware of the differences between actual insanity and its portrayal in literature. The madman of literature is, to some extent, modeled on the actual one, but his differences from such a model are at least as important as are his resemblances to it: he is rooted in a mythical or literary tradition in which distortion is a generally accepted mode of expression; furthermore, the inherent aesthetic order by which his existence is limited also gives his madness intrinsic value and meaning. A mad literary character must thus be approached on his own terms, through the verbal, dramatic, and narrative symbols that convey the unconscious processes he portrays and reveals. Even when a writer draws on his own experience of insanity as the subject or emotional source of his work, what is of most interest in this study is his adaptation of delusion, dissociation, or other aberrations to the creation of a unique view of his society, his art, and his own mind.

In exploring such processes, I rely on certain basic psychoanalytic formulations of mental and psychic experience, as I do on historical and anthropological data. My purpose is neither to consider literary works as the psychological autobiographies of their authors nor to diagnose the psychic complaints of fictive madmen, tedious procedures that add little to our knowledge of psychology or literature. Nor do I seek to reveal the anthropological or historical significance of the literature of madness. My method is to employ all areas of knowledge relevant to a comprehension of the types of symbolic transformation that characterize madness in literature.

Whereas attempts at diagnoses of the pathology of fictive characters by literary critics are often anachronistic, not to say absurd, and those of authors generally as unconvincing, it would be shortsighted in any study of literary madness to ignore psychoanalytic theories of mental functioning and psychopathology when they provide essential clues to the symbolic nature and expression of such characters. In probing the meanings of ancient mythical prototypes of madness, one discovers narrative structures of psychic experience, some of them primordial symbolizations that persist in both ancient and later literary forms. Certain ancient Greek myths of madness reveal with remarkable clarity the evolving mental processes of particular stages of human phylogenetic development; even relatively late literary versions of such myths—Dionysiac frenzy, the pursuit by the Erinyes, prophetic raving—elucidate the archaic thought processes characteristic of states of madness. The figures of Dionysus, Pentheus, Agave, Orestes, and Cassandra, even depicted from the point of view of a playwright living in the Greek world of the fifth century B.C., convey the mental and emotional experience of human beings in much earlier stages of social and religious development. The madness of Ajax, on the other hand, portrays the pressures of emerging democratic institutions on a mind that clings to earlier adaptive mechanisms inappropriate to the rapid changes he cannot assimilate. Unconscious thought processes generally accepted as characteristic of the insane are reflected and illuminated in the action, conflict, suffering, and achievement of the mad gods, men, and women of ancient myth. These myths dramatized in ancient tragedy also express the inextricable connection between psychic experience and social conflict; the mad influence and sometimes rule the state; or, as prophet or suicide, they become its victims.

The numerous adaptations of these mythical prototypes of madness throughout literary history disclose the presence of archaic thought processes remaining within the context of changing social, economic, and political life. For Nietzsche, the god Dionysus symbolizes the efficacy of frenzy as a means of returning to primordial psychic freedom. In *Dionysus in 69*, the Performance Group's version of Euripides' *Bacchae*, the actors explore their own conflict and rage in reaction to the war in Vietnam, political power and corruption, the current sexual revolution, and their individual inhibitions, by acting out a psychic merging with the primitive god and the madness and violence he inspires. Commenting on Euripides' *Bacchae*, which he adapted in 1973, Wole Soyinka calls it "a prodigious barbaric banquet" based on a "class-conscious myth." His own version, which reflects his view of the Dionysiac as "an extravagant rite of the human and communal pysche,"[12] depicts Dionysus as ancient and modern, Greek and African, an embodiment of social and psychic destruction and renewal perennially merged.

Psychoanalytic formulations of mental processes also serve as guides to the particular modes of thought and feeling expressed by mad characters not directly related to such mythical prototypes. Sometimes this frame of reference points up resemblances between the symbolic language and action of legendary or realistic mad characters of later literature and those of myth; at other times it provides insight into the oblique communications of highly individualized mad figures. In much of twentieth-century imaginative literature, overt psychological and psychoanalytic allusions are commonplace, often referring to particular Freudian, Jungian, or

Laingian theories, which actually become part of the symbolic structure of novels, plays, and poems.

The broad application of psychoanalytic theory to literary analysis and especially efforts to follow Freud's own example of observing the operation of "the unconscious mechanisms . . . familiar in the 'dream work' in the processes of imaginative writing"[13] have developed into various structuralist approaches to symbolism. Recent critical interest seems directed more to the application of rhetorical theory to traditional psychoanalytic methods of analyzing symbolic structures than to the more common Freudian or Jungian interpretations of literary characters, plots, or language. Psychoanalytic uses of rhetorical or linguistic theory as a structure for the interpretation of dream and symbol have in turn become models for literary analysis. Among the best known of the psychoanalytic-linguistic structuralists is Jacques Lacan,[14] whose adaptations of Freudian concepts to language and rhetorical theory in his analyses of dream and literary symbolism are based on his principle: "dans le langage notre message nous vient de l'Autre, et pour l'énoncer jusqu'au bout: sous une forme inversée" (p. 9). Lacan's concept of "l'Autre" as the unconscious locus or source of symbolic thought and expression ("l'inconscient, c'est le discours de l'Autre," p. 379) is one of the most controversial aspects of his system. Defining "l'Autre" as "le lieu où se constitue le je qui parle avec celui qui entend, ce que l'un dit étant déjà la réponse et l'autre décidant à l'entendre si l'un a ou non parlé" (p. 431), he views its functioning as crucial to the laws of language. "L'Autre" is the locus of signifiers, both their contents which derive from memory traces and their linguistic form as metonymy, metaphor, or symbol, which he views as the essential structure of both language and the unconscious mind. Thus, "l'Autre" is the locus of dreams; summarizing Freud's conception of the process of "secondary revision" on the part of the dreamer, Lacan concludes that interpretation of the resultant images depends upon linguistic laws (pp. 267-68). This is, of course, hardly a new idea, but Lacan's discussions of metaphor, metonymy, and the relationship between "le langage" and "la parole" are efforts to clarify the presence of primordial emotions within sophisticated symbolic expression: "La fonction symbolique se présente comme un double mouvement dans le sujet: l'homme fait un objet de son action, mais pour rendre à celle-ci en temp voulu sa place fondatrice" (p. 285).

Lacan's conception of the extensive functions of "l'Autre" and his many applications of this principle cannot be briefly summarized, since these result from a radical adaptation of philosophical ideas to a combined psychoanalytic-linguistic theory. One basic point, however, must be mentioned since the very notion that the most fundamental instinctual desires derive from and are experienced—whether in dream or waking consciousness—as messages from an Other inevitably alien to the self seems to me unconvincing as he applies it both to actual human beings and to literary figures. In an essay on *Hamlet*,[15] for example, Lacan says: "There is a level in the subject on which it can be said that his fate is expressed in terms of a pure signifier, a level at which he is merely the reverse-side of a message that is not even his own" (p. 12). Lacan's development of this assumption in relation to Hamlet is connected with another fundamental concept: the subject "must find again in the discourse of the Other what was lost for him . . . the moment he entered into this discourse. What ultimately matters is not the truth but the hour [*l'heure*] of truth" (p. 16). Hamlet's "structure," according to Lacan, consists of two essential "factors": "his situation of dependence with respect to the desire of the Other, the desire of his mother," and the resulting circumstance that "he is constantly suspended in the time of the Other, throughout the entire story until the very end" (p. 17). Lacan's Hamlet is distinguished from Oedipus and other ancient heroes in that he *"knows"* and accepts his own psychological dilemma and "is forced to feign madness in order to follow the winding paths that lead him to the completion of his act." In this respect, Lacan goes on to say, he exemplifies "the strategy of the modern hero" (pp. 19-20).

Lacan develops this thesis in detail, illustrating the ways in which Hamlet's relationships with Ophelia, Claudius, and other characters reveal that he "is always at the hour of the Other." Hamlet is the hero who "sets everything up so that the object of his desire becomes the signifier of" his own "confrontation" with the inevitable "impossibility" inherent in human desire (p. 36).

Applied to Hamlet or other literary or real figures, Lacan's concept of "l'Autre" seems both overextended and reductive. The figure of Hamlet, even as an exemplar of the internalization of what Lacan would call the Other is infinitely more complex in its depiction of the symbolic transformation of events and relationships than Lacan's scheme allows. His view that the Other, as the desire of Hamlet's mother, prevents Hamlet from choosing between his exalted father and the despised Claudius reduces perhaps the most complex figure in English literature to a one-dimensional signifier of the Other's commitment to the "sacrosanct genital object" (p. 12). Furthermore, in this essay, as in parts of *Ecrits*, Lacan does not always differentiate clearly between the Other as internalized and as an actual figure. His discussion of Hamlet's pretended madness does not come to terms with either pretense or madness, but is merely a generalized and currently fashionable equation of special knowledge with aberrant thinking and behavior. He never makes clear the role he suggests pretended madness plays in the realization of the "desire" or the "hour" of the Other. But perhaps the essential shortcoming of Lacan's central concept as applied to Hamlet and to actual human beings is that it limits signifiers of unconscious desire and conflict to the expression of alienation from the self. As I hope this study of the literature of madness will indicate, symbolic representations of such unconscious experience reveal that the self cannot be separated from its internalizations; the infinite adaptations of the Other signify the victories as well as the hazards in the psychic struggle for autonomy.

At best, Lacan's analysis of Hamlet points up some possible symbolic routes of instinctual desire and frustration, but his delineation of these Freudian concepts in linguistic terms does not enrich the concepts themselves. It merely converts them into reductive philosophical ideas about the nature of desire, power, and truth. His most useful contribution to the study of the relationship between language and psychoanalytic theory is his explication of many of the techniques that have long been used by both psychoanalysts and literary critics for the analysis of symbols. But he has not created a comprehensive scheme for such analysis. For the study of literature, especially the theme of madness, his work, particularly *Ecrits*, merely points up some of the ways in which psychoanalytic methods can disclose conflicting meanings and emotions conveyed by symbols, the oppositions between past and present, unconscious desire and conscious knowledge, the imaginary and the real.

Another, more recent, effort to describe methods of interpretation used in psychoanalysis by the use of linguistic structures is Marshall Edelson's *Language and Interpretation in Psychoanalysis*.[16] Edelson's approach depends on his view that "Psychoanalysis as a science is essentially a study of symbolic systems, relations among them and the use of symbolic systems in symbolic functioning" (p. 19). In attempting to explicate the bases of psychoanalytic interpretation by "a theory of language and symbolic systems" (p. 73), he applies the rules of transformational-generative linguistics to Wallace Stevens' "The Snow Man," which he approaches as "a linguistic object" (p. 118). Edelson's discussion of the poem is no doubt illuminated by his use of certain concepts of Freud, such as condensation and displacement; his analysis of its sound, though unnecessarily technical, is nonetheless interesting. Still, the results of his effort "to reconstruct how and what operations have been used" in the creation of the poem are not new to literary critics. His use of linguistic theory in this extended analysis provides little more than a means of identifying some standard methods of literary interpretation of sound patterns, symbols, and images.

Edelson's method of describing "the relation between a symbolic object and its meaning" oversimplifies what he calls the "significant relation between psychoanalysis and trans-

formational-generative theory" (p. 5). Furthermore, it overlooks the important differences between literary symbols and
those in dream, free association, or ordinary discourse. In
defining psychoanalytic theory as "primarily . . . about symbolic systems and symbolic functioning, and especially about
language and the use of language" (p. xii), Edelson, like Lacan, sets unnecessary limits on the range of physiological,
emotional, and intellectual experience it encompasses and on
its usefulness when adapted to the interpretation of the arts.
On the one hand, psychoanalysis, even as "a study of symbolic systems," employs techniques other than linguistic
ones. On the other, the analysis of a literary text cannot de-
pend merely on psychoanalytic techniques—however similar
or adaptable to linguistic theory. Even when literary and
psychoanalytic methods of interpreting symbols overlap,
they are never quite the same, for the complications of symbolic meaning can be fruitfully explored only with an awareness of the differences as well as the similarities between actual people, their unconscious conflicts and their dreams, and
the creation of these or of personae in aesthetic form. Insofar
as literature is concerned, it is only in conjunction with all the
other disciplines that clarify the individual and collective
roots of a work of art that psychoanalytic concepts can contribute to a theory of symbolic structure. In helping to reveal
the processes of personal inner transformation of the external
reality of societal, historical, and cultural events, it is certainly
indispensable.

Certain psychoanalytic theories I have adapted to my own
approach, such as Freud's delineation of the primary
processes—displacement, condensation, substitution by the
opposite, and compromise formation—and his view of the
dream as a "psychosis of short duration"[17] (a concept at least
as old as Plato and long familiar in commentaries on madness[18]) are widely known and accepted, and thus require
only brief explanation. Others, however familiar, are at
present either commonly distorted in popular usage or so
controversial that in referring to them I find it necessary to
indicate my own position.

In interpreting symbolic expressions of madness, the function of the primary processes in producing "overdetermined" symbols—that is, representations with many disparate references which "fulfill at once a number of emotional needs"[19]—is particularly important. Of course, overdetermined symbols also occur in literature that has no connection with madness, but a special function of such symbolic operations in the literature of madness is to convey, through displacement and condensation, unconscious motivations overwhelming conscious perception, selection, and ordering. Meanings of what are apparently disconnected, bizarre associations are sometimes elucidated as much by literary and social history as by the particular background of a character or persona established within the work itself. Allusions to mythical and literary creations of mental aberration or to traditional conceptions of its causes and effects can be fused with highly individual references in portrayals of overdetermination.

Since the term "ego" is often misused even by critics who cite psychoanalytic sources, it seems necessary to indicate that in this book the word refers to those cognitive processes that produce a continuous and integrated recognition of one's own physical and mental existence in relation to time, the external world of nature and society, cause and effect. The ego can be regarded as the mediation among the manifold expressions of the self—unconscious, conscious, impulsive, rational—which allows for the discovery of the possibilities and limits of external reality.[20]

Central, and at present still highly controversial, issues regarding the mental functioning of both the mad and the sane revolve around the popular dichotomies: instinct or learned reaction, biological inheritance or environmental adaptation. In this connection no concept has raised more dispute in psychological and anthropological literature than the Freudian theory of the undifferentiated psychic energy that exists at the first stages of human life and which in the normal course of development is channeled in two major instinctual aims, libidinal and aggressive. Yet no explanation of the pervasive human impulses that Freud, "after long hesitancies and vacillations," finally classified as "*Eros and the destructive instinct*" (*SE* xxiii, 148) has been more fruitful in producing further speculation and understanding. Although Freud's theory of the instincts changed from its early appearance in *Three Essays on Sexuality* (1905) through its extended development in his later works, it can be said that he never relinquished his view that an instinct is "a concept on the frontier between the mental and the somatic, as the psychical representative of the stimuli originating from within the organism and reaching the mind, as a measure of the demand upon the mind for work in consequence of its connection with the body" (*SE* xiv, 121-22). The editor of *The Standard Edition* suggests that there is an ambiguity in Freud's use of the term "instinct," pointing out what he sees as an essential difference between this as well as earlier similar descriptions of an instinct as a "psychical representative" and later definitions in "The Unconscious" and elsewhere which seem to indicate that Freud draws "a very sharp distinction between the instinct and its psychical representative." Thus, he quotes Freud in "The Unconscious" as saying that "an instinct can never become an object of consciousness—only the idea [*Vorstellung*] that represents the instinct can. Even in the unconscious, moreover, an instinct cannot be represented otherwise than by an idea. . . ." (*SE* xiv, 112). Perhaps the contradiction can be resolved by considering Freud's further comment: "Although instincts are wholly determined by their origin in a somatic source, in mental life we know them only by their aims" (*SE* xiv, 123). Instinctual drives can be known only as they are transformed into and appear as "ideas," or, as Edelson puts it, as "a particular kind of symbolization."[21] Freud's concept of instinctual aim eliminates the body/mind duality.

Thousands of pages have been written developing, justifying, and, more commonly, objecting to the concept of the instincts and to the language Freud used to describe these and other aspects of mental functioning. There is little doubt that the mechanistic terminology and spatial descriptions he adapted from contemporary scientific and metaphysical usage can seem inappropriate today, conveying a literal rather than the intended metaphorical meaning. But it is a mistake to conclude that his assumption of a biological factor in certain basic mental and emotional developments necessarily results in a mechanistic approach to human psychology. The division that Harry J. S. Guntrip[22] observes "throughout Freud's work between the physicalistic type of scientific thought in which he had been trained and the need for a new type of psychodynamic thinking that he was destined to create" (p. 45) seems more essential to the development of Guntrip's own theoretical position than inherent in Freud.

Feelings of love and aggression, whether assumed to be instinctual in origin or entirely acquired, are dominant subjects of literature; in the literature of madness the symbolic expressions of such feelings in hundreds of intricate ways are the surest clues to the mind in confusion or conflict. Thus, it seems necessary briefly to explore Freud's delineation of these as instinctual in relation to Guntrip's and other recent objections, and also to glance at more sympathetic amendments of Freud's conception.

Guntrip sees what he calls Freud's "physicalistic" or "process" approach as "enshrined in his instinct theory" (p. 45). But Guntrip's interpretation of the Freudian instinctual drives is a common oversimplification: Eros to him is "sex" and aggression is merely "an innate drive to hostile, attacking behavior" (p. 12). Regarding Eros as "sex," Guntrip interprets it narrowly as "an appetite" (p. 12), merely one manifestation of the drive that Freud describes as coinciding "with the Eros of the poets and the philosophers which holds all living things together" (*SE* xviii, 50). Eros is "the preserver of all things," including the self (*SE* xviii, 52). Its "aim" is "to establish greater unities and to preserve them—in short to bind together" (*SE* xxiii, 148). Freud is even more explicit in defining the broad meanings of "love" as he sees it: its "nucleus" is "sexual love with sexual union as its aim. But we do not separate from this—what in any case has a share in the name 'love'—on the one hand, self-love, and on the other, love for parents and children, friendship and love for humanity in general, and also devotion to concrete objects and to abstract ideas." Freud sees "all these tendencies" as "an expression of the same instinctual impulses." Thus, he believes "that language has carried out an entirely justifiable piece of unification in creating the word 'love' with its numerous uses." Although he here refers to the term Eros as "genteel," he concludes that it "is in the end nothing more than a translation of our German word *Liebe*" (*SE* xviii, 90-91). He may have begun by using Eros "to soften the affront" (*SE* xviii, 91) to his society of his conception of sexuality as an instinctual force, but he retained it not as a concession but as a symbolic term that conveyed the unifying, creative powers within human beings manifested in civilization itself.

There is, of course, no demonstrable evidence that Eros in its broadest sense is biologically innate, but there is incontrovertible evidence that love in some form is necessary for survival of the infant, that the capacity to respond to the external world of people and objects with affection is a sign of maturation, that sexual desire is at least to some extent biologically determined, and that creating, unifying, and preserving are essential for the existence of even the most elementary forms of human society.

Perhaps because Freud viewed the aggressive or destructive instinct as inextricably connected with the highly controversial "death instinct," it has been even more vulnerable than Eros to social and moral repugnance and the chief target of attack in persistent questioning of the instinctual determinants of mental processes. Yet even those who would explain human aggression on entirely cultural grounds find that some variation on this concept is difficult to avoid in the face of historical evidence of its simplest physical and most complicated psychological bases.

Aggression, as Freud describes it, has broad and apparently contradictory manifestations. He uses the term to designate "hate" in contrast with love (*SE* xix, 42); its "aim" is "to undo connections, and so destroy things" (*SE* xxiii, 148), but it is essential for self-preservation as well as for reproduction. Furthermore, aggression as an instinctual component, like Eros, is generally expressed in dynamic fusion. Freud's "assumption indispensable to our conception" that the "two classes of instincts" are "fused, blended, and alloyed with each other" (*SE* xix, 41) aids in and is itself validated by the investigation of symbolic expressions of mental processes. In his description of "every instinctual impulse that we can examine" as consisting of "fusions or alloys of the two classes of instinct" he explains that these operate "in the most varied ratios" (*SE* xxii, 104-105), a theory that conveys the multiplicity of their appearances and disguises. Thus, in fusion with Eros, aggression can be seen in "the act of eating," which is "a destruction of the object with the final aim of incorporating it" (*SE* xxiii, 149). "Self-preservation," which is a manifestation of Eros, "must nevertheless have aggressiveness at its disposal if it is to fulfill its purpose" (*SE* xxiii, 209).

The hypothesis of the fusion of drives suggested to Freud the relation of the "defusion of the various instincts" (*SE* xix, 30, 41) to pathology: "fusions may also come apart, and we may expect that functioning will be most gravely affected by defusions of such a kind" (*SE* xxii, 105). I shall refer to this theory in later chapters; as Freud anticipated, it has been further developed and applied to the study and treatment of psychopathology. In the literature of madness, one observes dramatic representations of defusion as the "complicated defense" described by D. W. Winnicott, "in which aggression becomes separated out from erotic experience after a period in which a degree of fusion has been achieved."[23]

One of the most fruitful avenues of approach to the instincts is through their basic functions or, as Freud says, their "aim." This concept has been explicated and further developed in the theory and practice of ego psychology. In discussing "instinctual drives as motivations," David Rapaport illuminates not only the nature of intrapsychic motivation itself but the complexity of the role of instinctual forces in combination with many other internal and external causes of behavior.[24] Roy Schafer has also clarified Freud's point that in their production of psychic energy, instincts, which "behave in qualitatively different ways in mental life," are actually "all qualitatively alike and owe the effect they make only to the amount of excitation they carry. . . ." (*SE* xiv, 123). Although Schafer "does not minimize the significance in psychic life of the powerful libidinal and aggressive infantile drive aims and their derivations in the ego and superego systems," he questions the notion of "kinds of psychic energy," which Freud often seems to assume, as the introduction of "quality or direction into a quantitative concept." Schafer, justifiably, it seems to me, prefers to distinguish drive energy by its "motives" or "aims" rather than by its quality.[25] This is actually less a modification than a clarification of basic Freudian concepts; it does not alter the meanings of Freud's terms, Eros and the aggressive instinct, which are particularly useful in the present study. They are employed here to designate not qualitative entities but rather psychic motives, which are almost always ambivalent in nature.

More recently, Schafer[26] and others have raised stronger objections to metapsychological concepts as irretrievably rooted in mechanistic thinking, and the issue remains controversial in current psychoanalytic theory. Although it seems to me entirely possible to employ such terms as "drive" and "libido" without reification, in fact necessary to realize the enormous advantages these abstractions offer in delineating nonphysical processes, it must be admitted that the objections of the most thoughtful of such commentators oblige one to revaluate and define these terms, even if they seem as yet irreplaceable. Certainly, the new terminology proposed by members of the antimetapsychological school does not even approximate the signification of the energy metaphors. For example, "to wish," which they would substitute for "drive," inevitably excludes the amorphous yet exigent quality of affect that "drive" connotes. The problem of defining unconscious experience conceptually is not solved by substituting terms that cannot evoke it. Whatever the limitations of metapsychological language, its virtue is that it mediates between unconscious process and conceptualization. As Paul Ricoeur points out, "the energy metaphors replace the inadequate language of intention and meaning. Conflicts, formations of compromise, facts of distortion—none of these can be stated in a reference system restricted to relations of meaning to meaning. . . ." Ricoeur is well aware of the limitations of such metaphors: "it may be that the entire matter must be redone," but he underlines the necessity of retaining the concept of psychic energy as he goes on to say, "possibly with the help of energy schemata quite different from Freud's." Ricoeur's essential point is that both unconscious sources and their various representations must be included in a theoretical descriptive language: "The intersection of the 'natural' and the 'signifying' is the point where the instinctual drives are 'represented' by affects and ideas; consequently the coordination of the economic language and the intentional language is the main question of this epistemology and one that cannot be avoided by reducing either language to the other."[27]

Speculation on the biological roots of instinctual drives continues. A biological explanation for what could easily be identified as Eros, or a primitive basis for at least some of the aims Freud attributes to Eros, is suggested in a consideration of "altruism" by Lewis Thomas: "Maybe altruism is our most primitive attribute, out of reach, beyond our control. Or perhaps it is immediately at hand, disguised now, in our kind of civilization, as affection or friendship or love, maybe as music. I don't see why it should be unreasonable for human beings to have strands of DNA, coiled up in chromosomes, coding out instincts for usefulness and helpfulness."[28] Thomas's avoidance of technical language and the simplicity of his examples should not blur his implied distinction between physiological and psychological processes. The seriousness of his point is clarified by just such a distinction made earlier by David Rapaport: "It is not questioned that motives, just like any other psychological processes, have a (neuro-) physiological substrate in the organism. What is denied is that motives can be equated with this substrate. Motives are concepts derived from observations of behavior, and any observed correlations between them and physiological conditions can indicate at best that one of the necessary conditions of their operation has been discovered."[29]

This comment also clarifies Thomas's observation, in a discussion of protozoa and bacteria, that "there is a tendency for living things to join up, establish linkages, live inside each other, return to earlier arrangements. . . ."[30] As the first three of these tendencies suggest the biological roots of the Freudian Eros, the last reminds one of Freud's conception of the "final aim" of the "destructive instinct": that is, "to lead what is living into an inorganic state" (*SE* xxiii, 148). Dying, says Thomas, "is, after all, the most ancient and fundamental of biologic functions, with its mechanisms worked out with the same attention to detail, the same provision for the advantage of the organism, the same abundance of genetic information for guidance through the stages, that we have long since become accustomed to finding in all the crucial acts of living." Although Thomas does not make a connection between "the biologic functions" of dying as intrinsic to life and aggression as an instinctual force, his discussion of this "coordinated, integrated physiologic process"[31] clarifies the physiological basis of Freud's theory of aggression as the "diversion" of the destructive instinct "outwards . . . for the preservation of the individual" (*SE* xxiii, 150). Such diversion is endlessly complicated, accounting, at least in part, for the simplest biological functions, such as eating, as well as complex psychological mechanisms, such as the formation of the super-ego, and the enormous diversity of human activities involved in the conquest of external nature. The unfortunate term "death instinct" obscures Freud's conception of aggression as a drive against self-destruction which adapts and integrates the fundamental processes of biological dissolution into the very thrust for survival.

Perhaps because Freud described the instincts in symbolic and sometimes in mythical terms[32] (as, incidentally, Thomas describes biological functions[33]), certain elements of his theory are extremely useful in apprehending the mental conflict, confusion, and struggle for illumination recorded in imaginative literature. Particularly, it is the dynamic nature of the instinctual drives and the manifestations of their delays and detours, as Freud conceived them, and which are often overlooked or underestimated by his detractors, that elucidate much that may seem obscure in the symbolic communication of literary characters.

Freud's own associations with the term "drive" and other metaphors he used derive not only from the natural and physical sciences but from imaginative literature. In describing the "driving factor" of an instinct, he quotes from Goethe: *"ungebändigt immer vorwärts dringt"* (*SE* xviii, 42). It is in such symbolic form, which conveys the consumption of physical and mental resources in the encounter with and transformation of external reality, that love and aggression can be known by the human mind. In reading autobiographical accounts of the experience of insanity, one is struck time and again by the writer's acknowledgment of such feelings through metaphors of driving forces: "An inconceivable urge to destruction rose in me, an urge to annihilate myself at all costs," says Renée, the author of *Autobiography of a Schizophrenic Girl*.[34] She speaks of herself as "pursued by the impulses to self-destruction, impulses lacking any element of feeling or emotion" (p. 80). The only opposition to this aggression turned on herself are the pathetic signs of an impulse toward love, denied, repressed, but communicated symbolically even in "torpor and mutism" (p. 79).

Autobiographical narratives and imaginative literature also depict the psychic reality of another concept originating in Freud's work and later elaborated: the "attempt at recovery" which is manifested in delusions and hallucinations. *"The delusional formation,"* he says, *"which we take to be the pathological product, is in reality an attempt at recovery, a process of reconstruction,"* which is only partly successful. The most important function of such delusions is that they express a renewed effort on the part of the psychotic to recapture "a relation, and often a very intense one, to the people and things of the world," although this connection is now a "hostile one" (*SE* xii, 71).

In "violent hallucinations" Freud sees "a struggle between repression and an attempt at recovery by bringing the libido back again on to its objects" (*SE* xii, 77). Another and later discussion of hallucinations considers the possibility that they are a means by which forgotten material "forces its way into consciousness." Freud here suggests that "the delusions into which these hallucinations are so constantly incorporated," thus "the turning away from reality," may actually be a process of regaining memories long repressed in the unconscious. "The essence of it," he says, "is that there is not only *method* in madness, as the poet has already perceived, but also a fragment of *historical* truth" (*SE* xxiii, 267-68).

Although it may not always be possible to discover efforts at restitution in the delusions and hallucinations of psychotics, it is certainly true that both autobiographical accounts and imaginative representations of madness provide evidence that such bizarre constructions cannot be viewed merely as signs of withdrawal from reality. The very contents of the delusions and hallucinations of both literary figures and actual persons express symbolically an inner transformation of the world experienced through the deprivation, anger, pain, and guilt that have become the only emotional means of engagement with it. Paul Federn's objections to Freud's explanation of hallucinations on the basis that "the psychosis is no defense but a defeat"[35] sets up a false dichotomy. Defenses themselves may spell defeats of any expectations of fulfilling the self's cravings, but they may also express a struggle to maintain mere existence, however limited the possibility for any victory beyond that may seem. M. A. Sechehaye, commenting on her schizophrenic patient's description of the most dangerous stage of her illness as one in which she became "dumb," explains:

> "Dumb" signified: total indifference, a state in which delirium is not active. Our patient was perfectly right in saying that it is worth more to be given insight (to be delirious) than to be "dumb" (demented), because the period of her illness which seemed the most hopeless was that in which the delirium and the hallucinations lost their affective substratum, and where indifference gained ground and led the patient toward affective dementia.[36]

Ernst Kris has demonstrated how "the representational creations of psychotics, being attempts at restitution, follow the laws of the primary process, the 'language' of the id."[37] Literary representations of madness often go further in their depiction of the processes of restitution, revealing the ways in which the mad distort reality in accordance with their unique psychic deprivations and requirements, yet, in so doing, create an emotional environment for the reconstruction of a self image. The means may seem irrational and bizarre, but they are coherent within their own framework, and, in this respect, they illuminate the inner world of actual psychosis. In a recent medical study of insanity, the schizophrenic is described as "trying to come to grips with a threatened loss to his total being" and thus "grappling with some of the most fundamental questions that man can ask. Who am I? Why do I exist? What is the meaning of my life? Of any life? What is the ultimate reality? Who is God? Am I God?"[38] These are the ancient questions that entered into the creation of myth, ritual, religion, and literature, and to the mad they remain fundamental for survival and for the recovery of the self. The inner confrontation with these questions recorded in myth and literature exposes the drive of unconscious impulses against denials and controls, individual demands overwhelming social constraints and conditioning, the mind observing and struggling with its own nature and its apprehension of external reality.

The reader may well ask how a fictive character can reveal unconscious mental processes: how can one probe a mind that, strictly speaking, does not exist? Furthermore, how can one separate a fictional being from the mind that is responsible for its creation? In regard to literature based on mythical narrative, the answers are apparent: no matter how original the approach of the individual playwright or poet, the collective and social origins of mythical structures can be traced through historical, archeological, and anthropological evidence. The mind of the ancient author responds to and transforms revelations of psychic experience that both encompass and exceed his own. To some extent, moreover, this process is involved in the creation of all literary symbolic forms, for all works of art are both social and individual manifestations. Discussing the artist "projecting the forms of feeling into vis-

ible, audible, or poetic material," Susanne Langer suggests
that the "image" he creates

> serves two purposes in human culture, one individual,
> one social: it articulates our own life of feeling so that we
> become conscious of its elements and its intricate and
> subtle fabric, and it reveals the fact that the basic forms of
> feeling are common to most people at least within a cul-
> ture, and often far beyond it, since a great many works
> do seem expressive and important to almost everyone
> who judges them by artistic standards. Art is the surest
> affidavit that feeling, despite its absolute privacy, repeats
> itself in each individual life. It is not surprising that this is
> so, for the organic events which culminate in being felt
> are largely the same in all of us, at least in their biologi-
> cally known aspects, below the level of sentience.[39]

The creator is, of course, always present in his product,
but, without separating him from his creation, it is possible to
view a literary work or character as an aesthetic construct of
the psychic, historical, and social forces which together determine the intricate mental processes of human beings. "A
poem," says the poet and critic Octavio Paz, "is an object
fashioned out of the language, rhythms, beliefs, and obsessions of a poet and a society."[40] The same could be said of the
creation of any significant literary work, and certainly of the
literature of madness. In a writer's depictions of mad personae and characters, his revelations of his own deep knowledge of psychic pain and terror or of his empathy with individuals struggling to communicate such experience include
what Eric Erikson calls "the panic emanating from his
group."[41]

Both anthropological and historical data help to elucidate
such "panic" as well as less dramatic but equally important
cultural effects on inner conflict. In records of attitudes toward madness in tribal societies still in existence and of customs regarding its treatment, one discovers remarkable parallels with ancient myths. Anthropological data also help to
elucidate the relationship between individual modes of psy-

chic expression—dreams, fantasies, compulsive ritualistic behavior—and societal myths and rites. In studies of contemporary mechanized cultures, analyses of the intricate links between the psychoses and the "modalities of social life"[42] disclose patterns of oblique communication of rage, despair, confusion, and alienation that are reflected in literary characterizations and expressions of madness.

Historical data, an essential source of information regarding social attitudes toward madness and their representation in literature, are often contradictory and difficult to interpret. One has only to compare the interpretations of these data in medical surveys of psychiatric theory and practice, such as Alexander and Selesnick's *The History of Psychiatry* or George Rosen's *Madness in Society*,[43] with that of the philosopher Michel Foucault in *Madness and Civilization*[44] to observe vast differences in evaluation and perspective. Whereas Alexander and Selesnick describe Bethlehem Hospital as "originally far different from the snake pit that later became known as Bedlam," and go on to mention the "concern" and kindness with which its patients were treated,[45] Foucault sees all medical justifications for confinement as social hypocrisies:

> Before having the medical meaning we give it, or that at least we like to suppose it has, confinement was required by something quite different from any concern with curing the sick. What made it necessary was an imperative of labor. Our philanthropy prefers to recognize the signs of a benevolence toward sickness where there is only a condemnation of idleness.   (p. 48)

The overwhelming evidence of mistreatment of the insane in asylums throughout Europe in the seventeenth and eighteenth centuries leads to general agreement that fear and superstition determined reactions to madness during these periods, but, whereas medical commentators value the efforts of eighteenth- and nineteenth-century reformers, such as Philippe Pinel in France, Vincenzo Chiarugi in Italy, and William Tuke and his descendants in England, "to apply reason and observation" to the study of human conduct and its envi-

ronment,[46] Foucault views such methods as merely a more
subtle form of cruelty. He regards Tuke's establishment of
York Retreat in 1792, an asylum based on Quaker principles,
as no "act of 'liberation' '" but the substitution "for the free
terror of madness the stifling anguish of responsibility; fear
no longer reigned on the other side of the prison gates, it now
raged under the seals of conscience. Tuke now transferred
the age-old terrors in which the insane had been trapped to
the very heart of madness" (pp. 196-99).

Foucault's evaluation of Tuke's own description of his
methods of treating the insane discloses implications previous commentators have missed: the religious and moral strictures imposed, the insistence on work as "a constraining
power," the effects of "observation" by the staff, which, together with formal social occasions, were calculated to stimulate "the need for esteem" but clearly could be both inhibiting
and frightening (pp. 199-201). He also clarifies the differences
in the atmosphere and the methods of treatment in Tuke's
Retreat and in Salpêtrière and Bicêtre, where Pinel was
physician-in-chief during approximately the same period,
differences resulting largely from Tuke's religious values and
Pinel's secular moral ones. Foucault is most effective in indicating the relationship between the values Pinel established
within the asylum and those of bourgeois society, especially
its emphasis on transgression, guilt, and punishment, which
ultimately led to the "internalization of the juridicial instance" (pp. 213-14).

But Foucault's evaluation of Pinel is incomplete; it emphasizes only the inevitable limitations of the moral standards and rational principles of the Enlightenment. What he
omits is Pinel's effort to transcend the rigid approach to the
mind characteristic of his time and his profession. Observing
"so many errors to rectify, and so many prejudices to remove,"[47] Pinel ignored what he called "general principles of
treatment," which he found useless, and concentrated on individual symptoms, giving "attention to the state of the mind
exclusively" (p. 108). He describes in detail various symptoms, ranging from delirium and "maniacal fury" to

"idiotism," all "so different, and all comprehended under the general title of insanity." These he observed and studied with compassion and as much objectivity as he could achieve. His description of his purpose, "to endeavor, as far as possible, to divest myself of the influence both of my own prepossessions and the authority of others" (p. 2), indicates his awareness of his own limitations. His consciousness of those more generally to be found in his profession is justly even greater. Describing the practice of bleeding the insane, to which he objected only when he felt it was abused, Pinel does not exclude the medical authorities from the condition of those to whom they minister: "The blood of maniacs is sometimes so lavishly spilled, and with so little discernment, as to render it doubtful whether the patient or his physician has the best claim to the appellation of a madman" (p. 251). Pinel's "philosophical" approach to mental disturbance does reflect a neoclassical emphasis on reason, order, and authority, but his repeated attacks on prejudice, his conviction that the study of insanity is "intimately connected with the history and philosophy of the human mind" (p. 3), and his reports of his efforts to learn about madness from the mad themselves suggest that his attitude was less dogmatic and his practice less rigid than Foucault would have us believe.

Furthermore, the vast conclusions Foucault draws from Tuke's and Pinel's principles and practice are unjustified by historical and psychological evidence, which is broader and far more complicated than Foucault apparently would admit. Thus, describing Tuke's system of observation, from the point of view of the insane, as a "passage from a world of Censure to a universe of Judgment," Foucault concludes: "thereby a psychology of madness becomes possible." Observation, actually "Surveillance and Judgment," according to Foucault, continues into the present as a pervading technique, though it was modified to some extent by psychoanalysis, which relied on "the powers of language." But, he hastens to add, "psychoanalysis doubled the absolute observation of the watcher with the endless monologue of the person watched—thus preserving the old asylum structure of non-reciprocal observation but balancing it, in a non-symmetrical reciprocity, by the new structure of language without response" (pp. 201-202). The phrase "endless monologue" may reveal Foucault's own "judgment," but it certainly does not indicate the function of speech—to convey free associations—in psychoanalysis; even more telling, his phrase "language without response" excludes the psychic partnership that makes such communication possible.

Foucault believes that the notion of "mental disease, with the meanings we now give it," is directly related to the ideological structures first developed by Tuke and Pinel, "whose spirit and values," he says, "are so different," yet "meet in" the conception of the *"medical personage"* as healer of the insane (p. 216). The portrait he draws of this medical personage—the psychiatrist practicing both within and outside of institutions from the end of the eighteenth century to the present—is as oversimplified and distorted as his caricature of the patient subject to his treatment.

The revolutionary changes in psychological theory and practice instituted by Freud are dismissed by Foucault as modifications of techniques used by Tuke and Pinel—especially Pinel's use of silence as an inducement to humiliation and guilt: "When Freud, in psychoanalysis, cautiously reinstates exchange, or rather begins once again to listen to" the "language" of madness, "henceforth eroded into monologue, should we be astonished that the formulations he hears are always those of transgression?" (pp. 210-11) Neither Freud's interpretations of his patients' dreams and associations nor the moving revelations of some of those patients themselves suggest that transgression in the usual sense of the word had much to do with the spirit or language of psychoanalytic treatment. The whole theoretical structure of Freudian psychoanalysis is in opposition to such religious or moralistic standards. Determined to view psychoanalysis as an outgrowth of methods introduced in the asylums of the eighteenth and nineteenth centuries, Foucault omits or distorts out of recognition the very techniques that define it: free association, the reporting and interpretation of dreams, and transference.

Furthermore, in his effort retrospectively to rescue the mad from the moral and social ideologies that dominated the asylums of the late eighteenth and nineteenth centuries, Foucault idealizes the condition of madness as essential freedom constrained. The sharp analytic intelligence and skepticism which enable him effectively to probe the social and religious determinants of the organization of the first asylums seem to desert him whenever he turns to the subject of madness as an inner experience. At such times he becomes vaguely mystical. One of the reasons I have dealt at some length with Foucault's work on madness is that in this respect it represents an approach that has currently become all too fashionable: an idealization of madness that actually confuses compulsion with freedom, anarchy with truth, suffering with ecstasy.

Medical historians, in their certainty of the steady progress in the development of psychiatric theory and treatment, have too often ignored the participation of the physician in the social and moral crimes of history. The correction of such an approach, however, is not another kind of simplistic distortion that views all of medical history as a paradigm of prescribed inhibition and alienation. Both positions finally ignore an essential source of enlightenment: the varied and subtle commentaries on historical and medical data of the mad themselves, in their own accounts of their inner experience or in literary interpretations.

Foucault's rhapsodic descriptions of the "free terror" the madman could experience through "the dungeon, the chains, the continual spectacle, the sarcasms," which were "the very element of his liberty," bear little relation to historical records of the painful and debasing existence the mad endured in such institutions as Bedlam. Nor does Foucault define the "truth" he insists the mad could communicate to the hostile society of the dungeon through "the dialogue of delirium" (pp. 209-210). Words such as "truth," "freedom," and "glory" too often blur the actual messages of the mad—in art and in life—with superimposed philosophical significance, as does the assumption that the mad are all alike in their vision of a reality unknown to the sane. The varieties of communication among the mad include muteness, violence, and suicide, as well as verbal and pictorial symbols, all of which convey inner experience of enormous range and complexity.

Despite this variety, patterns of communication do emerge, in literary as in actual madness. Tracing such patterns in literature, one finds revelations of suffering more often than of achievements of freedom or glory. One discovers, moreover, a symbolic language that discloses the intricate ways in which the mad incorporate the very conflict and suffering of the world from which they have withdrawn.

II

Dionysiac Frenzy and
Other Ancient Prototypes
of Madness

The similarities between actual symptoms of insanity and the
conduct of the mad protagonists of certain Greek myths have
long been apparent and sometimes grossly appropriated in
both scientific and imaginative analogies. A recent example,
Jules Henry's generalization regarding the people whose behavior he analyzes in detail in *Pathways to Madness*, "I perceive these families as Greek tragedies without gods," is
based on a parallel between the complex relationships among
the various members of these families and the relationship of
the mythical figure of Orestes with his sister, his mother, and
"his father's soul." Henry, however, makes one significant
modification: "But just as the configuration of the *Oresteia* is
spun from the totality of Greek culture, so the threads that
have been taken up and woven into their own destiny by my
families come from their *culture*."[1] Henry's main point is in-
disputable, but he, like many others who draw on myths
from literary sources as analogies for actual symptoms of
madness, generalizes too readily about the symbolic figures
to which he alludes. What does he mean by the "totality of
Greek culture?" Even the comparatively small body of extant
Greek myths of madness is by no means the product of a uni-
form and settled society. Dionysus, the Erinyes, and other
major mythical prototypes reveal evidence of their origins in
and transmission from cultures far older than those that pre-
served them in literary form. Orestes existed as a mythical

prototype long before he figured in Aeschylus' trilogy. He is older than the *Odyssey*, in which he is repeatedly mentioned as an example of virtuous conduct. Aeschylus interprets Orestes' prototypical attributes and experience in the light of his own time and place in history.

If Orestes and other mad mythical protagonists remain relevant to an exploration of the psychology of madness from a scientific, cultural, or literary point of view, it is not only because they reveal the effects of social and political forces on familial attitudes of a certain period in history, but also because the narratives in which they figure express primordial and continuous inner experience. The "Destiny" by which they are "controlled," like that of the mad people whose suffering they have come to symbolize, is older and more complicated even than what Henry sees as its modern equivalent—a "family's history."[2] A study of the mental processes communicated through the stylizations and distortions of ancient myths of madness indicates that for many of the figures involved in these narratives destiny is a symbolic expression of the inevitable individual and social effects of adaptive processes within the human psyche in its phylogenetic development. In both ancient and later literary versions, the primordial symbolizations of developing mental processes inherent in these myths remain, like primitive layers of the mind itself, responding to internal and environmental pressures. Susanne Langer's premise that "not only the processes but also the products of art become starting points for the understanding of mind, and, indeed, for fundamental inquiries into its entire evolution from primitive biological traits and tendencies" is particularly applicable to ancient tragedy, in which those primitive traits persist in the very plot structure, which is chiefly based on traditional mythical narratives. These narratives, especially myths of madness, reveal not only "the morphology of feeling,"[3] but the strange and devious ways in which it was communicated in the very process of its evolution and development.

It is impossible (and hardly desirable) to separate the exploration of mental processes revealed in these myths of madness from a critical study of the literary works in which they are delineated. Previously unrecognized thematic elements and character traits emerge through a study of a playwright's interpretation of traditional narratives, with their primitive remnants, in relation to contemporary problems and conflicts. Furthermore, such an approach helps to explain the persistence of these prototypes of madness throughout literary history into the present, and to elucidate the continuous relevance of their symbolic communications.

Although the mad gods and characters of ancient myth have permeated psychoanalytic and imaginative literature of the twentieth century, the essential meanings of their attributes, their conduct, and their characteristic forms of expression have remained largely unexplored. The study of myths of madness as symbolic expressions of adaptive psychic mechanisms is especially relevant to current psychoanalytic interest in "aberrant symbolic processes."[4] It is a commonplace of psychoanalytic theory that many of the symptoms of psychoses indicate a regression to archaic cognitive and emotional patterns, which provide a mode of escape from unbearable conflict and tension and thus a form of survival, however painful and limited. The correspondences between such symptoms—conviction of the magic properties of words and objects, ritualistic movement and utterance, obsessional guilt represented as an imagined pursuer, the fantasy of incorporation of a god—and the narrative structure of ancient myths of madness suggest that certain of these characteristic expressions of psychosis reveal a regression to earlier stages of psychic adaptation. At least some of the "aberrant symbolic processes" of the schizophrenic seem to express a desperate detour to psychic mechanisms that once, early in human history, developed as stages of evolution toward greater degrees of mental differentiation and consciousness of motive and conduct. The psychotic regression for survival can thus be viewed as a retreat to survival mechanisms of human phylogeny itself.

The symbolizations that suggest a connection between such seemingly disparate stages of inner life may help to explain both the pervasive general interest in madness reflected in literary representations and the periodic nostalgia to return to organized expressions of extreme forms of psychic experience, such as Dionysiac frenzy, which recurs throughout history and is abundantly evident in social manifestations and literary products of the twentieth century.

DIONYSIAC FRENZY

The greatest extant literary work centered on Dionysus, Euripides' *Bacchae*, evokes and clarifies the primordial qualities of the god, especially the frenzy that characterizes him and his worshipers. For the modern world, Euripides' drama has itself become a source of Dionysiac power—in Nietzsche's view, straining against Euripides' very intention to set limits upon it; the god of the *Bacchae* was identified with Christ by Hölderlin and Yeats, and, more recently, the play has served as a model for Auden's and Kallman's *The Bassarids*, the Performance Group's *Dionysus in 69*, and Wole Soyinka's *Bacchae*, which attempt to revitalize Dionysiac frenzy as a psychological, social, and political force. Classified as an irrational element in society and treated as a curious phenomenon within religious history, this frenzy has elicited distaste, approval, or both at once, from scholars, critics, and poets, but it has never been satisfactorily explained as a ritual expression of psychological responses to social and environmental determinants.

In this study, I shall attempt to show that myths of Dionysiac frenzy and the remnants of ancient rites present in their narrative structure retain in literary representations certain symbolic expressions of evolving processes of the human mind which determine its elemental and continuous nature. That such psychic developments occurred in conjunction with changes in the physical environment, which were undoubtedly determining influences, is unquestionable. In presenting a new view of Euripides' *Bacchae* as the chief extant source and interpretation of a long tradition of Dionysiac worship, dating back to prehistory, my main effort is toward analyzing and defining the mental processes that constitute Dionysiac frenzy. Such an approach, it seems to me, illuminates the fundamental tragic conflict portrayed in this drama, which has not been explored from this point of view.

In his Introduction to his edition of Euripides' *Bacchae*, E. R. Dodds says that the play is "about an historical event—the introduction into Hellas of a new religion. When Euripides wrote, the event lay in the far past, and the memory of it survived only in mythical form; the new religion had long since been acclimatized and accepted as part of Greek life."[5] Both this edition and Dodds's *The Greeks and the Irrational* have done more than any other commentary on the subject to elucidate the "historical" nature of the play and of the myths that compose its plot. Yet further analysis of myths and rites of Dionysiac ecstasy and madness, and especially of their depiction in the *Bacchae*, suggests that Euripides' play also contains traces of a much earlier historical event reflected in these myths of Dionysus' relations with human beings, an event more significant and far-reaching than the god's introduction into Hellas, for it is a crucial episode in the history of the development of the human mind. In fact, there is reason to believe that ancient myths of Dionysiac frenzy both express and portray in ritualistic narrative form some of the early stages in the development and functioning of the conscious mind, adapting controls over older biological and psychological processes. The story of Dionysiac power, fertility, pleasure, and madness conveys the efforts of human beings to regulate their own feelings and conduct; indeed, it delineates the mental and emotional tracks of that precarious inner route.

It is important to recall that Dionysus, the god known for his power to inflict madness on others, was himself once afflicted with madness by Hera; myths record that in this state he wandered through Egypt and Syria until he was healed by Rhea in Phrygia and initiated into her mysteries. As an infant, moreover, Dionysus was the victim of *sparagmos* and *omophagia*: he was torn to bits and consumed, but he is also, in one of his manifestations, Ὠμάδιος, the "devourer of raw flesh."[6] In his double role of victim and executor of madness and violence, he is a primordial mythical construct of the growing human capacity to conceptualize perception, emotion, motivation, action, and, most important, control. Dionysus' experience of the very madness he was to arouse in his victims, his endurance of and participation in cannibalism, his dual powers—to bind with frenzy as Βάκχος and to free the spirit from that affliction as Λύσιος, to cause destruction and death and to promote fertility and growth— are a projection of his creators' conflicting instinctual drives on a being who is both subject to and master of these forces. These ambiguous qualities of the god, moreover, are not local, or even merely Greek, conceptions. There is a good deal of evidence to support Euripides' view that the cult of Dionysus was "a sort of 'world religion,' carried by missionaries (as no native Greek cult ever was) from one land to another."[7]

A great body of excellent twentieth-century scholarship[8] convincingly demonstrates that Dionysiac myths were introduced into Greece from at least two, or possibly more, independent sources, and that they served an important function in early Greek religious practice. There is no need to repeat or summarize the historical material easily available in the works cited above, but certain details regarding origins and transmission must be emphasized, for they help to elucidate the nature of Dionysiac frenzy. Furthermore, an analysis of the mental processes involved in the formation of these myths in relation to the background of their syncretic nature leads to the conclusion that they or their prototypes are among the earliest narrative structures in the prehistory of humanity.

Dodds suggests that Dionysus "may in fact have reached mainland Greece by two independent routes—overseas from the Asiatic coast by way of Cos, Naxos, Delos, and Euboea to Attica, and by land from Thrace to Macedonia, Boeotia, and Delphi," and he cites a good deal of evidence to indicate that the Greeks were aware of the god Dionysus by "the thirteenth century B.C. at latest" (p. xxi). Further evidence of the "Asiatic and non-Greek origins of the [Dionysiac] religion" is provided by W.K.C. Guthrie, whose discussion of Euripides' references in the *Bacchae* to the ancient and far-reaching background of Dionysiac myth is of extreme importance. Most significant is Guthrie's consideration of the "syncretism" revealed in the first choral ode of the *Bacchae*, in which, he says, "Phrygian, Lydian and Cretan [elements] are invoked side by side, and names like Satyrs, Kuretes, Korybantes, Dionysos, Bacchos, Mother-goddess, Kybele, Rhea, infant Zeus and Tmolos come tumbling in profusion from the lips of the inspired women." Guthrie discusses the attribution of the worship of Dionysus to both Thracians and Phrygians, which, he points out, were originally one race, whose tribes moved "from Thrace across the Hellespont to settle in Asia Minor," and he indicates the close connection between the "religions of Dionysos and of Kybele, the Asiatic Mother-goddess with her young attendant Attis, [which] were of the same orgiastic type, and by historical times had become inextricably mingled." He further considers the ways in which the Korybantes, the attendants of the Phrygian Great Mother-goddess (an orgiastic band, whose very name became the verb κορυβαντιᾶν, "to be in a state of divine madness in which hallucinations occurred"), were also connected with Dionysus. Guthrie points out that the parodos of the *Bacchae* refers as well to the Cretan Kuretes (ll. 119-34), who in fifth-century Greece were identified with the Korybantes; both are here related to the Satyrs. "Thus Phrygian and Bacchic religion are intermingled with Rhea and the birth of the Cretan Zeus in one gloriously catholic stanza."

One of Guthrie's most interesting theories is that the introduction of Dionysus into Greece is closely related to the religious practice that had existed "from time immemorial" in Crete. The god of Crete, like Dionysus, symbolized fertility and creation; he was worshiped ecstatically in dance, and was offered the flesh of a bull. "Behind this similarity is in all probability an initial prehistoric identity."[9]

There has been a good deal of speculation on the characteristics and functions of the prehistoric Dionysus prototype,[10] and on the social environment in which this figure emerged. The most convincing view is Jean Bayet's, who suggests that "Le Prôto-Dionysos" belongs to a period before man clearly distinguished between himself and the animals he hunted with: "Car nous sommes là au berceau des compagnonnages entre hommes et bêtes; non domestications ni domptages (quels mots affreux!): mais sentiment de communauté, qui adoucit les fauves en ensauvageant les hommes."

Bayet believes that there are two subjects of investigation ("avec tous leurs risques") necessarily related to the origins of Dionysus: the prehistoric formation of a "complexe" which predetermined the Dionysus of the Greeks, and the "capacity that this god inherited and conserved to draw to himself a multitude of unofficial aspects of Greek religion." He goes on to say that the clues to probability in these two areas of investigation "seront de sociologie historique et de continuité psychologique."[11] The myths of Dionysiac frenzy that remain in ancient Greek literature express important stages in human beings' psychological development, which were both decisive and continuous in determining their social history; furthermore, the mental processes these myths reveal indicate the nature of the Dionysus prototype and elucidate the attributes that assured both his continuity and his evolution.

The strikingly ambiguous characteristics of Dionysus all point to a prototype who enacted in ritual form an advance in the evolution of the human mind toward a greater degree of differentiation between unconscious and conscious processes than had been achieved in earlier psychic history. Myths of Dionysiac frenzy are a record both of archaic processes and of the self-regulatory functions that Jean Piaget has shown to be crucial to human development.[12] In literary adaptations of such myths it is possible to perceive the continuous relation of the human mind to its ancient past persisting in its very adaptations to a changing environment, and the dynamic struggle between violence and creation, madness and reason, which is a condition of human existence.

The causes, characteristics, and results of Dionysiac frenzy—itself a mental state in which different levels of consciousness are hardly differentiated—symbolically express an advance in psychic controls over inner and external reality, a progression from predominantly aggressive responses, such as literal and symbolic incorporation, to the more sophisticated operations that comprise internalization of both actual and fantasied qualities of the environment, and an emerging perception of human existence as separate from the mind's omnipotent projections. Incorporation, the taking in or consumption of an object, or at least its potency or meaning, is easily understood in Dionysiac myth and rite, in which it is literally enacted in cannibalism. Internalization, a more complicated series of operations, has been variously defined. The most useful definition I have found is Schafer's: "Internalization refers to all those processes by which the subject transforms real or imagined regulatory interactions with his environment, and real or imagined characteristics of his environment, into inner regulations and characteristics."[13]

It is the nature of this transformation that Dionysiac myth particularly clarifies, for it is itself a product of the processes of association, synthesis, and representation by which environmental and social demands are integrated with the primary material of dream and fantasy. The structure of such myths indicates how the symbolic narrative contents of this material are converted into concepts in the experience of learning manifested in the regulation of behavior. In Dionysiac myths of madness, the god, his adherents, and his victims sometimes simultaneously express unregulated libidinal and aggressive aims and enact the tentative steps toward their fusion. The integrating and controlling operations—developing ego functions—are evident in the very midst of, or immediately after, the mad and violent acts; they account for the paradox so often present in these myths, in which self-knowledge emerges through violence and destruction, reason through madness. In this symbolic fusion of instinctual drives, moreover, libidinal aims predominate over aggressive ones; the projected god who afflicted human beings with madness and violence becomes the god of fertility, the principle of creation in nature.

In many of its adaptations to literary form, the narrative and symbolic structure of Dionysiac myth retains evidence of some of the earliest efforts at socialization, the achievement of soundness of mind, temperance, self-control in its most basic sense, and, with this control, a degree of self-knowledge. One of the most important words in Euripides' *Bacchae* is the verb σωφρονέω (to be sound of mind). Some form of it, or of the morpheme φρήν (the heart or mind),[14] recurs throughout the play, and it is a key not only to the meaning of the tragedy but to myths of Dionysiac frenzy in their many forms and appearances. Clues to the ambiguous psychic processes symbolized by Dionysiac madness also exist in both earlier and later literary references to the god, and it is useful to glance at a few of these before turning to the fullest development of the myth in Euripides' play.

The earliest literary allusions to Dionysus depict the extraordinary ambiguity of his nature; in the *Iliad*, Zeus, enumerating the women he has loved and their offspring, says that Διώνυσον Σεμέλη τέκε, χάρμα βροτοῖσιν, literally, "Semele gave birth to Dionysus, a source of joy to mortals" (xiv, 325). The word χάρμα is itself an ambiguous term, related to χάρμη, the joy or lust of battle, and χαίρω,[15] which can express both greeting and renunciation; furthermore, χάρμα itself can mean "a source of malignant joy."[16] An earlier reference in the *Iliad*, moreover, reveals a deeper ambiguity in the god's nature: here Diomedes tells of how Lycurgus, the Thracian, drove μαινομένοιο Διονύσοιο τιθήνας ("the nurses of mad Dionysus") down the sacred mountain Nysa. Frightened, they let their wands fall to the ground, while Dionysus plunged into the sea. For this deed Lycurgus was hated by the gods and was punished with blindness (vi, 130ff.). Thus, the god who is a source of pleasure as ambiguous as the primary term contained in one of his epithets is also a mad god who takes vengeance on those who oppose him.

This is one of his most common roles in myth, and most frequently the punishment is madness. In myths recorded by Apollodorus and Hyginus and depicted in vase-painting,[17]

Dionysus inflicts madness on Lycurgus; in this state, believing that he is cutting off the branch of a vine, Lycurgus dismembers his own son Dryas. Only after he has committed this violent act is he restored to sanity. The Lycurgus myth expresses the characteristic cause of Dionysiac frenzy—the refusal to accept and worship the god;[18] furthermore, the version recorded by Apollodorus (*The Library*, III, v, 1) and Hyginus (*Fabulae*, 132) depicts typical effects of this denial: delusion leading to violent action, especially dismemberment of one's own child, followed by recognition of the dreadful act and the restoration of sanity.

Aeschylus' conception of the story, which can be only partly derived from the brief fragments of his Lycurgus-trilogy,[19] contains some of these characteristic features as well as other significant elements of Dionysiac frenzy. Fragments of the first play, *Edoni*, indicate that it dealt with the appearance of Dionysus and his followers at Lycurgus' palace, and the rejection of the god by the king. A few surviving lines suggest that Dionysus is addressed contemptuously by Lycurgus or one of his subjects: the god is referred to as a "woman-man" and his clothing is mocked. Even more interesting is a choral passage describing the music that induces Dionysiac frenzy among his followers. This is part of the "holy rites" or orgies (the word ὄργια used here had both meanings), which doubtless were one and the same experience for those involved in Dionysiac worship. The orgiastic rite depicted in this passage seems designed to elicit fear and wonder: the sound of the pipe arouses μανίας, "madness"; mimes with voices of bulls give answer to the clang of the strange music; their bellows arouse fear as does the sound of the timbrel, echoing, like thunder, from under the earth. Another fragment depicts the house itself as filled with the god; the roof βακχεύει, "celebrates the Bacchic rites."[20]

The second play of the trilogy, the *Bassarides*, expresses the conflict between Dionysus and Lycurgus through the traditional association of the god with the bull, which seems about to butt with its horns the goat (Lycurgus). The *Bassarides* dealt with Dionysus' anger at Orpheus, who refused to accept him as a deity and instead worshiped Helios whom he called Apollo. For this neglect, Dionysus ordered the Bassarides, his followers, to dismember Orpheus and scatter his limbs.[21]

Sparagmos is, of course, an important element in both Orphic and Dionysiac rites, but its meaning has not been fully explored. Clearly, the *sparagmos* of the god is directly related to that of his victims. The literal and symbolic meanings of the tearing and scattering of limbs should be considered in relation to the function of *omophagia*, which often followed *sparagmos* and was probably the more important act in Dionysiac myth and ritual. Furthermore, both must be examined as ritual expressions of elemental processes in the development of the human mind.

Many of the myths concerning those who resisted Dionysus describe the god's victims in their madness participating in these acts of murder and cannibalism, often of their own offspring. One such mythical narrative is that of Dionysus' effect on the daughters of Minyas, who, in their madness, "craved human flesh" (ἀνθρωπίνων ἐπιθυμῆσαι κρεῶν). When they drew lots for their children (διαλαχεῖν περί τῶν τέκνων), Leucippe's son Hippasus was chosen to be torn apart (διασπάσασθαι) and, no doubt, consumed. From that time the Minyads were named "Oleiae," murderesses. Plutarch remarks that even in his own day their "descendants" were given this name, and at the festival of the Agrionia they were pursued by the priest of Dionysus, who might kill any one of them that he seized.[22]

This is but one of many Dionysiac myths that tell of mothers tearing to pieces and consuming their children. Apollodorus relates similar tales about Dionysus' effect on women who resist his influence: in Thebes, the delusion of Agave which leads her to dismember her son Pentheus (discussed at length below) and the madness of the women of Argos, who eat the flesh of the infants at their breasts.[23] There are many other mythical stories[24] so similar in their basic structure—which contains some or all of the following elements: resistance to the god, madness, murder or dismemberment of one's own offspring, often accompanied by cannibalism—as to suggest a pattern of actual behavior or symbolic action or both. Certainly, there is evidence for the enactment of this pattern in ritual ceremonies that symbolically repeated the acts of the god's victims, and for a similar pattern in the various rites in which Dionysus himself was dismembered and consumed.

"The culminating act of the Dionysiac winter dance," says Dodds, "was the tearing to pieces, and eating raw, of an animal body, σπαραγμός and ὠμοφαγία." The ὠμοφαγία is clearly a ritual eating of the god incarnated in his "beast-vehicle," and, further, there is a strong possibility that this was "a still more potent, because more dreadful, form of communion—the rending, even the rending and eating, of God in the shape of man." Dodds provides a good deal of evidence from recorded rituals and myth to support his suggestion that cannibalism actually took place, and he convincingly relates such ritual acts to the essential nature of the god, but his explanation of the origins of the cult of Dionysus is utterly unconvincing: "His cult was originally an attempt on the part of human beings to achieve communion with [the god's] potency. The psychological effect was to liberate the instinctive life in man from the bondage imposed on it by reason and social custom: the worshipper became conscious of a strange new vitality, which he attributed to the god's presence within him" (pp. xvi-xx). Dodd's explanation of the attraction of Dionysiac myth and cult may well apply to the sophisticated Athenians of the fifth century, or even to earlier periods for which there is said to be evidence of the "introduction" of the god's worship. But, as was indicated above, there is a good deal of more basic evidence (some of it provided by Dodds himself) that Dionysiac myths—or at least their prototypes—originated in prehistoric times, long before men's and women's "instinctive life" was regulated by "social custom"; in fact, one contention of this study is that what is regarded as the "introduction" of Dionysiac worship in historical times is actually a *reintroduction* of ritual acts that originated earlier in human development. Whether such rites were practiced by the aboriginal pre-Hellenic inhabitants of the Greek mainland cannot be known, but the Cretan Dionysus figure certainly provides evidence of primordial Mediterranean worship of an ecstatic type that closely resembles that of the historical Dionysiac religion. Dodds himself mentions the possibility suggested by Nilsson of "a missionary movement in the Archaic Age which was in fact a reintroduction from abroad of ideas and rites that had been familiar to the Minoan world" (p. xxi, note 3).

If one approaches the mythical tales of Dionysiac frenzy and the rites enacting them as an expression of an emerging stage in human mental history, marked by an increasing consciousness of self-regulation and social responsibility, some of the bizarre acts that make up the pattern of these rites are illuminated. One must begin by asking what is the relationship between the god and those who resist him and, as a consequence, are compelled to repeat his very experience in madness and violence. Dionysus' ambiguous nature is clearly a projection of the turbulent and conflictive inner experience of the generations who created and recreated his story. As an infant, Dionysus is a victim of *omophagia*, an extreme expression of aggression, the aim of which is literal incorporation. The cultural and psychological roots of infanticide and cannibalism are inextricably connected, but their occurrence from very early times to the present indicates certain basic causes common to various stages of mental and cultural development. Infanticide, of course, persists in the present even in highly developed societies; cannibalism remains a custom of some primitive tribes.

Dionysus, in the form of Zagreus (great hunter), was dismembered and eaten by the Titans at the instigation of Hera, the wife of his father.[25] As Dionysus, he was nursed by the daughters of Lamos, but barely escaped being eaten by them when they were afflicted with madness.[26] In many of the Dionysiac myths that tell of mothers who are the god's victims killing and consuming the infants at their breast, the pattern that emerges in relation to both the god and those possessed by him is of the female protector, the ostensible guardian or nurse (often literally), who is also the devourer.

There is no better example of the operation of the conflicting drives of libido and aggression in their most elemental form of love and hate. The cannibalistic act is also the most primitive and most violent confusion of the two impulses; the incorporation of the loved child takes place at the moment that it is being devoured. It is the most primitive form of merging with an object, an act in which love and violence are not distinguished, in which libido does not mitigate the drive of aggression.

Dionysus' identification with the wildness and potency of many animals—especially the goat and bull—is significant in relation to his role as the projection of these undifferentiated human drives. Bayet's suggestion that the Dionysus prototype emerges from a time before man could make a clear distinction between himself and the animals with which he hunted sheds light not only on the god's capacity to transform himself into various animal forms but also on the apparent identification of animals and human infants by those engaged in Dionysiac rites, first suckling and afterward devouring the young of animals, and then performing identical acts with their own offspring. Most important, it helps to explain the constantly shifting concept of the self characteristic of the Dionysiac initiate, who is at once a devouring animal, a reverent worshiper, and finally a god, as he merges through ritual violence with the feared and adored Dionysus.

The contents of the various myths of madness centered around Dionysus, along with what is known or can be reconstructed regarding early Dionysiac rites, indicate that both spring originally not from human efforts to release their unconscious drives but rather from their need to control and direct them. Only in historic times did human beings return to such rites out of a desire to release emotions inexpressible through socially accepted patterns. Paradoxically, conduct and action that express civilized people's reversion to older and more primitive forms of feeling and behavior originally constituted a major movement toward conscious judgment and deliberate control.

In attempting to reconstruct the prototypes of Dionysiac

myths and rites of madness as expressions of phylogenetic development, it must be assumed that three major factors are inextricably connected: the nature of primitive man as a member of a species, the nature of the family or tribal organization to which he belonged, and the external environmental conditions in which he existed. According to Bayet, "Les formes rituelles plus évoluées, du dionysiasme retiennent encore des traces nettes d'un très long temps de 'civilization de chasse.' "[27] Both Bayet and Henri Jeanmaire emphasize the vestiges of "la chasse primitive" in extant Dionysiac myth. Certainly, the association—and identification—of Dionysus with the bear, the lion, the bull, and the goat, as well as his form as Zagreus and his role of great hunter,[28] accompanied by the maenads who also pursue animals and human beings in a wild but purposeful hunt, reflect not only human beings' psychic development but the physical and economic conditions that helped to determine it.

There is a good deal of evidence to suggest that the earliest elements of the myth and ritual of the proto-Dionysus derive from the Mesolithic era,[29] when the chief activities of human beings were still hunting, fishing, and gathering. There are, moreover, clear indications in some of the details of the mythical narratives and ritual action of the great evolutionary changes characteristic of human beings during this period, as they gradually turned from the nomadic life of hunter and gatherer to the settled agricultural life of the Neolithic era. Farnell points out that Dionysus was "associated with the pasturing herds" and with the "aboriginal pasture-god . . . Pan" with whom Dionysus received "a common sacrifice . . . in the borders of Argolis and Arcadia" (v, 127). But the most significant clues lie in the most primitive details of Dionysiac myth—the frenzy that leads to cannibalism and the act of violence itself—which can be shown to reflect changes in the mental functioning and social mores of human beings adapting to new external conditions and internal necessities. In this aspect of the myth of Dionysus also lie clues to the god's prehistoric nature and the origins of his worship.

It is generally accepted by anthropologists that one of the

factors that drove Mesolithic man to seek new ways of obtaining food was a growing scarcity of animal meat. Even during earlier periods, hunting bands did not always find a sufficient supply of game. Thus, for early peoples, cannibalism sometimes satisfied both economic and psychological need: it supplied food for a desperately hungry nomadic band, and it expressed the ambivalence of conflicting drives and undifferentiated states of consciousness and identity. It is possible that in times of stress Paleolithic and early Mesolithic homo sapiens hardly differentiated between the animals and those (especially the young) of his own species that he devoured. In his irregular, unplanned existence, precarious in every respect, the direct release of aggression was a determining factor in mere survival. "The life of communities whose economy is based on hunting is necessarily one of tactics rather than strategy, of short-term decisions taken, perhaps rapidly, in relation to the movement and behaviour of the larger mammals which constitute the basic food supply."[30]

With the gradual shift to a new and more settled agricultural society, new attitudes and values inevitably emerged, which no doubt challenged and conflicted with older ones, even as they began to replace them. "When . . . animal domestication and plant cultivation are consciously envisaged as an essential part of the economy, a long-term view is immediately inevitable. . . . The achievement of this larger perspective is in itself a psychological advance of no mean order."[31] Later Mesolithic and Neolithic human beings, facing the necessity for self-control and therefore for a self-knowledge inconceivable earlier, advanced—however unevenly and incompletely—in their consciousness of their own development as social beings.

In attempting to delineate one manifestation of this complicated process, it is helpful to glance at the actual practice and mythical expression of cannibalism in a modern society which is primitive in structure and dependent upon hunting for survival. The attitudes toward cannibalism of several groups of Indians—Ojibwa, Montagnais-Naskapi, and Cree —living in Northeastern Canada have common features, which anthropologists label the "Windigo psychosis."[32] These Algonkian-speaking Indians, whose "technology is one of a stone age people,"[33] are obsessed with a fear of a giant spirit, the Windigo, whose attributes include a heart of ice and an insatiable craving to consume human flesh. Either through possession by a Windigo or transformation into one, a person becomes imbued with an overwhelming desire to commit acts of cannibalism.

The harsh environment of Northeastern Canada has sometimes, especially during periods of famine, driven members of these tribes to eat human flesh. Although the Indians find such behavior "revolting and reprehensible," they profess to understand the necessity for it under the threat of starvation. Nonetheless, they believe that, no matter what the provocation, once a person "has tasted human flesh, he develops an insatiable desire for more of it."[34] Furthermore, it is reported that among the Cree tribe "such a psychosis developed in men and women who had not themselves previously passed through famine experience."[35]

Among the "Windigo Cases" collected by Morton Teicher, moreover, there are some in which the compulsion to eat human flesh does not result from starvation. A particularly interesting story of this type is that of Shaywayko, which tells of a "mother who initiated murder and cannibalism in her family group."[36] The eating of children by parents is recounted in both factual sources and Indian folklore. In one folk tale, a woman who, when possessed by a desire for human flesh, consumed her husband and children, recovers her senses and realizes what she has done. The story tells of her horror at her past deeds and her pleas for death.[37]

The intense preoccupation with cannibalism among these Indian tribes cannot be explained on merely "environmental and cultural" grounds. The assumption that such an "unnatural" desire is an automatic "aftermath" of "the conflict between hunger and the rigid tribal taboo"[38] seems pure evasion of the evidence of a wish expressed in the psychosis to repeat a primitive instinctual satisfaction prohibited by law and custom but sometimes reluctantly sanctioned because of extreme physical circumstances.

There is no doubt that famine could be an immediate cause of cannibalism, but in itself it does not account for the most important cultural and psychological elements connected with the act. The very fact that a "rigid tribal taboo" against cannibalism exists indicates that it is not merely regarded as a practical, if dreadful, solution to the real problem of hunger. The taboo, the "profound horror of cannibalism,"[39] and the projections of cannibalistic giants are clearly prohibitions against inclinations deeper and more universal than those motivated occasionally by physical necessity. Such inclinations, moreover, are most vividly expressed in the particular form the Windigo psychosis takes: "a craving for human flesh."

The fact that men and women who had not endured the physical and psychological effects of famine, as well as those who had done so, suffered this craving further indicates that psychological and environmental factors are inextricably connected in the act of cannibalism. Wish may not lead to deed or even become part of conscious awareness when environmental conditions do not provide impetus or justification, but it is strong enough in many members of the group to result in delusion, terror, and physical deterioration. The cannibalistic giants are obviously projections of intense wishes to consume and merge with a fellow human being, as well as means of preventing the fulfillment of such wishes through fear of punishment. Accepting the existence of the Windigo, a person fears and shuns cannibalism; should he eat human flesh, he is condemned to a perennial craving for it as he is transformed into the superhuman being who personifies his forbidden cravings.

Teicher's main conclusion regarding the Windigo psychosis, that "belief controls behavior," is undeniable but rather disappointing, since it largely ignores the pressing psychological determinants of such belief. His statement that the "belief system reflects the social, economic, geographical, political and cultural conditions of man"[40] omits essential factors that must be explored in examining the Windigo psychosis: the inner drives and needs which are manifested in its particular aggressions and delusions.

There are striking parallels between the Indian folk tales of possession and madness, which convey deep psychological conflict, and Dionysiac myths of frenzy. One is reminded of the "craving for human flesh" afflicting those who refuse to worship the ancient god and of the identification with the "mad" god experienced by those who engage in *sparagmos* and *omophagia*. In addition, the Indians, though doubtless more highly developed mentally and further advanced socially than Mesolithic or Neolithic man, provide some insight into the manifestations and control of frenzy in which Dionysiac myth and rite originate.

Like the Windigo giant, Dionysus or his prototype is clearly a projection of both wish and prohibition. Adapting to the demands of new environmental conditions, late Mesolithic or early Neolithic man created a deity who enacted in frenzy his own primitive instinctual cravings for destruction and incorporation, and at the same time served as a curb on those very feelings. Though, of course, we know almost no details about the earliest rituals, it is possible to reconstruct their most salient features from anthropological, psychological, literary, and artistic evidence.

Two chief and undoubtedly very ancient rites connected with Dionysus recorded in literature and art and most graphically depicted in Euripides' *Bacchae* are those performed by his totally committed followers, the Bacchants, and those enacted in the stories of his opponents, the men and women who resist the god, are afflicted with madness, and recover as they recognize the power of divinity and the limits of their own human nature. Different as these may seem, they actually enact the same developing instinctual controls. Both, moreover, contain remnants of the old life of hunting tribes as well as evidence of the new and more settled agricultural patterns. The main difference between the rites performed by the established disciples, the Bacchants, and those who are to become reluctant initiates is that Dionysus and his "nurses" enact a rite in which conflicting instinctual aims are resolved in the ceremonial action, whereas the rites of those who deny the god explicitly reflect the psychic resistance to this process.

It is generally agreed that worship of Dionysus "was originally a women's rite with a single male celebrant,"[41] although there is evidence of later male participation in such rites. Certainly, in the myths that have come down in literature, the god's band of faithful followers is composed of women, sometimes described as "nurses." This is consistent with women's role in the early stages of human development. Even during the period when hunting was a chief means of survival, the female as bearer and nourisher of the young was often left behind to care for her offspring and to gather vegetable food.[42] Thus, it is likely that, prevented from diverting aggressive aims in the actual hunt, the female more readily than the male developed symbolic means of conveying the intensity of such drives and thus of regulating and redirecting them. It is significant also that females who resist the god's power in myth engage in the most barbaric act possible to their sex—the destruction and consumption of their own offspring.

Such females as well as males participate in the second ritual, which depicts those who, refusing to worship the god, are condemned to act out the frenzy of uncontrolled instinctual aims as a paradigm of the consequences of disobedience. In a state of delusion, they submit to their own most primitive impulses. At this point they are dissociated from the rational self that functions in a social context. The ultimate purpose of this rite, however, lies not in the expression of frenzy but in the enactment of human beings' achievement of a new apprehension of themselves, a recognition of their own potential violence and of their own capacity for insight and control, as they finally accept the power of the god.

The frenzy and ultimate control enacted in both these rites depict a psychological and mental phase of the human race, an inner drama of conflict between warring drives and an increasingly dominant rational ego. Not only the creation of the god but his subsequent development expresses his worshipers' increasing instinctual control: in Dionysus the libidinal predominates over the aggressive; the great hunter becomes the principle of creation in nature and in art.

In the many lands in which he was celebrated, Dionysus

gained various attributes as both traditional and later myths and rites were identified with his worship, but the essential ones, his frenzy, violence, productivity, and capacity to free and enlarge the mind and spirit, have remained intrinsic to his myth throughout its history. Turning from the most primitive manifestations of his worship to the most sophisticated ancient artistic work based on his myth, one discovers the perennial existence of his basic qualities in a new context.

In Euripides' *Bacchae*, Dionysus and his Bacchants return periodically to a life like that of Paleolithic hunting tribes—roaming over the mountains and associating intimately with animals. The play reveals how in a rite of revelry that reaches frenzy, both released and controlled by music and dance, and participating in a savage hunt culminating in *sparagmos* and *omophagia*, the worshiper, internalizing the god, expressed an awareness of the necessity of regulating instinctual aims. The apparently regressive behavior enacts the mitigation of aggression by libido as the participant in rite expresses these drives in symbolic acts of reverence for the creative and destructive powers in the universe, which are ultimately one in all things, including the self, and are so depicted in the figure of the god. To the Bacchants, Dionysus is Λύσιος, the god who frees humanity from domination by its most destructive compulsions.

The *Bacchae* has presented many difficulties in the way of interpretation, none more frequently alluded to than the ambiguity of the character of Dionysus. This quality results in part from the intrinsic nature of the god himself, manifested in almost all his appearances in literature, but, more significantly, from Euripides' sophisticated treatment of the oldest and most primitive elements connected with Dionysiac worship. Euripides reveals the key to the elemental meaning of Dionysiac frenzy even as he adapts the myth to the currents of feeling and thought of fifth-century Greece.

I mentioned earlier the extreme importance in this play of the morpheme φρήν and its cognate σωφρονέω, words that throughout the *Bacchae* express the idea of control implicit in the original myth and explicit in Euripides' dramatic version.

The theme of control in the play has, of course, been treated before, either in what has become the standard view, which considers the central concern of the play the conflict between the rigid controls Pentheus attempts to exert and the demands of the Dionysiac spirit, which, when repressed, emerges finally in violence, or, more recently, in an original and stimulating though questionable interpretation by Marylin Arthur of the chorus' emphasis on moderation as evidence of their role "throughout the play, as an apologist for bourgeois morality."[43] This discussion and many others also consider the significant occurrences of the words τὸ σοφόν (cleverness) and σοφία (wisdom). Arthur, unlike most other commentators on the play, finds no contradiction between the chorus' first use of τὸ σοφόν in l. 395 and their later use of it in the refrain of the third stasimon and in l. 1005.[44]

Behind all this attention to the themes of control and wisdom lies a central problem of the *Bacchae* that has not as yet been satisfactorily treated: that is, what is the relationship between the depiction of frenzy and control in the myth Euripides inherited from a prehistoric past and his own treatment of this subject in the play? It is striking that a drama in which frenzied violence is the central action should concentrate so intensely on the mind, and especially on its capacity for judgment, self-control, and temperance. Consideration of the nature and function of moderation is by no means restricted to the choral odes; as will be shown below, moderation is a major concern of the dialogues throughout the play. Even more revealing is the discovery that the terms expressing this preoccupation, such as σωφρονέω, σώφρον, τὸ φρονεῖν, τὸ σοφόν, and σοφία, which would seem to suggest an anachronistic rational approach to a primitive myth (and are consistently so interpreted by Euripides' critics), actually convey the complexity of the original primitive mythical construct operating within the framework of the comparatively advanced society of fifth-century Greece.

It is generally agreed that the *Bacchae* is Euripides' most "traditional" play,[45] and that its many ritual elements were derived, to some extent at least, from his observation of

Dionysiac cults in Macedonia, where worship of the god was no doubt closer to its primitive origins than in the festivals of fifth-century Athens. In the *Bacchae*, Euripides is concerned with the continuing function and meaning of these very ancient myths and rites in the personal and social lives of his contemporaries. His approach is neither judgmental nor propagandistic; for him the *sparagmos* of Pentheus is not an exemplary historical tale about a king's punishment by a god.[46] The *Bacchae*, like the myths on which it is based, cannot be reduced to a simple formula: if the Dionysiac is repressed, it emerges in violence; the Dionysiac is salutary or destructive, or both. Although it can be said that all these statements are valid, they do not finally deal with the essential meaning of the play. Euripides perceived the myth of Pentheus' conflict with Dionysus operating beneath the surface of daily existence, the σοφία contained in the myth conveying a deeper understanding of experience than its offshoot, τὸ σοφόν of the philosopher and the politician. Tiresias, the seer, exists within the soul of the fifth-century rationalist Tiresias,[47] and beneath Pentheus, the repressive leader of the polis, lies Pentheus, the ritual sacrifice. The theme of the play is concerned with the subtle relationship between these inner and surface elements and with the degree to which the forces and motivations expressed in the deep wisdom of myth determine the conflicts between rulers and citizens, and elucidate the disparity between state law and natural law, between philosophical theories and human drives, within Euripides' own society.

Throughout the play, Euripides' Dionysus explains the meaning of his own myth, the chief component of which—at least in this play—is frenzy. Even in his opening address, the god remarks on his appearance in mortal form, explicitly states the purpose of his arrival in Thebes, and describes in some detail the effects of the frenzy with which he has afflicted the women of Thebes. Dionysus' appearance as a mortal is itself significant beyond its dramatic function; Geoffrey Kirk suggests that Dionysus' "completely mortal form" at the beginning and the end of the play and the ambiguity of his role throughout much of the action help "to produce a mysterious uncertainty about where the natural ends and the supernatural begins."[48] This ambiguity in the god's form and his attributes is a remnant of one of his most primitive functions: the expression of early human beings' growing but as yet inconsistent ability to differentiate between themselves and their own mythical projections. The god's appearance as man is an inversion of the human ability to become one with the god in the performance of his orgiastic rites.

In explaining his purpose, Dionysus indicates that Thebes is but one of the many places in which he is to be worshiped; he has already established his rites throughout Asia and, once he has accomplished his mission in Thebes, he will move on to exert his powers in another land (ll. 48 ff.). Thus, Euripides makes explicit reference to the widespread appearance of the Dionysiac religion. Despite Dionysus' declaration of his special aim in Thebes—to punish those who doubted his divine origin and the honor of his mother—the god in his first appearance makes it clear that this is by no means his only purpose. Nor does he use an unusual method of punishing the sisters of Semele and the other women of Thebes. Driving people to a state of frenzy is Dionysus' characteristic means of punishing those who deny him. What is most striking, moreover, is the similarity of the effect of Dionysus on his faithful followers and on those whose faithlessness he would punish. Both the Bacchants and the afflicted Theban women are driven to frenzy, and both groups devote themselves to the god's orgiastic rites, the only difference—and it is a critical one—being that the followers of the god worship him with restraint and joy, whereas those who in the past denied him become his adherents only through violence and anguish. It is this similarity in the ritual action and this difference in the emotional experience of those engaged in it, that Dionysus clarifies in Euripides' play and, in so doing, reveals the essential meaning of Dionysiac frenzy.

In his first speech, Dionysus describes the women of Thebes, driven in frenzy to the mountains, obliged to wear the apparel appropriate to his rites (l. 34), sitting on rocks among the pines. They seem at first a band of Bacchants (the word Dionysus uses for them, ll. 51, 62), like the chorus, who in their parodos tell of their life as followers of the god. The heuristic function of the chorus of Bacchants is expressed in their description of the syncretic nature of Dionysiac religion as well as in their delineation of the purifying effects of his rites. Those who are blessed in knowing the rites of the god (ll. 72-73) are aware of his great antiquity and his widespread worship in Crete and Asia, evidence of his authenticity and power. Furthermore, his identification with the bull in his very birth (l. 100) suggests one of his earliest animal forms as well as the nature of rites in which the god's worshipers identify with his ferocity and potency.

The actual rites are described in some detail: the wild dancing, the chase of the animal, the eating of raw flesh; and their influence on the fertility of nature and the souls of human beings is clearly indicated. The ground flows with milk and wine and the nectar of bees—the verb ῥεῖ (flows) three times in one line (141) emphasizing the productivity of the earth. The Bacchants, moreover, led by Dionysus, experience rapture. The chorus here and throughout the play consistently evoke the most primitive and most essential content of the mythical narrative and ritual enactment of Dionysiac frenzy. They are figures outside time, a part of the natural world in which they belong and function.

Tiresias, Cadmus, and Pentheus, on the other hand, though traditional mythical figures bearing ancient associations, are depicted as also functioning within a historical framework, and involved in the problems of state. With the entrance of Tiresias in the first episode, the audience is moved rather abruptly away from the intense emotional atmosphere created by Dionysus and the chorus to a more commonplace level of existence. Tiresias sends for Cadmus in order to fulfill their agreement to worship the god, and the two old men discuss in factual terms the means and nature of such worship. The common approach to this scene as merely humorous misses its main point. Tiresias and Cadmus, in attempting to accommodate Dionysiac religion to their own needs, at first consider only the outward forms of respect, but their limitations of age and understanding are more touching than humorous. Furthermore, in this first scene, Euripides introduces two very important concepts—the nature of wisdom and the inextricable connection of primeval myth to present reality; in the development of these concepts, and the revelation of the essential relationship between them lies the theme of the play.

Cadmus begins by complimenting Tiresias, referring to "the wise speech of a wise man" (l. 179), and, a little later on, saying directly: "You are wise" (l. 186). His admiration for wisdom here is clearly based on his assumption that Tiresias will know the proper procedures for expressing devotion. When Cadmus asks him if they alone will dance in honor of Bacchus, Tiresias' response: μόνοι γὰρ εὖ φρονοῦμεν, οἱ δ᾽ ἄλλοι κακῶς, literally, "We alone think well, the others badly" (l. 196), expresses more than Cadmus seems to expect or to comprehend. These are words that remind us of the Tiresias of the *Oedipus Tyrannus* or the *Antigone*; they are the utterance of a seer, who perceives the minds of men behind their acts.

It is important to recognize so early in the play Euripides' association of Dionysiac worship with good thinking, especially as Tiresias clarifies his meaning in his continuing instructions to Cadmus: at line 200 he warns Cadmus: οὐδὲν σοφιζόμεσθα τοῖσι δαίμοσιν ("We do not argue subtly about the gods"), indicating that thinking well does not imply sophistic argumentation but rather acceptance of (l. 201ff.) "the traditional customs of our fathers, coeval with time. No subtle argument can overthrow them, not even the cleverness of the sharpest minds." In contrasting good thinking with τὸ σοφόν (l. 203), Tiresias is actually contrasting the traditional wisdom implicit in the primordial myths attached to Dionysus with the superficial rationalistic interpretations of the present.

Geoffrey Kirk's comment on this passage expresses a view that is commonly held: "Tiresias' professions of conservatism are odd for one who goes on to demonstrate sophistic cleverness and rationalism at its worst. He is part hypocritical, part confused."[49] This interpretation overlooks Tiresias' ambiguous role in this play, in which he wavers between ancient seer and contemporary rationalist. Tiresias' intuitive understanding of the validity of traditions as old as time does not express "conservatism" with its modern connotations, but a realization of the perennial vitality of these traditions in the lives of men. In his effort to persuade Pentheus, which follows this passage, Tiresias does offer some rather superficial rationalistic explanations of Dionysus' history, but interwoven with such clearly "modern" views is an intensely emotional expression of his deeper understanding of the god's meaning and function.

It is Tiresias who sees beneath Pentheus' objections to Dionysiac frenzy a more dangerous madness. Pentheus misrepresents both the intention and conduct of Dionysus and his followers. Insisting that they feign religious rapture to cover their sexual excesses, he argues for restraint and decorum. Tiresias' reply discloses the hollowness of Pentheus' claims. Once again he raises the subject of good thinking as opposed to mere sophistry; he begins with a general statement of some significance:

> ὅταν λάβῃ τις τῶν λόγων ἀνὴρ σοφὸς
> καλὰς ἀφορμάς, οὐ μέγ' ἔργον εὖ λέγειν.
>
> (ll. 266-67)

literally, "When a wise man takes a good basis for his thought, it is not a task to speak well." This translation, though somewhat awkward, conveys a meaning of the statement that is often obscured by more graceful approximations. The key words, καλὰς ἀφορμάς, refer to the origins or source of thought and words, more profound than the apparent rationalism of Pentheus. Tiresias then goes on to show Pentheus that he is not thinking correctly. Three times in the space of four lines (268-71) he attempts to do so: ὡς φρονῶν ἔχεις ("as if you had wisdom"); ἐν τοῖς λόγοισι δ' οὐκ ἔνεισί σοι φρένες ("in these words of yours there is no wisdom"); and θράσει δὲ δυνατὸς καὶ λέγειν οἷος τ' ἀνὴρ / κακὸς πολίτης γίγνεται νοῦν οὐκ ἔχων ("The man who is influential through audacity and is able to speak is a bad citizen, since he is without sense"). The last statement is a plea for sanity (νοῦν) as opposed to force, a point Tiresias repeats later on in the same speech: at line 310, he tells Pentheus, "Do not boast that might has power over men," and once again he warns him: (ll. 311-12) "Nor, if you form an opinion and your judgment is sick, hold that opinion to be wise." Tiresias contrasts Pentheus' inability to think properly, his lack of judgment, with the soundness of mind of the Bacchants: "Dionysus does not force women to be temperate" (σωφρονεῖν, literally, "to be sound of mind"); "but self-control (τὸ σωφρονεῖν) is·in their own nature, in all things forever. You must look at this. Even in the Bacchic rites, the woman of sound mind (σώφρων) will not be corrupted" (ll. 314-18). After repeatedly emphasizing soundness of mind or self-control as characteristic of the followers of the god, Tiresias concludes his argument by again referring to the sickness of Pentheus' mind (ll. 326-27): "You are most grievously mad. Neither can you be cured by medicines, nor is it for lack of them that you continue to be ill."[50]

The basic problem raised in this initial episode is developed throughout the play: how are sanity, soundness of mind, self-control to be achieved? Tiresias accuses Pentheus, the ostensible defender of morality and restraint, of intemperance—indeed of madness; the maenads, who participate in rites of frenzy, are his models for soundness of mind. The development of this paradox in all its complexity in the course of the play expresses Euripides' perception and interpretation of primordial functions of the ancient Dionysiac myths and rites persisting into his own time.

The question of the nature of sound thinking and of who is mad is probed throughout the play, involving all the major characters as well as the chorus. In this first scene, the chorus praise Tiresias, saying (l. 329), "you are sound of mind (σωφρονεῖς) in honoring the great god Bromius." Cadmus, reiterating Tiresias' arguments, also takes up the subject of sound thinking. He tells Pentheus that he is flighty: "you think nothing that is real thought" (φρονῶν οὐδὲν φρονεῖς,

l. 332), and reminds him of the fate of Actaeon, a victim of *sparagmos* resulting from his boast that he was superior to Artemis in hunting. The image of the hunt is a very important one in this play; as will be shown below, it is another reflection of the primitive world in which the myth originated, persisting in Euripides' treatment of Pentheus' *sparagmos*. Cadmus' words here have the force of a prophecy that he himself does not consciously apprehend.

In response, Pentheus returns to a subject Tiresias has raised twice before—sickness—but, unlike Tiresias, who had accused him of sickness of the mind, Pentheus uses this term to describe the effects of Dionysus on the conduct of the Theban women; this sickness, he says, results in their "dishonoring their beds" (ll. 353-54). His remarks provoke Tiresias to harsher comments on Pentheus' inability to think rationally; he declares: "You are raving mad now, who before were devoid of sense," and goes on to refer to Pentheus as a "savage" (ἀγρίου). Turning to Cadmus, Tiresias expresses the wish that Pentheus may not bring grief (πένθος, *penthos*) to his house. He insists that this is not to be taken as prophecy but as a comment on Pentheus' deeds (ll. 359-69). Tiresias' remarks brilliantly unite the traditional role of Pentheus as ritual scapegoat with his present dramatic role as a leader whose willful blindness leads to his destruction. The name Pentheus echoed in this warning seems intended to evoke a deeper understanding than Pentheus has yet revealed, an apprehension of the unconscious forces depicted in his mythical prototype, which Pentheus, king of Thebes, chooses to ignore.

The choral ode immediately following this episode suggests its implications beyond the immediate circumstances. The chorus begin by appealing to divine or natural law (ὁσία, ll. 370-71), which in their eyes are one, extending its power over both "the gods and the earth." It is this law that Pentheus violates in refusing to worship Dionysus; he has expressed "unholy arrogance" toward Dionysus, and he is also the man of "lawless thoughtlessness" (ἀνόμου . . . ἀφροσύνας, l. 387). He has violated not only ὁσία but νομός, the law or custom of man. Like Tiresias, the chorus foresee disaster for Pentheus. As opposed to his lawlessness is their own "calm life" and "reason" (τὸ φρονεῖν, l. 390) which "remain tranquil" and hold the home together. The chorus then take up the subject of wisdom as opposed to "mere cleverness." Their position is entirely consistent with Tiresias', the repetition here, and throughout the play, indicating the extreme thematic importance of this dichotomy. They state directly, τὸ σοφὸν δ' οὐ σοφία ("cleverness is not wisdom," l. 395), and then intensify their meaning by declaring: "and thinking beyond what is mortal (τό τε μὴ θνητὰ φρονεῖν) is to have a short life." Such are the ways of madness (ll. 396-401).

They then express a wish that they "might go to Cyprus, the island of Aphrodite, where the gods of love dwell, charming the minds (θελξίφρονες) of mortals" (ll. 402-405). They speak of the fruitfulness of Paphos, and the beauty of Pieria, seat of the Muses, on the "holy slope of Olympus," and ask Dionysus as Bromius to lead them there, for "there are the Graces and there is Desire. There it is lawful for Bacchants to perform their rites" (ll. 406-15). Commentators have explained the references to Aphrodite and the Muses in a variety of ways, none of which is entirely convincing. To be sure, there is no question of Aphrodite's association with Dionysus as a symbol of fertility; as Dodds suggests: "her association with Dion., the other great Nature-power, is rooted both in popular thought and in the imagination of poets and artists." But Dodds, in saying that Aphrodite here "is a symbol not of sensuality but of the happiness and liberation which comes from the gay and reverent acceptance of natural impulse" (p. 123), ignores her connection in the passage with Πόθος, Desire, though he does point out that both Πόθος and the Graces (Χάριτες) are widely connected with worship of Dionysus (pp. 126-27). Kirk merely suggests that both in the reference to Cyprus and "in the unusual association of Pieria, the home of the Muses, with Desire, sexual love is used to symbolize freedom and peace."[51] They and others[52] automatically treat this section as a typical Euripidean "escapeode" or "prayer," and explain its meaning variously on this basis.

Although the chorus do express a desire to go to idyllic and fabled places, it seems far more profitable to consider the meaning of such symbols within the context of the entire ode than to take their wish literally. Cyprus, Paphos, and Pieria symbolize not only the "calm life" the chorus has spoken of earlier, but the places where love and desire affect the minds of men. Fertility, love, desire, and their expression in poetry are associated with the worship of Dionysus, and thus are evoked in opposition to Pentheus, the man who cannot accept love and responds to their god with aggression and hatred. Aphrodite, the gods of love ("Ερωτες), the Graces, and sexual Desire all convey man's powerful libidinal drives at once fostering his reason and controlled by it, and thus subduing his violence and aggression. It is perfectly consistent for the Bacchants, who have repeatedly emphasized sound thinking and continue to do so throughout the play, to wish not so much for escape as for a life devoted entirely to love and productivity, untroubled by the conflict and aggression they have just encountered.

There seems little doubt that Euripides perceived in Dionysiac myths and rites intrinsic civilizing functions, answering not only a human need for emotional expression but for rational control as well. Without any unnecessary anachronistic claims for his understanding of human development, it is certainly reasonable to assume that the playwright whose extant works reveal a remarkably explicit psychological sophistication would sense the basic conflicting forces of love and aggression enacted again and again in these myths and rites, and would seek at once to understand and express the ways in which such impulses determined human thought and conduct. The choral ode ends with further evidence of his concern with the disparity between the decrees of the leaders of the state and the requirements of the "mind and heart" revealed in Dionysiac myth: the chorus say (ll. 427-31): "It is wise to hold back one's mind and heart from eminent men. What ordinary people have taken as their custom, this I would accept." This statement indicates Euripides' reliance not only on "the intuitive wisdom of the people,"[53] but on their more basic expression of the primordial heuristic meanings of the myth, which he incorporated into this play.

In the second episode, the image of the hunt is used to convey naked aggression against the civilizing influence of Dionysus. The image of the hunter and his prey, which is a dominant one throughout the rest of the *Bacchae*, has been traced in detail by several critics,[54] and it is unnecessary to repeat this process, but no commentator has discussed the significance of this image in relation to the problem of sound thinking and the self-control that results, which is at the heart of Dionysiac myth and of Euripides' *Bacchae*. The obvious point that hunter and hunted are reversed in the course of the action has been made many times, but the fact that Pentheus, the original irrational hunter, becomes the prey of his frenzied mother and her band of equally frenzied followers only after he himself has been crazed by Dionysus suggests an intrinsic connection between the image of the hunt and the contending forces of aggression and love, frenzy and control, which constitute the central inner conflict of this play. The hunt as it is depicted in the *Bacchae* is primitive and possibly cannibalistic; the extended images of man as prey that foreshadow the climactic action, itself a hunt, may well reflect Euripides' feeling for the primordial origins of the myth in hunting tribes developing self-control through ceremonial frenzy and disciplined worship of a "new" god who was both hunter and nourisher, the god identified with violent beasts and the civilizing skills of agriculture. Certainly in the *Bacchae* the hunt is used both to express frenzied aggression and to depict control of violence through its ritual enactment.

In their first dialogue, Dionysus attempts to subdue Pentheus' aggression with reason. Like Tiresias and the chorus, he dwells on the nature of wisdom and restraint; the words σοφός, φρονεῖν, and others denoting mental processes or their effects appear throughout their argument, in which Euripides applies the wisdom he perceives in this myth of Dionysiac power to the philosophic questions on the nature of thought current in his own time. When Dionysus remarks that "all foreigners dance in these rites," and Pentheus rigidly answers that "they have far less sense than Hellenes," Dionysus explains that "in this respect, they are wise, rather, though their customs are different" (ll. 482-84). Dionysus' praise of the foreign may well reflect "one of the advances in thought due to the sophistic movement," as Dodds suggests (p. 138), but it is also a comment on the nature of wisdom—here exemplified by participation in rites that express basic human impulses and conflicts. Dionysus equates Pentheus' ignorance with impiety (l. 490), to which Pentheus responds by accusing Dionysus of sophistic arguments (l. 491). Actually, it is clear that Pentheus persistently avoids understanding the nature of the god before him, preferring his own sophistic arguments to the challenge of a new view of himself and human nature. Here Euripides seems more critical of than indebted to the sophistic method; he counters clever but essentially destructive argumentation with the wisdom of myth.

When it becomes clear to Pentheus that he cannot frighten Dionysus, he turns to force and orders him seized. In warning Pentheus not to bind him, Dionysus declares directly that he is self-controlled, Pentheus is not (αὐδῶ με μὴ δεῖν σωφρονῶν οὐ σώφροσιν. l. 504), and then, when Pentheus persists in applying force, Dionysus responds by exposing Pentheus' total ignorance of his own nature: "You do not know how you live, what you do, or who you are" (l. 506). It is essential to observe that Dionysus' comment on Pentheus' aggression is a direct and comprehensive revelation of his inability or unwillingness to know himself. Even Pentheus seems momentarily stunned by this exposure. The only answer he is able to summon is his name and the names of his parents. In Dionysus' response, Euripides again recalls the meaning of Pentheus' name: "You are adapted in your name for misfortune" (l. 508). Countering Pentheus' refusal to understand his own motives and acts, Dionysus uses his very name to suggest the grief inherent in his willful ignorance; Pentheus is forever defined by his inner self, which he refuses to understand or accept.

The chief function of the choral ode following this episode is to emphasize the folly and arrogance of Pentheus in denying Dionysus, whose power is made to seem as inevitable as that of nature itself. This power is certainly in evidence in the next scene, in which he calls on the forces of nature—an earthquake and lightning—to shake the palace of Pentheus and cause flames to leap up around the tomb of Semele. Furthermore, the god escapes from Pentheus' prison, leaving only an animal form of his, the bull, to greet the astonished Pentheus. In the face of Pentheus' rage and violence in this scene, Dionysus remains calm, indicating his restraint as a model for human conduct: πρὸς σοφοῦ γὰρ ἀνδρὸς ἀσκεῖν σώφρον' εὐοργησίαν ("It is the nature of a wise man to practice restrained gentleness of temper," 1. 641). It is interesting that the word for gentleness of temper, εὐοργησία, contains the word ὀργή, "natural impulse," which is, of course, in its plural form, the word most commonly used for the rites of Dionysus.

When Pentheus and Dionysus come together, after the upheaval, they once again argue about the nature of wisdom. Pentheus (1. 655) accuses Dionysus of being wise except in that in which he should be wise, his implication being that Dionysus merely knows all the right answers in an argument, to which Dionysus responds that in what he should most be wise, there indeed he is. To provide evidence of his wisdom before attempting further persuasion, Dionysus urges Pentheus to listen first to the Messenger who has just come from the mountains to which the women of Thebes have fled.

Even the first Messenger suggests the difficulty of persuading Pentheus that the god's claims are valid; he asks if he may speak freely, for he fears the king's "swiftness of temper" (τὸ . . . τάχος σου τῶν φρενῶν, 1. 670) and his wrath. Given leave to speak, the Messenger describes the Theban Bacchants living among the trees and animals, neither drunken nor licentious, as Pentheus imagines, but (1. 686) "self-controlled" (σωφρόνως, once again). He emphasizes their closeness to nature—some of the women offer their breasts to fawns or the cubs of wolves—and the spontaneous fertility of the earth, from which they derive milk and honey. Their rites, though frenzied and ecstatic, are apparently in accord with the laws of nature, for the mountains and the wild animals join in the worship of Bacchus.

The Messenger goes on to describe the sudden shift in mood resulting from Agave's discovery of him and his followers, who seemed to her to be "hunting" the Bacchants. Addressing the women as "running hounds," she urged them on to violence and destruction. The self-controlled worshipers are now transformed into wild hunters, dismembering animals and stripping the flesh from their bones. They invade the Thebans' homes, snatching their infants. Impervious to harm themselves, they wound those who rush to attack them (ll. 731-68).

As if to underline the evidence he has provided for the necessity of accepting Dionysiac worship, the Messenger ends his account with a plea to Pentheus to receive this god who is so powerful and who gave man the vine. The scene he has described is consistent with the concept of Dionysiac worship developed throughout the play: when accepted, it fosters self-control and productivity; opposed, it results in violence. The reversion of the Theban maenads, in the face of opposition, to a wild and disordered hunting band indicates the powerful aggression that the Dionysiac rites had channeled. These are new and reluctant initiates; their control is only partial, for they have too long denied the god. This scene merely foreshadows the more violent and tragic hunt that is the climax of the play.

Far from being persuaded by the Messenger's report, Pentheus is more eager to seize the women by force. Although Dionysus is aware of Pentheus' obstinate refusal to yield, he persists in trying to warn him not to take arms against a god. Pentheus' response again reveals his unwillingness to learn: οὐ μὴ φρενώσεις μ' ("Do not teach me," l. 792). But Dionysus does continue to try to teach Pentheus to regulate his feelings through ritual enactment: (ll. 794-95) "Sacrifice to the god, rather than, in a rage, kick against the goad, a mortal against a deity." To Pentheus, however, the word "sacrifice" means only the expression of his rage in violence. Playing contemptuously on Dionysus' words, he echoes him: (ll. 796-97) "Indeed, I will sacrifice, stirring up much bloodshed of women—as they deserve—in the glades of Cithaeron." When Dionysus offers to bring the women back peacefully, without arms, Pentheus accuses him of plotting against him. Dionysus' last appeal is simple and direct (l. 806): "I wish to save you through my art," but Pentheus, just as directly, demands arms and orders Dionysus to speak no more, a clear choice of force over reason.

Neither the words nor the "art" of Dionysus can elicit gentleness from Pentheus to temper his aggression. His libidinal impulses emerge only in response to Dionysus' suggestion that he spy on the Bacchants and observe their forbidden rites. Euripides employs the traditional myth of the king who denies Dionysus and is thus maddened and destroyed by him in both its elemental and contemporary senses. Throughout Pentheus' appearance in this play, he is incapable of accepting love as a force that subdues and modifies the violent aggression that consumes him. Thus, he enacts a refusal to accept the earliest function of Dionysiac rite, and he retains certain qualities of the traditional sacrificial victim. But he is also Euripides' contemporary, expressing many layers of emotional as well as social and religious history in his complex and sometimes devious responses. His refusal to understand his own arrogance and his fantasies of omnipotence, his sophistic games with truth, and his attribution of his own prurience and lust to others are civilized man's various expressions of his inability sufficiently to control and direct his own instinctual drives. His pathetic delight in his prospective role of voyeur is a remarkable revelation of his inability to express joy and love, to achieve the soundness of mind explicitly designated as Bacchic in this play. The perversion of his libido is indicated in his fantasies of the obscenity he will observe. Pentheus is Euripides' version of those who have been incapable of self-knowledge and control in the most basic sense, beginning with the ritual prototype created by primordial man and continuing in various historical representatives to his own contemporaries who wasted Hellas with war and employed specious argumentation in the name of truth.

In instigating Pentheus' madness and death, Dionysus and

the chorus enact the operation of primordial feelings and conflicts in the continuous history of human beings. Instructing the chorus, Dionysus emphasizes their effect on Pentheus' mind (ll. 850-53): they are to "put him out of his mind" (ἔκστησον φρενῶν) and make him mad, for, "in his senses" (ὡς φρονῶν . . . εὖ) he would not put on women's clothing. If, however, "he is driven from sanity" (ἔξω δ᾽ ἐλαύνων τοῦ φρονεῖν), he will do so. Having indicated that this is the clothing Pentheus will wear when he goes to Hades after he has been slain by his mother, Dionysus goes on to speak of himself as (ll. 860-61) "a most terrible god, but kindest to men," designations that do not seem contradictory when one recognizes the nature of his gifts: self-control and productivity, the rejection of which results in madness and destruction.

As he approaches the climax, Euripides returns to the image of the hunt, employing it with a new intensity. The chorus, relieved to have escaped Pentheus' aggression, compare themselves to a fawn eluding its hunters. Turning once more to the subject of wisdom in the refrain, they now define it simply as the conquest of one's enemies, a view clarified in the antistrophe, in which it is evident that their enemies are those (ll. 885-87) "who honor senseless pride and, in their mad judgment, do not foster the efforts of the gods." This insane arrogance is in opposition to "law," which the gods defend; "they hunt the impious one, for a man must never judge or act beyond what is lawful" (ll. 890-92). The chorus' conception of "law" reminds one of Tiresias' earlier expression of respect for age-old custom: "What is divine and what is lawful for a great length of time," they say, "exists forever in accordance with nature" (ll. 894-96). Thus, in their view, Dionysiac religion reflects law that emerges from basic human attributes. This ode is the prelude to the last encounter between Dionysus and Pentheus, who, in defying the god, calls upon himself the natural and human violence this law was created to control.

Pentheus' hallucinatory state is merely a more obvious and more exaggerated form of the "madness" he has displayed and been accused of throughout the play. He has earlier referred to Dionysus as an animal—as prey; now he sees him as a bull (ll. 920, 922). His intense fear of and hatred for the Bacchants is here revealed as a cover for his prurient curiosity and envy of the licentious behavior he imagines they indulge in. His earlier self-deception and boastfulness are now increased to the point where he asks whether he could carry the glens of Cithaeron and the Bacchants themselves on his shoulders.

In encouraging these fantasies, Dionysus is indeed the "terrible" god he has admitted being, for his nature is determined by the ambivalent mind of man, struggling for self-knowledge and caught in delusion. In this last dialogue between Dionysus and Pentheus, the god mocks Pentheus' delusions with ironic praise for his μεθέστηκας φρενῶ (his "converted mind," l. 944); he says, "Before your mind was not healthy, but now you have one that befits you" (ll. 947-48).

Responding to the frenzy of Pentheus, the chorus call forth the "hounds of madness" (l. 977). Taking on the role of hunters, they cry out for the prey, suggesting that Pentheus is the offspring not of a woman but of a lioness or of Libyan gorgons. Yet they are constantly mindful of the discipline Dionysiac worship demands; in the refrain of this ode they declare that Pentheus must be killed by justice (ll. 991f., 1013f.) because he is a man, ἄθεον ἄνομον ἄδικον ("without god, without law, without justice," ll. 995, 1015). Furthermore, in this ode, as throughout the play, they emphasize the necessity for control and sound judgment as conditions of human life. The text of lines 1002-1004 is disputed,[55] but it is evident that in these lines the chorus attempt to express a reasonable justification for the plan to kill Pentheus: religious law, based on sound judgment, demands the death of the violent man, Pentheus, who opposes that law and the god who requires its fulfillment, "but, unhesitating, to accept those things that belong to the gods is right for mortals and brings about a life without grief." The "things that belong to the gods" clearly involve laws of behavior that emerge from deeper impulses and more urgent needs than τό σοφόν, which the chorus say they do not "grudge" (l. 1005), but they recognize its limited meaning in the lives of men.

If one is aware of the original function of Dionysiac myth and rite persisting in the climactic *sparagmos* of Pentheus, then there is no contradiction between the chorus' repetition here of its earlier concern with "soundness of judgment" and the intensity of its rallying cry to Dionysus in his various animal forms of bull, snake, and lion. The rite that expresses the integration of instinctual aims includes the violent and aggressive as well as the tender and loving, and enacts both the refusal and final acceptance of inner control. In the *Bacchae* the savagery of the primordial hunt is used both to recall this rite and to indicate its symbolic expression of continuous human conflict. This is the knowledge that goes beyond τὸ σοφόν, which Pentheus denies and which Agave finally acquires at a dreadful cost.

In the second Messenger's report of the violence of the Theban Bacchants there are many details connected with traditional ritual: Agave in the role of "priestess" begins the slaughter of what she takes to be a lion cub; the other women join in a typical ritual *sparagmos*. Even the fact that Pentheus is actually the son of Agave does not necessarily place this scene outside its traditional context. As is well known and has been discussed above, this is but one example of many ancient mythical tales in which a parent who has denied Dionysus is maddened and kills his own offspring.

Yet this scene is not merely a literary depiction of traditional myth and rite. The shrieks of Pentheus and especially his pleas to his maddened mother to recognize him as her son as well as the dramatic expression of Agave's delusion and violence reveal the psychic conflicts that produced this ancient pattern. Furthermore, Pentheus' arrogance and violence throughout the play have provided a realistic background against which his punishment takes on a contemporary as well as a perennial meaning. The comment with which the Messenger concludes his dreadful tale, "Self-control and reverence for the gods are best" (τὸ σωφρονεῖν δὲ καὶ σέβειν τὰ τῶν θεῶν / κάλλιστον, ll. 1150-51) reiterates the exhortations of the chorus, Dionysus, and Tiresias throughout the play, and points up the social meaning of Dionysiac worship. Pentheus, who, as ruler, has represented the inherent violence of the rigid, has become the victim of his own unwillingness to understand himself and other human beings.

Pentheus as a character is less moving than his fate; Agave, on the other hand, is almost unbearably touching in her struggle to know herself and in the agony of achieving this knowledge. In murdering her son, she acts out a pattern of untamed aggression and psychic confusion repeatedly expressed in myths recounting *sparagmos* and intended or actual *omophagia*. As she moves from the role of primordial hunter, offering as food for a banquet the son she has slain, to that of a tragic protagonist gradually recognizing her own deeds and the forces symbolized in the god who motivated her, she transmits the pain of human beings' perennial struggle with the conflicting drives that determine their nature. The dignity of her final acceptance not only of what she has done but of the consequences of her acts reflects her achievement of that integrity or soundness of mind that is the goal of Dionysiac worship.

It has been pointed out that "in the state-cults, at Athens at least, much of the original madness of Dionysiac worship was purged away, though Dionysus could never be pressed into the Olympian mould. . . ."[56] Perhaps Euripides first perceived even in these stylized ceremonies the turbulent quest for inner harmony that created such depictions of ritual madness. It is also possible that, writing the *Bacchae* in Macedonia, where the rites were closer to their original form, he saw a connection between the opposing aims they depicted and the conflicts that determined the character of his own society—the debilitating wars among the Greek states, the struggle for control of the Athenian Assembly, the often puerile philosophical disputes over the nature of wisdom, law, and justice. In the *Bacchae*, Euripides is neither in favor of nor opposed to Dionysus or, for that matter, any of the other characters; nor does he warn against the danger of repressing sexual or other feelings. Employing a myth that early man gradually formed to portray his unconscious strivings to internalize the changing conditions of his environment and to regulate the demands of his own nature, Euripides recreated its drama as a continual conflict of the human spirit, never entirely resolved, but ever producing more devious and more powerful vehicles of expression.

OTHER ANCIENT PROTOTYPES

THE *Oresteia*

Like Dionysus, the Erinyes, the pursuers of Orestes, emerge from a primitive tribal conception. Like him, also, they inflict madness as a form of vengeance. Probably the Erinyes were originally conceived as curses, and there is evidence to suggest that they were potent forces in the Aegean area long before the Greek settlers arrived.[57] Farnell's discusson of the Erinyes confirms his judgment: "For the study of early ethical-religious ideas, as of the special evolution of Greek religion, no personal forms are of greater significance than those of the 'Ερινύες." He provides convincing evidence to identify them as "originally the personal curse" or "the curse-force externalized." His explanation of this phenomenon elucidates the role of the daemon or "evil spirit" in Aeschylean tragedy: "The strong mental emotion is conceived as 'demoniac,' and being projected into the unseen world without is identified with some vague 'numen' of divine causative power." "Personifications," such as the Erinyes are thus "by no means a mark of later reflective thought, but a primitive habit of mind."[58]

Since the Erinyes take vengeance chiefly, though not exclusively, on those who have murdered their kindred, they are of some importance in the study of primitive and ancient conceptions of mental disturbance resulting from familial conflict and its consequences. Their relationship with Orestes, moreover, is critical to the theme and action of Aeschylus' *Oresteia*.[59] The Erinyes are alluded to in Homer[60] and appear in many ancient works, but it is in the *Oresteia* that they have a major role. It has long been recognized that in this trilogy Aeschylus reconstructs primordial symbolizations of curse and pollution that result in madness: "In Aeschylus himself, fortunately, we still find the materials from which these deities were constructed, and the various stages of the method by which they caused madness."[61]

Aeschylus treats the Erinyes both as inner voices and as externalized projections, thus representing different perceptions of them, each of which enlarges the other. Both elucidate the ways in which these primitive symbolizations became intrinsic to the functioning originally of the family and later of the state. The ancient symbols retain their original causal connections with the concepts they externalize even when they are later employed in the service of rational and productive ends.

Madness in the *Oresteia* descends from the past, infects the present, and is finally controlled by communal action that looks forward to the future. The madness caused by the Erinyes is not the personal affliction of an isolated individual but the disease of the ruling house of Argos and therefore of the state itself, a concept that is clarified by John Jones's definition of the term "House" as "a psycho-physical community of the living and the dead and the unborn."[62] Jones's emphasis on the role of the *"oikos"* or "House" is salutary in counteracting commentaries that dwell on the supposed personal motivations of the protagonists, which simply do not exist in the trilogy. In his generally useful discussion of the communal, *oikos*-centered determinations of the action, however, Jones sometimes views the central conflict as merely the outgrowth of social and economic institutions. What Jones calls the "psycho-physical force" (p. 135) of the Furies must be explored not only in relation to the economic and social arrangements it enters into, but also as a manifestation of psychological determinants. One can only applaud his efforts to discredit commentaries on Aeschylus' "conscious archaising" and on the dramatist's "intention to oppose civilized principles of equity and morals to the savagery of blood-guilt, pollution, and ritual purgation," but his conclusion that in the *Oresteia* the "sophisticated and primitive worlds are both fictions" (pp. 106-112) is open to serious question.

Inherited guilt and the daemon pervading the family and

the house, the very notion of the "psychic impregnation of material objects," which Jones mentions (note 2, pp. 92-93), and the physical appearance and savagery of the Furies themselves are all primitive concepts. To be sure, there is no evidence to suggest that Aeschylus viewed these primitive elements from a superior "civilized" point of view, but one can hardly therefore conclude that his trilogy is a mere representation of "psycho-physical pollution" (p. 107). Primitive guilt, vengeance, and madness are intrinsic to the mythical narrative of the *Oresteia* and thus to its subject and theme: a concept of justice at once rooted in and evolving out of these ancient sources.

Justice, explaining her function, in a fragment of a lost tragedy by Aeschylus, declares: ". . . in the reckless I engender a temperate mind."[63] As Hugh Lloyd-Jones points out, *Dike*, which means not only justice but "the order of the universe,"[64] is inextricably connected with the Erinyes, who protect her (p. 83) or help to enforce her rule (p. 93). In the *Oresteia*, as in the *Bacchae*, justice is associated with divine promotion of madness, the very means of producing the σώφρονασ . . . φρένας to which the fragment refers, the soundness of mind that is the ultimate aim of the creation and the mediation of symbols of irrationality and violence.

The Erinys or Erinyes are mentioned several times before the murder of the king in *Agamemnon*, in connection with Paris and Helen and in a general warning by the chorus that the "black Furies" bring "to darkness" a man who has prospered "unjustly" (ll. 462-69). The most remarkable allusion to "the Fury" in this play is made by the chorus after Agamemnon's triumphant return to Argos. In spite of their desire to rejoice and to deny the fears that beset them, the Elders reluctantly acknowledge the revelations of their own souls: "And yet my soul within, without a lyre, self-taught, sings the dirge of the Fury" (ll. 990-92). Thus, long before the Erinyes appear as personified avengers, the chorus express their awareness that the Furies come from within; the madness they inflict is "self-taught," the individual response to familial and social discord. Yet soon after, responding to Cassandra's vision of "a net of Death," the chorus ask her "what Erinyes" she calls upon the house of Agamemnon (ll. 1114-20). Later, in Cassandra's prophecy (ll. 1189-90) and in Clytemnestra's and Aegisthus' justifications (ll. 1580-82) for the murder of Agamemnon, the Erinyes are clearly avenging spirits who inhabit the house and, in the last instance, are said to have spun the robe in which Agamemnon was entangled, a combination of the symbolic and the literal material of the drama.

Before the Erinyes appear to Orestes in the *Choephori*, he reveals his fears of these spirits, who, according to the oracle of Apollo, will overwhelm him if he does not avenge his father's death. Here, as in Homer and Hesiod, the Erinyes are described as emerging from the earth, to inflict hideous diseases, madness, and terror on man. This speech (ll. 269-306) undoubtedly retains some of the most primitive fantasies involved in the concept of the curse of the unavenged dead. Certainly its details suggest that the curse in its origins was a means of conveying largely unconscious and conflicting feelings regarding murder, guilt, and responsibility—the emergence of conscience in images of violent aggression against the offender.

The imagined afflictions are both physical and mental: "the wrath of the malignant spirits" (δυσφρόνων, the root of which is φρήν; thus they are literally opposed to the mind) brings ulcers and sores that eat away at human bodies, and, in the form of the Erinyes, madness and "empty" or groundless terror in the night. The fear of the dead themselves, who lie in the earth and who reappear at night in "empty" dreams and fantasies, and the conflict and guilt associated with the murder of a blood relative are projected onto shadowy, threatening fantasy figures. These not only provide evidence of the "involuntary" nature of primitive imagination, and the connection of this process with "image-making,"[65] but also indicate the role of externalized fantasies in the development of a sense of guilt and responsibility. Aeschylus himself recreates this development in the dramatic evolution of the Erinyes in the *Oresteia*.

In this evolution, Orestes' conflict and madness are crucial. Vengeance is demanded of him by a primitive concept symbolized in a threatened curse of madness on those who refuse this obligation; also, as he himself says, even if he distrusts the message of the oracle, he is driven by the loss of the kingdom, his grief, and his rage against the murderers. Nonetheless, vengeance demands that he himself become a murderer and, worse than that, the slayer of his own mother. His conflict is most dramatically portrayed in the scene in which, determined to kill Clytemnestra, he wavers, turns to Pylades for confirmation of his obligation, finally commits the matricide, and is then confronted with the Erinyes, who demand retribution for her death.

Referring to the matricide, Orestes says that his "victory is a pollution" (l. 1017); soon after, he describes his mind or wits (φρένες) as overpowered and carried away. In images that suggest a reference to ancient rites, which are remarkably similar to twentieth-century primitive rituals of mourning,[66] he declares, "In my heart, fear is ready to sing and dance in wrath" (ll. 1023-25). When he cries out in terror at the appearance of the Erinyes, whom he compares with Gorgons, the members of the chorus ask "what fancies" trouble him, for they do not see the Furies. But to Orestes, "these are no fancies of calamity." The chorus attribute the "fancies" to pollution: "It is the blood still fresh on your hands. From this a disturbance attacks your mind" (ll. 1055-56). The question of the imagined or actual presence of the Erinyes is left open. Orestes' direct statement: "You do not see them, but I do see them; I am driven from here and can no longer stay" (ll. 1061-62) suggests that, even if these are inner visions, they are to be accepted as sufficient cause for seeking the prescribed cleansing of Apollo. Actually, there is no clear distinction in the *Oresteia* between the Fury who sings within the soul of the chorus or sings and dances within the heart of Orestes and the externalized pursuer. The threatening fantasy figure is both a personified force incorporating social prohibitions and punishments and an internalized agent of control by guilt and fear.

Orestes describes the Erinyes in their first appearance as "malignant hounds" (l. 1054), a phrase Clytemnestra had used earlier (l. 924) in warning him to beware the avengers of a mother. This is but one of many animal images employed throughout the *Oresteia* in connection with the pervasive metaphor of the hunt,[67] which reaches its greatest intensity in the Erinyes' pursuit of Orestes in the *Eumenides*, where they are compared to a pack of savage hounds tracking their human prey by the scent of blood on his hands.

Orestes' madness is depicted and implicitly defined as the guilt and suffering resulting from this pursuit. At the beginning of the *Eumenides*, he is discovered by the prophetess of Delphi at the *omphalos*, his hands dripping with blood, holding a sword and the olive-branch of the suppliant, the signs of his role of murderer and of his efforts to find release from the Erinyes, who lie before him, asleep. The ghost of Clytemnestra enters the dreams of these monstrous creatures (*Eumenides*, l. 117) and demands that they put this dream of violent chase into action (ll. 131-32), a dramatic portrayal of the primitive fusion of dream or fantasy with reality. Once the Erinyes are accepted as inevitable pursuers of the polluted, neither Orestes' speech nor his actions can be regarded as irrational. In fact, in Aeschylus' conception of the mythical character, they are exemplary. In both the *Odyssey* and the *Oresteia*, Orestes' vengeance on the murderers of his father is the fulfillment of an inherited code. But there are important differences: in Homer, Orestes is not depicted as troubled by doubts before the act of vengeance or pursued by the Furies after it; Aeschylus' Orestes not only hesitates before committing the prescribed murders, but afterward is pursued and tormented like a "bleeding fawn" (ll. 247-48).

Orestes is, however, not only the executor and victim of the code of blood vengeance; he is finally its challenger. "Taught by suffering" (*Eumenides*, l. 276), as he describes himself, he has been cleansed and declared free of pollution by Apollo. Nevertheless, he is pursued by the Furies, who insist that they will continue to feed on him and consume his strength. In the anomaly of his position lies the challenge to the principle of inherited blood vengeance. Although Apollo has purified Orestes, the god realizes that the threat of the Furies still hangs over him, and he sends him to Athens, where, he says, Athena will take up his cause. Orestes defends himself on two bases: he committed matricide in accordance with an inherited code, and he has endured the harsh discipline of seeking expiation. Still, when he pleads for the help of Athena, although he insists that he is no longer a suppliant requiring purification, he asks the goddess to judge him. Thus, his long search for release from the cruelty and violence of the Furies and his insistence that he comes unpolluted before a new code of law finally lead to his trial, his vindication, and, more important, the transformation of the Furies, through the persuasion of Athena, into the Gracious Ones.

He is condemned to madness by a primitive code of vengeance; he is released from the last vestiges of this pollution by a jury trial. The images of the hunt throughout the trilogy, and especially in the dreams of the Furies and in their pursuit of their prey, Orestes, recreate the inner world of the victim of the curse in which the Erinyes originated. But if the Erinyes project processes of mind that do not quite differentiate the self from the bestial, the dead, or the imaginary, they also personify an early quest for social justice, however primitive, in which the murderer, in his madness, internalizes the emerging tribal demand for regulation of impulsive violence.

In *Phaedrus* (244D-E), Plato suggests that one of the benefits of madness is its conversion of guilt into prayer and expiation. Although he does not mention Orestes, the example he gives of families who have endured "disease and the greatest suffering from some ancient bloodguilt" would certainly include the House of Atreus. So too would his conception of how madness has appeared within them, and, through prophecy, has led them to "purification and sacred rites" and thus brought them "a means of release." Madness is both a manifestation of guilt and an avenue of deliverance from its ravages.

The role of the Erinyes in the *Oresteia* is as ambiguous as Orestes'. Throughout the *Eumenides*, they cry out for justice, the very word seeming an outrage within the context of their bloodthirsty hunt. Even more striking, before the trial by jury in the *Eumenides*, they speak of the danger of *hubris*, and of the "health in the mind" from which "dear and longed-for prosperity comes" (ll. 532-37). Ironically, the goddesses whose influence has been described as a disease throughout the play instigate the struggle for a health of mind, a form of justice, which only their own conversion can bring about. Within the curse lie the seeds of conscience; the perpetrator of vengeance is also the suppliant, seeking not only release from the madness of guilt but a concept of justice more objective, more removed from the influence of dream and fantasy than the family or clan can administer. Aeschylus is explicit in thus commemorating "the first trial for bloodshed" (*Eumenides*, l. 682) by the council of Areopagus, a court that exemplifies the substitution of state law for the primordial concept of vengeance.

Yet, even as he commemorates this institution, he depicts its first jury as divided, for half would not free Orestes. The influence of the Erinyes is persistent and is mitigated only by Athena. It remains so to the end of the *Oresteia*. The old goddesses are persuaded by Athena to bestow the blessings of fruitfulness on the land, for they have not been vanquished (ll. 795-96), and their power remains mighty (ll. 950-51). It is, moreover, Athena who issues the warning that the evils of the past bring a man before these goddesses and destroy him (ll. 934-37). Identified with the Semnae at the end of the *Oresteia*, the Erinyes nonetheless remain symbolizations of instinctual aggression turned upon the self, binding human beings to their own history, even as these goddesses, and the sense of guilt intrinsic to their function, are adapted to controlling, civilizing, and productive aims.

The intricate connections among aggression, guilt, madness, and conscience are objectified in the *Oresteia*. Although the Orestes of Aeschylus' trilogy is never as explicit as Euripides' Orestes in identifying his terror of the Erinyes as "his conscience" (*Orestes*, 1. 396), too much has been made of this obvious difference in the treatment of this figure by the two dramatists.[68] In Euripides' *Orestes, Electra,* and *Iphigenia at Tauris,* the Erinyes pursue Orestes, as they do in the *Oresteia,* both as inner visions and as externalized beings. Euripides may be more direct in indicating their function as inner forces, but it is their objective dramatic role in the *Oresteia* that most graphically conveys the very morphology of the feelings that entered into their creation as mythical figures—unconscious aggression and guilt expressed in dreams and fantasies, channeled through the formation and internalization of a tribal belief in pollution, which evolved into a conception of justice.

CASSANDRA

A second type of madness in the *Oresteia,* the prophetic frenzy of Cassandra, is also a dramatic version of a very ancient and influential social institution. Although the prophetic powers of Cassandra herself are first mentioned in Pindar (*Pythian* xi, 33), the tradition and practice of "ecstatic prophecy," which her character reflects, go back to much earlier times. Dodds suggests that "prophetic madness is at least as old in Greece as the religion of Apollo. And it may well be older still." He makes the further point that "If the Greeks were correct in connecting μάντις with μαίνομαι—and most philologists think they were—the association of prophecy and madness belongs to the Indo-European stock of ideas."[69] The tradition of prophecy is widespread and complex, not only in Indo-European societies but throughout the ancient Near East, involving cults, gods, or, for the ancient Israelites, God, rites, and a variety of customs and attitudes that cannot be discussed here, but one of its essential features—its reliance on processes of mind generally associated with madness or at least a type of frenzy—is particularly relevant in connection with the prophetic role and utterance of Cassandra.

There is abundant evidence that the ancient Greeks, like the Hebrews and other ancient peoples, accepted and even encouraged the bizarre conduct and expression of the prophet because these served a social function. Prophecy was regarded as a special form of madness, a perception of reality unavailable to the rational mind. In the vast literature on the prophets of the Old Testament, there is much disagreement on the question of the mental stability of these Biblical figures. Like the shaman, the prophet has been examined—most often retrospectively—in accordance with the standards of mental health of mechanized societies of the twentieth century. A less rigid approach is taken by George Rosen, who expresses his indebtedness to Ruth Benedict, Melville S. Herskovits, and other anthropologists who have demonstrated the effects of cultural attitudes on evaluations of extreme psychic manifestations. Rosen emphasizes the basic connection of the Hebrew prophets' psychic experience with "communal traditions and problems."

In discussing the mental experience manifested in the prophetic madness of the Old Testament prophets, Rosen is more concerned with exploring their use of unconscious processes than with determining the exact degree of their mental stability:

> Apparently in various human populations, perhaps in all, there are numbers of individuals who are capable of experiences such as possession and trance. These experiences, which may occur under a variety of circumstances, are characterized in current psychiatric terminology as dissociative states, that is, conditions where there is a division of consciousness with a segregation of mental processes and ideas to such an extent that they function as unitary wholes as if belonging to another person. These states and the experiences associated with them are not innately religious in character, but religious interpretations and values may be attributed to them, thus endowing them with special significance for a given group.

Rosen's emphasis on the "socio-cultural milieu"[70] in which such mental states are induced and employed illuminates the ways in which prophetic frenzy functioned in ancient societies.

Certainly, one of the central questions to be raised in connection with the nature of prophetic madness is its method of seeking insight and enlightenment for the communities in which it functioned. The best ancient analysis of the relationship between madness and insight is Plato's in the *Timaeus* (71E-72A), where he describes the divine gift of prophecy as a vehicle of "truth." No one, he says, achieves prophetic powers when he is rational, but only in the mental states brought about by "sleep" or "disease" or by the "inspiration of a god." He goes on to make a vital distinction between the functions of two states of mind: that in which prophetic powers emerge and that of the more rational condition proper to interpretation of prophecy. Only "when he is rational should a man recollect and meditate on what has been spoken in a dream or waking vision by the prophetic and inspired nature and the many visionary images seen." One can interpret such products only "by reason," distinguishing what is significant and "judging for whom the prophecies are bad or good in the future, the past, or the present." Plato insists that "it is not the task of the person who has been frenzied and continues to be so to judge the appearances and voices by himself; for it was well spoken of old that only for the sound of mind is it proper to do and to know his own affairs and himself."[71]

Plato describes a deliberate use of what would now be called unconscious processes for the purpose of self-knowledge and understanding of events—not only in the future but in the past and present as well. The passage reveals a complex attitude toward the "frenzied" mental state in which prophetic visions and utterances occur: dreams, fantasies, inner voices are valuable, often divinely inspired, and potential sources of great wisdom; the mind, however, when producing them, is not "sound" and therefore not fit for rational interpretation of their significance. Prophecy is thus the application of reasoning or conscious processes to the products of unconscious ones—dreams or visual and auditory hallucinations—however occasioned, by sleep, sickness, or divine inspiration.

Plato's remarks clarify many characteristic features of the dramatic portrayal of prophecy in ancient Greek tragedy and are of particular interest in connection with Cassandra in the *Agamemnon*, who is divinely inspired, experiences anguish as she perceives dreadful visions of the past and future, and combines the roles of frenzied recipient of prophetic knowledge and rational interpreter. Unlike the Pythia at Delphi or the priestesses at Dodona and other oracular centers, Cassandra does not perform established rites as a prelude to prophecy. These priestesses, moreover, did not interpret their own oracles; this art was left to specialists to whom the recipient brought the prophetic riddles. Nonetheless, there is a relationship between the prophetic frenzy depicted in the *Agamemnon* and what is known regarding the conduct of these priestesses as well as more spontaneous prophets in ancient society. Most authorities would agree with H. W. Parke that it was not vapors or drugs that induced oracular powers but the priestesses' "own state of mind which was the determining factor."[72] At Delphi, a "simple peasant woman was brought up from childhood with the current local belief that once seated on the tripod in the inner sanctuary inspiration would come from Apollo,"[73] a tradition that reflects a long history of reliance upon access to irrational or unconscious processes for communal purposes. Cassandra's frenzy is a dramatic creation of the quest for extraordinary experience and insight within one's own being, which is then communicated in verbal symbols.

The first descriptions of Cassandra by the chorus as "like a wild animal" (l. 1063) and by Clytemnestra as "mad" and as "hearing her own frenzied thoughts" (l. 1064) indicate that the prophetic mood is upon her. Soon after, she calls out to Apollo, the traditional divine source of her oracular powers. Accepting the god as the agent of both suffering and wisdom, who induces the irrational mental state in which unconscious knowledge is released, Cassandra allows herself access to the painful memories of and violent associations related to her family's and nation's destruction and her own deprivation of all that she valued. These emerge in the disordered images produced by self-induced trance and, accompanying them, rage against and fear of the destroyer of her people and now her own master—Agamemnon, whose past with its "primal guilt" (l. 1192) and violence she dares to face unflinchingly, although it has determined her own fate. The traditional acceptance of the "unsound" mind, as Plato puts it, as the vehicle through which prophecy emerges removes the normal inhibitions—which the chorus convey—against reliving suffering that has, at least to some extent, been suppressed, and enduring the knowledge of its further implications.

In the series of images in which Cassandra's prophecies emerge, the violence of the past is interspersed with that of the present and the future. First she envisions the children of Thyestes lamenting over their murder by Atreus and their consumption by their father. This is followed by an image of Clytemnestra reaching forth her hand to slay Agamemnon, and then an even more graphic one of the murder itself. To the chorus, these visions are evidence that Cassandra is "frenzied of mind, possessed by a god" (l. 1140) and, as she continues to rave about her imminent death, the ruinous love of Paris for Helen, her own childhood, and the destruction of Troy, the disordered chronology and the combination of exact details of the past with threatening images of the future—a relentless Fury, a bull trapped by his mate—do suggest a mind incapable of sequential associations or self-control. But in her frenzy Cassandra expresses a wisdom beyond conscious or reasoned logic; the images she sees convey the inevitable emotional and moral relationships among past, present, and future. They indicate the intrinsic connection between the fall of Troy and the violence inherent in the house of Atreus, between corruption in the state and individual suffering and death. In fact, her wild visions articulate for the chorus the warnings repressed in their own souls, "the dirge of the Erinys" they have refused to hear.

After her intense emotional portrayal of these inner visions, Cassandra attempts more rational communication with the chorus. She becomes her own interpreter as she tells them: "I will no longer teach you through riddles" (l. 1183). Now she warns them directly of the Erinyes, chanting their song of "primal guilt" within the house of Atreus (ll. 1188-97). Although she is soon overcome again by the "terrible suffering" of prophecy (ll. 1215-16), she continues to interpret her own images of the violent past and future, and the chorus confess their terror at the "truth" (ll. 1243-44) she imparts.

It has been demonstrated that "Dionysiac possession has much in common with mantic possession," a similarity more apparent in the Cassandra of Euripides' *The Trojan Women* [74] than in Aeschylus' character, for Euripides' Cassandra is more clearly and directly "possessed" [75] by a god. Unquestionably, although Apollo is named as the god who inspires her, the "mantic frenzy" of Euripides' Cassandra "is described in Dionysiac terms." O'Brien-Moore suggests that the "connection of Dionysus and the Bacchic frenzy not only with mantic possession and its madness but with madness of any sort haunts Euripides' mind," and he indicates the many instances in *The Trojan Women, Orestes, Iphigenia in Aulis*, and other plays in which Euripides' very language reflects this association. Thus, for example, in *The Trojan Women*, the chorus respond to Cassandra's hymeneal ode by referring to her as βακχεύουσαν (l. 342), and Cassandra herself tells Hecuba that although she is possessed by the god (ἔνθεος), she will cease from Bacchic raving to prove that the Trojans in their defeat are more fortunate than the victorious Greeks (ll. 365-67). [76]

Euripides' view of prophetic insight as essentially Dionysiac is most apparent in Cassandra's wild ode and dance in celebration of Hymen. Like the god's followers in the *Bacchae*, the possessed woman is remarkably aware of the meaning of her bizarre conduct. Her strange "marriage-song," ostensibly about love and desire, includes recollections of fallen Troy and her slain father and brothers. Later, like the Cassandra of the *Agamemnon*, she interprets her own frenzy: her celebration of her "marriage" to her conqueror is actually a cry of vengeance, which she plans to take for the deaths of her father and brothers. Her ecstatic song is finally a prophecy of impending destruction to the Greeks. This ironic celebration points up a further irony: the conquerors in war face the dreadful consequences of their victory. The association of prophetic with Dionysiac frenzy in this play and elsewhere is based on more than the similar effects attributed to possession by a god, such as the wild physical manifestations that ensue. Both Dionysiac and mantic frenzy are actually social and religious adaptations of the products of unconscious mental processes: the deliberate use of trance, vision, fantasy, memory, and the concomitant intense emotive responses, in ceremony and rite that regulate and interpret their symbolic content.

AJAX

In ancient Greek tragedy, the types of madness discussed thus far—Dionysiac and mantic frenzy, and the obsessive guilt inflicted by the Furies—are not portrayed as resulting primarily from personal or idiosyncratic causes. The symptoms of such madness emerge as mental and psychological manifestations that were instrumental in determining and were themselves channeled by very ancient religious and social institutions. The first literary work in which madness is treated as essentially individual, a personal alienation from accepted social and political conduct, is Sophocles' *Ajax*.[77] Although Ajax himself has mythical roots as a cult hero in Athens and the Troad, and the "cult name of Athena Aiantis"[78] suggests an early ritual connection with the goddess who deludes him in Sophocles' drama, madness is probably a late and purely literary element of his story.[79] Certainly in Sophocles' tragedy, Ajax's conflict evokes the myths and legends of a heroic rather than a primitive era. As Bernard Knox suggests, "Ajax belongs to a world which for Sophocles and his audience had passed away—an heroic, half-mythic world which had its limitations but also its greatness, a world in which great friendships, and also great hatreds, endured forever."[80]

Concentrating on the famous speech (ll. 646-92) in which Ajax views his present ignominious role in relation to the inevitable change wrought by time, Knox discusses Sophocles' dramatic development of Ajax's character within the context of fifth-century Athenian democracy. Essentially, Knox views him as a figure whose traditional attitudes and values render him "unadaptable" to "political institutions which impose rotation and cession of power, which recognize and encourage change." He is a hero whose stubborn adherence to "the old code and its claims for permanence" lead to his renunciation of life itself. Knox's sensitive treatment of Ajax's isolation elucidates Sophocles' interpretation of the meaning of a heroic myth to a "society of equals" (pp. 54-60), but, in seeking the "key" to the drama in the apparently reasonable and moving speech Ajax delivers between two expressions of violence—one against the herds and the other against himself—Knox neglects or underestimates the two dramatic events that constitute the main action: Ajax's initial delusion and his suicide. In fact, Knox, like other commentators, does not perceive the relationship between the delusion and the suicide, the first, the most prominent symptom, and the second, the culminating act, of Ajax's madness.

Ajax's delusion itself has generally been regarded as a temporary aberration or a brief confusion of vision: "it consists only in his mistaking animals for men; the madness affects his vision more than his mind,"[81] an oversimplification that divorces the delusion and its consequences from the character itself. Actually, the delusion that causes Ajax to mistake animals for men is but an extreme expression of the mental and psychological alienation that characterizes all he says and does within the play.

In a warning to Odysseus near the beginning of the play, Athena explicitly says that Ajax's madness is a consequence of his pride. She tells Odysseus to express no boasts against the gods, to avoid pride, and to know that "the gods love those who are self-controlled (σώφρονας) and hate evil men" (ll. 127-33). Ajax's past arrogance in denying his need of the gods' help, and particularly his rejection of Athena's, is recalled in the play (ll. 766-77), but these episodes, which link Athena's present anger at Ajax to his past history, do not in themselves explain the subtle connections among his pride, anger, alienation, and madness.

Ajax's delusion and his consequent slaughter of the animals taken as booty are precipitated by his murderous wrath against the Atridae and Odysseus, who denied him what he justly deserved—the arms of Achilles. The role of Athena, the external agent who "sends" the delusion, is best described by Cedric Whitman, who points out that she "motivates nothing," but "illustrates much. . . . She merely confirms Ajax in his madness and Odysseus in his sanity." Whitman's further comment, "It is wholly in keeping with the plasticity of Greek polytheism that the figure of Athena can be used here to symbolize the inner being of the two men, painted large and timeless at the beginning of the play,"[82] is certainly valid, but it raises rather than solves the central problem of the play: the nature and dramatic function of the "inner being" of a mad protagonist who is also heroic and tragic.

Ajax's initial act of madness reveals much about his character and especially about his inner transformation of external circumstances and experiences. In torturing and murdering animals, whom, in his delusion, he envisions as the Greek leaders, he expresses his combined feelings of impotence and rage. Athena's diversion of his wrath from the chiefs to the animals is a symbolic expression of his inability to destroy the forces that deny his exalted concept of himself; thus, he lashes out at the helpless creatures that cannot oppose him but serve as the objects of his fantasy and his uncontrolled fury. His pathetic acceptance at this point of Athena as his "ally" (ll. 116-17), when he has rejected her aid at the appropriate time, in battle, indicates that the inner world he has created is an inversion of the reality he has known; as a traditional source of power becomes the agent of his wild fantasy, the scorned warrior enacts a mock victory, which is actually a revelation of his utter defeat.

Ironically, the man Ajax most detests, Odysseus, responds to his condition with compassion. He regards Ajax, bound to *ate*, his inner blindness, as an example for himself and all mortals, who are, he says, "empty shadows" (ll. 121-26). In reply to Odysseus' observation on human beings' fragile hold on reality and life itself, Athena emphasizes moderation and self-control, the qualities that characterize him and, throughout the play, are the standard by which Ajax's extravagant fantasies and violent acts are judged. Ajax and Odysseus represent two potential responses of human beings to the recognition of their own precarious condition. Odysseus, the most rational of men, can nonetheless identify himself with the raving Ajax, but Ajax, even when he emerges from his delusion, is totally enclosed by his outraged pride and his vision of heroic fame.

Ajax's emotional condition throughout the drama—the obvious madness of his delusion and his subsequent withdrawal from other human beings as he contemplates suicide—is described as νόσος, sickness, a state of mind that ultimately leads to his suicide. This final enactment of his μανία or νόσος results from various external circumstances and inner forces[83] operating together to convince him that self-destruction is his one avenue of self-assertion.

Certainly the precipitating cause of Ajax's rage—the awarding of Achilles' arms to Odysseus—sets off a complex reaction to his allies, to his own fame, and to life itself, which must be explored in connection with his suicide. A definitive characteristic of Ajax, the pride that compelled him to scorn the aid of Athena, is the essential motivating force for this act of violence against himself. His pride manifests itself in more than an exalted view of his own powers as a warrior; it conveys his conception of himself as a personification of the immortal fame that is the implicit promise of the heroic code. Until he is forced to recognize his terrible vulnerability by madness itself, Ajax has regarded himself as omnipotent. The extremity of his anguish upon realizing that his vengeance was taken only on helpless animals results not merely from shame but from the exposure of his own impotence to contend with the forces that now control his destiny—the hostile Greek leaders and their attendant goddess.

This assault to his image of himself increases his characteristic alienation from ordinary humanity. Tecmessa and the chorus realize that his "sickness" renders him inaccessible to their efforts to assuage his pain. For Ajax the only alternative to life on his terms, as the all-powerful hero, dependent on

neither human beings nor gods, is death. Thus, the only comfort he asks of the chorus is that they slay him. Dwelling obsessively on his humiliation, he cannot at this time see beyond it. The contrast between Odysseus' compassion for
Ajax and Ajax's fantasy of Odysseus' gleeful satisfaction in
his downfall points up the narrowness of his vision; he
wishes only to kill Odysseus and then to die. Ajax's dedication to immortality has been converted into a passion for
death.

His two great speeches—the one on time (ll. 646-92)[84] and
the farewell preceding his suicide (ll. 815-65)—are soliloquies.
Together, these speeches are a climactic expression of his
psychological and moral alienation from the current social
and political order, based on expediency and rapid alteration
of power and rule. Ironically, his symbolic transformation of
these emerging conditions for human realization through the
focus of his own pride and consequent extreme humiliation,
his wounded self-image, his alienation from other human beings, and his obsessive concern with personal immortality
yields extraordinary insight into his character as well as into
the psychological and philosophical roots of the heroic code.

For Ajax, time, the enemy, has always been subject to conquest by heroic accomplishment which assured personal continuity; in the first of these speeches he says that it now signifies change itself. Neither social bond through "awesome
oath" nor individual force of "stubborn will" can withstand
its capacity "to bring forth the unknown and to conceal what
appears." Considering his own role within this altered view
of reality, he goes so far as to imagine transforming his own
character: he says he will bury his sword, the accursed
weapon of his enemy, Hector, and yield to the powers of the
gods and the rule of the Atridae. Such behavior would con-
form to the laws of the universe: the seasons, day and night,
are subject to natural law. "Shall we," he asks, "not learn to
control ourselves?" Ajax's use of the word σωφρονεῖν here is
striking, since it seems to echo Athena's advice to Odysseus.
It is, moreover, not the first time he has used it. Earlier, when
Tecmessa, in trying to comfort him, had asked what he

planned to do, his response, σωφρονεῖν καλόν (l. 586), demanded that she exercise the self-control of which he was incapable. Now, somewhat reluctantly, he acknowledges that self-discipline is compliance with natural law. For himself, this is also a recognition of the impermanence of ties of friendship—the alliances of heroes—that he had earlier considered immutable. It is a truth he acknowledges but cannot accept. He turns from his inner thoughts, briefly addresses Tecmessa and the chorus, and goes off to seek his "release."

In this play, as in the *Bacchae*, irrationality and violence are explored in relation to the meaning of soundness of mind, that is, control of the self in adapting to social requirements. In the *Ajax*, as we shall see, the word σωφρονεῖν is an ambiguous one, and is used, as it sometimes is in the *Bacchae*, to justify political repression, but it also designates an acceptance of individual limitation, of mortality, a subjection to the law of ceaseless change. For Ajax, self-control means an acknowledgment that the heroic code, by which valor, and thus, ironically, death itself, can overcome human vulnerability to time, is now but an outworn symbol. He has responded with the violence of delusion to a public demonstration that the code no longer functions. Now, obsessed by a need to deny how shaky the basis of his self-image is, a frailty exposed by his own irrational conduct, he seeks death as an alternative to such an admission. In the *Bacchae*, the example of self-control is a chorus of maenads engaging in a rite that expresses communal union in productivity; Ajax, the isolated man, arrives at a concept of self-control in despair and alienation. For him it is a denial of individual aspiration, a conformity to social and political standards that demand the annihilation of his heroic image of himself.

The soliloquy preceding his suicide reveals a curious attitude toward death; he calls upon Thanatos to come to him, as if death were already an old friend, with whom he will have time to converse at length in the future. As if by his own death he can obliterate all that has shattered his vision of himself, he invokes the Erinyes to exact vengeance on the Atridae and finally to destroy the whole Greek army. His farewell to Helios, to his home Salamis, to Athens, and finally to "the rivers, springs, and plains of Troy," is a farewell to the way of life that fostered him, whose values and rewards, he believes, can now survive only in the realm of the dead.

Ajax could not have imagined the breadth of vision that prompts Odysseus to defend his right to burial as a hero. Ironically, the rigidity of Menelaus and Agamemnon, in their demand for vengeance, would have been more comprehensible to his unyielding (στερεόφρων, l. 929) mind. Menelaus, in the name of law and self-control, defends his own arrogance. He refers to the *hubris* of Ajax and declares it is now his turn for pride. Actually, Menelaus' petty satisfaction as he gloats over the body of Ajax has little resemblance to Ajax's pride. However narrow Ajax's vision and intense his reaction to insult, his pride is an attribute of the courage and dignity that led him to his final challenge—a prospect of mortality more dreadful than any danger that battle had offered. To Menelaus, self-control is a function of political power, a disciplined army (l. 1075); to Ajax, it is an inner assent to natural law, which inevitably leads to compliance with the unjust decrees of leaders such as the Atridae. Neither Menelaus nor Agamemnon, who also uses such words as "law" and "self-control" as justifications for refusing burial, has any conception of the heroic ideal Ajax could not relinquish. Odysseus alone among the Greek leaders defends Ajax's right to burial, and he does so on the basis of his noble example, which at this point is more important than their long enmity. The identification with Ajax that Odysseus experienced at the beginning of the drama again emerges in his comment that he too will require burial one day. His defense of Ajax is more than "enlightened self-interest,"[85] though it is that. Observing Ajax in the madness of delusion, Odysseus saw himself as a "shadow," an apprehension of mortality he shared with Ajax and retains now even as he reminds the callous Atridae of the hero's nobility. Odysseus can make the political and social compromises that Ajax could not tolerate, but his vision encompasses the tragic ideal of Ajax, whose cult he celebrates with Sophocles' contemporaries, as he demands initial rites for him.

Sophocles' Ajax represents an ideal of nobility that precludes personal and social compromises. His delusion, the obsessive ruminations of his soliloquies, and finally his suicide express the frailty and loneliness of a human being committed to a symbolic conquest of mortality, a remnant of an ancient code of conduct, now but an individual torment.

III

Reason in Madness

•

Edgar's exclamation, "O! matter and impertinency mix'd; Reason in madness" (*King Lear*, IV, vi, 176-77),[1] in response to Lear's ironic exposure of the "great image of Authority," has become a proverbial comment on the remarkable insight that can emerge in conjunction with the symptoms of insanity. The breakdown of social and personal inhibitions that can characterize mental derangement has sometimes illuminated not only the bases of organized hypocrisies but the psychic roots of the insane person's own symptoms. "Every psychotic who is not feeble-minded," says Paul Federn, "has enough intelligence to grasp and to accept the explanation of his own mechanisms. His mental disease brings him nearer to intuition and understanding; normal persons, laymen and psychiatrists alike, have greater resistance because of the logical, emotional, and ego components."[2]

Reason in madness has been interpreted in various ways in imaginative literature from ancient dramatic portrayals of Dionysiac harmony with natural law and prophetic revelation to contemporary depictions of psychoses as expressions of the "true" self, explicit revaluations of "reason" or sanity that exclude traditional norms of logic, order, and judgment. Whereas in ancient Greek myths reason emerging in madness conveys the development of intrapsychic controls, the adaptation of mental processes to survival through tribal cohesion, in later literature the insights of madness generally occur in psychic diffusion and social alienation. Within this diversity one persistent element, already discussed in the particular context of Greek tragedy, is the portrayal of a struggle to apprehend and define the self in its dynamic relation to external reality. The very effort toward self-recreation opens new perspectives on inner transformations of familial, religious, and political authority.

In a further exploration of the psychic processes disclosed in literary depictions of the manifestations of reason in the very enactment of madness, I have restricted myself in this chapter to two writers who develop this idea explicitly. My aims are to elucidate the ways in which madness appears in their work as a level of psychic experience that produces an enlargement of perception and understanding for the persona or character and hence for the reader, and to indicate how differently each reveals the unconscious determinants of the concept of the self.

The social and cultural milieu of the medieval poet Thomas Hoccleve's confessions of madness would seem to offer little inducement for his effort to apprehend this condition through observation and reason. Yet, within a context in which madness was equated with sin, to the extent that witchcraft was soon to become the paramount expression of madness for both the victims of mental disturbance and the authorities who denounced such states as moral corruption, the persona of Hoccleve's poetry explores his inner experience, discovering within a rigid symbolic framework a narrow but fruitful avenue for self-liberation. A century later, when scientific investigations of madness barely mitigated superstitious condemnations, Shakespeare created in Lear a prototype of the mind in madness observing and commenting on its own functioning and on the individual and social history its very processes reflect.

If the pervasive influence of the church's condemnation of madness as evidence of sinfulness throughout the Middle Ages in Europe did not preclude scientific inquiry into its causes, it was the chief determinant of social, legal, and aesthetic responses to the symptoms and effects of mental aberration. Historians of the theory and treatment of psychopathology during the Middle Ages have disclosed the various ways in which medieval philosophers and physicians sought to understand and provide remedies for madness, from the drugs and simple forms of psychotherapy employed by the

Arabs of the eighth through the twelfth centuries to the surgical means used by the doctors at Salerno.[3] No doubt, efforts were made by both priest and physician to distinguish between daemonic possession and other causes of madness—physical as well as psychological. Nonetheless, the cultural effects of the assumption that the roots of madness are sin cannot be underestimated.

This assumption underlies the apparently enlightened approach of Bartholomaeus Anglicus, the thirteenth-century friar and professor of theology, whose discussion of mental disturbance in his encyclopaedia *De proprietatibus rerum* is concerned not only with the physical or humoral causes but with medical, surgical, and psychological cures. Bartholomaeus' descriptions of the symptoms and suffering of the mad and his speculation on the effects of the humors and the functioning of the brain itself indicate his dependence on classical authorities[4] rather than a genuine effort to explore and understand abnormal mental processes in scientific terms. The common medieval view of the connection between physical and mental states should not be regarded as similar to modern theories of endocrine imbalance or other physiological disorders as causes of insanity. The moralistic bias that lies beneath the assertions that soul and body interact, to be found in Bartholomaeus, in the *Secreta Secretorum*,[5] and in other works dealing with the "passions," determined that investigation of mental aberration would inevitably lead to the discovery of immorality or evil. Still, in Bartholomaeus' work, as in that of Arnauld of Villanova, a professor at the University of Montpellier, and other medical authorities, the classical influence, particularly the Hippocratic theory of the humors, as adapted by Galen, at least to some extent modified the rigid moral approach.

But neither the humoral nor any other physiological theory could mitigate the widespread and growing effects of the belief that the devil exerted a direct influence by possession or an indirect one on human beings' natural propensity to sin, and thus was the most pervasive cause of madness. It is simplistic to say that the "major difference . . . between the medieval and the modern response to insanity is that what the theologian of the Middle Ages called sin, we call sickness."[6] The conception of madness as sickness or disease is as medieval as it is ancient or modern, but the notion that disease, both physical and mental, is punishment for moral corruption is characteristically medieval. Increasingly during the Middle Ages, both observation of the mad and application of ancient classifications and humoral theories led merely to the predetermined conclusion that madness is caused and can be cured only by supernatural intervention.

English imaginative literature of the fourteenth and fifteenth centuries generally reflects the assumption that madness, a sign of inner corruption, is inspired sometimes by God and more commonly by the devil.[7] Madness often results in "death and damnation,"[8] but it can also appear as a test, "serving as penance and leading to self-knowledge, confession, and reform."[9] Many of the symptoms of madness in medieval literature—alienation, sometimes to the extent of a retreat to the wilderness, violence, identification with animals, suicide and other forms of self-destructiveness— resemble those of the ancient prototypes discussed in the previous chapter, but they differ widely from these in their aesthetic and thematic functions. If the medieval literary character or persona seeks self-knowledge in his very delusions and regressions, it is a compulsion to define the self in relation to God and the dogma of the church that determines his quest and his discovery.

Within the rigid conventions of this literary framework, however, one occasionally senses an effort—or perhaps a deep need—to express more personal feelings about the strange inner processes and overt reactions that are assumed to constitute madness. Certainly the poetry of Thomas Hoccleve, whom Penelope Doob describes as "the first writer I know of to write at length *in propria persona* of a madness that could be real,"[10] not only discloses the poet's preoccupation with the subject of madness itself but suggests that the experience of madness was a formative element in the personality he depicts as his own. The question of the autobiographical nature of Hoccleve's work, which has perplexed commentators,[11] is significant beyond any historical value it may have, for the unique quality of his poetry results in large part from his ability to convey an individual transformation of accepted medical and religious attitudes toward madness and to describe what at least seems to be personal experience through the conventional literary themes and techniques used in connection with this subject.

In the Prologue to the *Regement of Princes*,[12] a conventional debate, Hoccleve describes symptoms of madness long familiar to the medieval reader: his "troubly dremes, drempt al in wakynge," his "wyt dispoylyd" (ll. 109-111), his feelings of worthlessness, and his longing for death. The Beggar, who offers himself as a model of moral reformation and consequent spiritual health, gives him conventional advice: that the poet accept the poverty of which he complains as an avenue of repentance. Hoccleve's rejection of the Beggar's efforts to convince him of the salutary effects of poverty and despair, and his acceptance of a more worldly solution—the writing of the *Regement of Princes*—seem the only expressions of individual experience within the traditional mode in which the Prologue is cast.

Yet one cannot be certain. Hoccleve was not an original thinker; he could conceive of madness, possibly his own, only through the intellectual and verbal constructs—medical, religious, and literary—of his time. The symptoms he describes, however conventional the terms he employs, are, after all, authentic manifestations of mental disturbance. The Beggar's advice that the poet talk about the causes of his melancholy as a means of overcoming it—one of the accepted treatments—may be expressed in the form of a typical debate, but it leads to a practical solution that is also a way to personal fulfillment.

The individual or personal adaptation of conventional concepts and modes emerges more clearly in another of Hoccleve's poems, the *Complaint*,[13] in which Reason, the traditional philosophical and religious guide, helps the writer to come to terms with a period of madness he has endured in the past. Furthermore, by revealing the motives of the God who sent this affliction, Reason alleviates his suffering over the persistent effects of his insanity on himself and on those who continue to scorn and avoid him. In the *Complaint*, Hoccleve describes a recurrence of his mental illness some five years before, again emphasizing his insomnia, confusion, melancholy, and feelings of aloneness. Although God "voydyd" him of the "grevous venyme" that "had enfectyd / and wildyd" his "brayne" (ll. 234-35), he remains deeply distressed by his former friends' ill-treatment and especially by their assumption that he still is mad. Their view of him weakens his confidence in his own sanity and makes him despair.

Hoccleve examines what he calls his "sycknesse" or "dissease" for its effects on his perception of his society and of his own physical and emotional being. He tells of his feelings of loneliness, knowing that others discuss his symptoms without compassion. When people predict a recurrence of his madness, despite the fact that his symptoms have abated, Hoccleve comments ruefully on their arrogance in pretending to know what no man can predict, and implies that they too can become victims of the same disease:

and no wight knoweth / be it he or she,
whom, how ne whan / god wole hym visete;
It happethe ofte / whan man wene it lite.

(ll. 103-105)

The emotional effects of his friends' gossip have physical manifestations; he describes his sensations of extreme heat and cold in response to this cruelty. Most touching is his description of examining his face in the mirror at home, to see if it reveals signs of madness. Comforted at first by the assurance that he can make himself appear sane, he then wonders whether he is blind to his true condition.

He then tells of reading a "lamentacion / of a wofull man" in a book of "consolation," and of discovering therein "the speche of Reason," with which he was "well fed" (ll. 309-315). The writer, overwhelmed by his own "wyckednesses,

. . . vexation of spirite / and torment," prays for death, until
Reason persuades him that suffering is the common lot of
human beings, a means of "clensynge" their "gylt" which ultimately "them inablethe / to Ioye evarlastinge" (ll. 320-52).
A. G. Rigg[14] has identified the "boke" in which Hoccleve
found consolation as the *Synonyma* by Isidore of Seville, and
has explored the extent to which Hoccleve followed this
source in the contents and organization of the *Complaint*. Plac-
ing similar passages side by side, Rigg shows that lines 318-71
of the *Complaint* draw most heavily on the *Synonyma*; he also
suggests that "at least one later section of the *Synonyma* may
have influenced [Hoccleve's] conception of the pattern of suffering, purgation, and divine justice" (p. 570).

As Rigg points out, Hoccleve's *Complaint*, like the
Synonyma, belongs to the popular "genre of *Consolatio* or
Trostbuch," the most famous example of which is, of course,
Boethius' *Consolatio Philosophiae*. Although there is no doubt
that the "boke" to which Hoccleve refers is the *Synonyma*, it
seems to me that he is closer to Boethius than to Isidore of
Seville in his descriptions of his mental disturbance as disease
and in his effort to assimilate a religious concept of Reason by
adapting it to his personal circumstances in his struggle for
self-acceptance. The subject of Boethius' *Consolatio* is the
ways in which Philosophy, his "physician" (I, iii, 2), uses
"divine reason" (I, vi, 53) to "cure" him of his inner "sickness" or "disease";[15] her chief discourse is "de nostrae men-
tis perturbatione" (I, i, 51), the confusion and grief that prevent his accepting his own nature and the conditions of his
life. Philosophy tells Boethius that the "greatest cause" of his
"sickness" is that he has ceased to know what he is (I, vi, 39-
40). It is reason that leads him to recognize his inner freedom:
happiness lies within man's own being (II, iv, 72-73), and ignorance of oneself is vice ("Nam ceteris animantibus sese ig-
norare naturae est; hominibus vitio venit," II, v, 88-89). If in
the *Consolatio* reason demonstrates the goodness of God, it
even more forcefully indicates the way to turn its own light
inward ("In se revolvat intimi lucem visus"), where one can
possess the treasures of his own mind (poem, III, xi, 1-6). In

the personal struggle for inner peace that emerges through the philosophical dialogue of the *Consolatio* philosophy and reason are finally internalized, as is God himself.

The concept of Reason as a source of consolation that Hoccleve found in Isidore's *Synonyma* no doubt derives at least in part from Boethius, but it is more remote from the persona and more explicitly a theological agent. Reason in the *Synonyma* is the traditional *logos* or *ratio* of the classical philosophers, especially Plato, Aristotle, Cicero, and Seneca, syncretized and adapted to Christian theology as the faculty by which human beings can approach and ultimately know the good and God himself. Its function is to interpret God's purpose in sending spiritual suffering as a penance for the writer's sins and to open the way to relief through the acceptance of God's will.

The persona of Hoccleve's *Complaint* accepts this lesson from the Reason he finds in Isidore's "boke," but in so doing he attempts to transform a theological concept into a psychological vehicle. Having learned from the "speche of Reason" to "wrastle" (1. 342) with his feelings of sinfulness and his suffering, he realizes that those "to whom god[de]s stroke is acceptable" (1. 355) are purged by this very torment and thus cured of mental distress and confusion. For the Hoccleve of the *Complaint* this interpretation of the inner conflicts and external manifestations of madness offers a way to self-acceptance. The irrational guilt and aggression that characterized his "sycknesse" seem alien and unacceptable—"the wyld infirmytie . . . whiche me owt of my selfe / cast and threw" (ll. 40-42)—until Reason persuades him to bear his own nature patiently. He ends his summary of the book of consolation by echoing its cry of repentance and plea for mercy.

At this point, he says that he would have continued to read in this book, but was obliged to return it to its owner. As Rigg points out, "it seems more likely . . . that Hoccleve simply used those parts of the *Synonyma* which he needed for his own purposes (having read, or skimmed, the remainder of at least the first book), and that he continued the fiction of the temporarily borrowed book (a fiction suggested by Isidore's *Prologue*) as a convenient way of ending his extract" (p. 573). The relinquishing of the book, moreover, seems to me Hoccleve's way of turning from his model back to the circumstances he has been describing as his own. He has, as he says:

> cawght
> sume of the doctryne / by reason tawght
> to the man / as a-bove have I sayde,
> where-of I hold[e] me / full well apayde.
>
> (ll. 375-78)

and now he is less troubled by his friends' comments on his sickness. More important, he is determined to "unpick . . . the lock" of his "disease" and suffering:

> with pacience / I hens-forthe thinke vnpike
> of suche thowghtfull dissease and woo / the lok,
> and let them out / that have me made to sike. . . .
>
> (ll. 387-89)

As a psychic intermediary among his suffering, his efforts to understand it by observation of his behavior and experience, and the accepted dogma that madness is inflicted by God as a test, Reason penetrates his melancholy, his irrational impulses and guilt, converting them to healing agents of penitence. Thus, he no longer condemns these manifestations in himself, as people condemned and shunned him in his madness.

In submitting to the Reason that guides him, the persona of the *Complaint* reiterates the conventional wisdom that his suffering and his salvation have come from God, but his feelings of sinfulness, and with them his fear of madness, have yielded to his individual observation and his effort to discover restorative powers within his own being. Furthermore, in the *Dialogus cum Amico*, clearly a sequel to the *Complaint*, reason is entirely internalized. The *Dialogue* begins with Hoccleve's decision to read the *Complaint*, which he has just completed, to his friend, who then advises him not to publish it, since people have by now forgotten about his insanity. In insisting

on his decision to make his poem public, Hoccleve returns to
an examination of the symptoms of his earlier disturbance, as
if compelled. In the light of both the classical and Renaissance
literature of madness and certainly that of the modern period,
Hoccleve's inner explorations and his apparent self-revelations seem meager indeed, but in the face of the heavy religious, social, and literary constraints a fifteenth-century
poet must have felt, his efforts to understand mental states
that he depicts as his own and to confront the threat of madness some time after he says he has been relieved of its
symptoms are remarkable. In the *Dialogue*, the threat within
is externalized in the warnings of his friend, but the surer
voice is that of the poet, who accepts his own predisposition
to insanity, insists on making his experience of madness public by releasing the *Complaint*, and estimates his capacity to
live and to work in relation to the self-knowledge he has
gained through inner conflict.

The casual tone of the *Dialogue* should not disguise the fact
that Hoccleve and his friend are engaged in an argument
about a fundamental issue of human life: can a man who has
been insane henceforth trust his own judgment? Insisting
that he has nothing to be ashamed of, Hoccleve says that he
wants people to know that Jesus has cured him. Madness, he
says, is not a crime. He is not a robber or a coin-clipper but
merely subject to human frailty. God, he goes on to say, has
given man liberty to choose "for to do well or no" (ll. 73-75),
and he now feels certain of his own choice.

Turning from himself, he looks at the injustice in the world
around him and inveighs against current crimes, especially
coin-clipping, which hurts the poor, with whom he clearly
identifies himself. An Act of Parliament, he says, has made
the weighing of coins mandatory, and "Reason axith / that it
obeyed be" (l. 138). He speaks with the authority of Reason,
criticizing the rich who, he says, ought to be punished, and
exposing injustice with the sensitivity of one who has endured it.

His own plans are to continue writing, to translate into
English a Latin treatise, "Learn to die," and thus to teach

other men how to face up to their sins. Although he deals
with his approaching old age, the infirmities of his mind and
body, the sorrow and suffering inevitable in life, and the
transitory nature of beauty, pleasure, and power, his mood is
not one of despair. Instead, he seems to accept the limitations
of mortal life with equanimity.

His friend, however, misunderstands him, and fears for his
sanity. Echoing the common notion that the poet's madness
resulted from writing and too much study, he urges him to
give these up, but Hoccleve vigorously denies that his involvement with these pursuits disturbed him, and offers as
evidence of his soundness of mind the *Complaint*, which he
has just read to his friend. He further explains that his madness was caused by his "long seeknesse," an apparent re-
dundancy but probably an attribution of the overt symptoms
of insanity to an inner state of "disese" (ll. 421-27). Urged to
show prudence by accepting his friend's judgment rather
than his own, Hoccleve defends his capacity to know what is
reasonable. "Haue I nat seid reson / to thyn thynkynge?" (l.
472). The Reason that led to acceptance of the very experience
of madness in the *Complaint* is now the inner faculty that provides confidence in his own judgment. Hoccleve goes on to
say directly that no one can judge a man's condition as well as
he himself can (ll. 477-83), an insistence on the autonomy of
the individual mind reminiscent of Boethius. This conclusion,
while convincing his friend, seems also intended to allay his
own fears and the suspicions of those who had observed and
commented on his states of madness.

In its portrayal of particular episodes and homely details of
the poet's struggle to come to terms with inner confusion,
Hoccleve's poetry can certainly be regarded as autobiographical. Wiser than his commentators, who wish to draw a
sharp division between madness and sanity in determining
his state of mind,[16] Hoccleve in the *Complaint* describes his attempts to observe himself and his environment during a period when his hold on reality and confidence in his judgment
are shaky, an effort that results in a rational assessment of his
personal limitations and of his power to alleviate his melan-

choly by exploring the lingering effects of his sickness. In the reactions of his neighbors and friends, he conveys the general superstitious avoidance of madness, attitudes and conduct that point up his own directness. For him, moreover, madness is an experience that he can only partly comprehend, that he submits not only as an offering to God but as his dues to the society in which he must survive. Many of the images he uses to portray his disturbed state of mind are conventional ones—men compared him with "a wilde steer" (*Complaint*, l. 120) and said "full bukkyshe is his brayne" (*Complaint*, l. 123)—but his tone is new. The episodes recounted and the inner conflict portrayed in the *Complaint*, and the questioning of the self depicted as a dialogue with a beggar in the *Regement of Princes* and with a friend in the *Dialogus cum Amico* communicate the feelings of a man struggling to achieve a personal definition of inner forces over which his society and church have claimed moral jurisdiction.

It has been suggested that "in treating conventional ideas freshly by using himself as an exemplum, in creating the appearance of tortured introspection, in illustrating dramatically the destructive moral tensions experienced by a would-be man of virtue living in the world, and in presenting a detailed study of the melancholic as more than just a sinner," Hoccleve "looks forward to the Renaissance."[17] These are large claims for a poet whose efforts at self-examination are finally blocked by a prescribed moral conclusion. Still, it can be said that Hoccleve's depiction of madness as a condition that deprives a man of self-control only to lead him to a deeper apprehension of reason, and his implication that the irrational is a perennial determinant of human nature and experience, to be continually borne "paciently" and reexamined courageously, foreshadow the bolder explorations into the meaning of madness as an inner drama of both suffering and revelation that appear in technical and imaginative literature of the Renaissance.

The assumption of sin that underlies Hoccleve's tentative efforts to understand a troubled mind continues, however, throughout the late Middle Ages and Renaissance, to counter the growth of rational approaches to the nature and treatment of mental illness. "The puzzling but undeniable fact remains that medical psychology toward the end of the fifteenth century became welded with so many abstract theological and legal questions that it seemed for a while to be beyond redemption." Medical and ecclesiastical documents support Zilboorg and Henry's contention that during this period "Galen and Hippocrates were paid lip service only, and their clinical theories were ingeniously interwoven with considerations of sin and the Author of all Evil."[18] Certainly one of the richest sources of psychopathological symptoms and of their interpretation and exploitation as sin by religious authorities is the notorious *Malleus Maleficarum* written by the German Dominicans, Jacobus Sprenger and Heinrich Krämer, who were appointed official Inquisitors by order of Pope Innocent VIII. Determined to destroy witchcraft, Sprenger and Krämer zealously report on the characteristics and crimes of those accused of practicing it, as well as on the means of detection, exorcism, and punishment. The work, which first appeared in 1486, is an important, if hideous, revelation of the extreme consequences of the commonly accepted notion that illness, and especially madness, results from sin, an assumption that served devious political and social purposes. For the student of psychopathology, the book is especially interesting for its portrayal of neurotic and psychotic personalities in complicity with their accusers, providing through their fantasies and their conduct the very evidence of evil inspired by the devil that the Inquisitors demanded. The bizarre disclosures of the so-called witches express an identification with the church's craving for victims: sexual yearnings, repressed aggression, terror, conflict, and, above all, feelings of guilt, become the material of sin, the devil inhabiting the human soul.

In one of the most sensational "confessions," a woman confirms Sprenger's and Krämer's view that the killing and eating of infants is an essential part of the "profession" of witchcraft. Whether or not Sprenger and Krämer report an actual case is irrelevant. Such confessions were made, and their significance lies in their revelation of the individual transformation of unacceptable and conflicting desires, confusion, and shame into the current mythology of witchcraft. Accepting the role her age has assigned her, the young woman says that she was converted to witchcraft by her aunt. She then tells of how "she had been severely beaten by her aunt because she had opened a secret pot and found the heads of a great many children." Sprenger and Krämer's apparently innocuous comment, "And much more she told us, having first, as was proper, taken an oath to speak the truth,"[19] has sinister implications to those who have read their descriptions of the torture employed to exact confessions.[20]

An interesting example of the victim's complicity with his torturers is the case of a male "witch" who was so convinced of his inner corruption that, when he was told that repentance would result in complete pardon, "joyfully resigned himself to death." In order to achieve this state of bliss, he confessed not only his own crimes, but those of his wife, also imprisoned as a witch. Despite her husband's unquestioning acceptance of the decision of the authorities, the woman refused to confess to any crime "either under torture or in death itself,"[21] a moving exception to the general identification with the church's judgment.

Other reports reflect a pathetic capitulation to Sprenger and Krämer's view of women as particularly susceptible to corruption and thus an enticement to evil. Quoting from Ecclesiastes 7:26, "And I have found a woman more bitter than death, who is the hunter's snare, and her heart is a net, and her hands are bands," they go on to conclude: "All witchcraft comes from carnal lust, which in women is insatiable." Thus, they find it "no matter for wonder that more women than men" are "infected with the heresy of witchcraft." Considering the type of women most likely to be guilty of witchcraft, they conclude "that three general vices appear to have special dominion over wicked women, namely, infidelity, ambition, and lust" (p. 47).

The assumption of Sprenger and Krämer that both the sexual desires and appeal of women are intrinsically evil results in an image of woman as a destructive combination of the enticing and the monstrous: "Hear what Valerius said to Rufinus: You do not know that woman is the Chimaera, but it is good that you should know it; for that monster was of three forms; its face was that of a radiant and noble lion, it had the filthy belly of a goat, and it was armed with the virulent tail of a viper. And he means that woman is beautiful to look upon, contaminating to the touch, and deadly to keep" (p. 46). The belief that the sin of women is "more bitter than death" had a pervasive influence on both the conduct and treatment of many of the tormented "witches" whose symptoms are viewed in the *Malleus Maleficarum* as additional data to support the evidence of inherent female corruption recorded in the Bible, in history, and in ancient literature.

By the fifteenth century the assumption that insanity resulted from sin was so widely accepted it is not surprising that Sprenger and Krämer conclude that "Lunatics" are ultimately victims of devils, who are "themselves deeply affected by certain phases of the Moon" (p. 31). Others—"frantic men" and those who "have the appearance of irrational beasts"—are also possessed by the devil "at the instance of witches" (p. 129). Of course, involvement in witchcraft was only one of the bizarre fantasies of those troubled by delusions, obsessions, and other forms of mental disturbance; madness during the Middle Ages, as always, expressed itself in a variety of ways. Still, both medical and literary evidence of the period point to a consistency of interpretation of insanity both by those afflicted and by those who described its symptoms and effects: madness is a sign of possession by supernatural powers.

Widespread ecclesiastical and popular belief in witchcraft developed later in England than on the Continent.[22] The appearance of five English editions of the *Malleus Maleficarum* between 1584 and 1669[23] is but one sign of the growth of fear of the mad as daemonic agents in the sixteenth and seventeenth centuries. Yet, during this same period, a great number of religious, scientific, and legal works appeared in England as well as on the Continent which made at least tentative efforts to explore the symptoms of madness as manifestations of physical disorder or expressions of processes of mind. Considerations of madness occur in works on melancholy, which, as Lawrence Babb[24] points out, "embraces all irrationality." Although in general one can agree with Babb that there is "no discoverable line of distinction in the old psychiatry between melancholy and madness" (p. 36), and as one disease they are usually traced to humoral dysfunction, in literature at least melancholy more often appears as a "fashionable psychic malady" (p. vii) than as the extreme mental derangement and anguish of madness. Babb's useful survey of the chief scientific studies of irrationality of the late sixteenth and early seventeenth centuries reveals the diversity of symptoms classified under the terms melancholy and madness, and describes current medical and psychological methods of treatment: "Evacuation of the offending humor," the application of various drugs and diets, and efforts to distract the patient through sports, gaiety, and moral instruction (pp. 38-41).

For an examination of madness in *King Lear* most sixteenth-century theoretical studies of madness have only a peripheral interest. Still, Shakespeare's "pervasive but undoctrinaire use of psychology"[25] does reflect not only the broad interest of the Renaissance in human physical and psychical nature, but also current speculation on processes of mind that determine emotion and conduct.[26] In both Continental and English commentaries on madness of the sixteenth century, especially the second half, one sometimes finds, within the context of traditional deductions from the Aristotelian theory of the faculties of the soul and the Galenic model of the humors, unexpected curiosity regarding or insight into the actual experience of mental aberration.

One of the most widely known of Continental works in which the discussion of madness draws on observation as well as on the usual authorities is the "Divine of Zurich, Switzerland," Ludwig Lavater's *De spectris, lemuribus et magis*

(Geneva, 1570). Originally written in Latin, it was translated into French in 1571, and appeared in an English translation in 1572 under the title *Of Ghostes and Spirites Walking by Nyght.* . . .[27] Although Lavater assumes that spirits exist and that these are "either good or euill Angels" (unpaged "Authours Epistle"), he attempts to show that often people "falsly persuade themselues that they see or heare ghostes: for that which they imagin they see or heare, proceedeth eyther of melancholie, madnesse, weaknesse of the senses, feare, or of some other perturbation" (p. 9). Lavater defines madmen as those "which haue utterly loste the vse of reason, or are vexed by Gods permission, with a Diuell" (p. 13). Although he accepts the general belief in the devil's capacity to madden human beings by appearing to them in "all shapes and fashions" (p. 96), he is particularly concerned with the "vayne imaginations" that result from emotional disturbances and physical illnesses. He reveals a sympathetic understanding of the deluded and obsessive: "They take on them maruelous things, eyther bycause they haue mused long time on some matter conceiued in their minds, as cunning Artificers often times do: or bycause they haue ben long weried with sicknesse, or else bycause they loue extremelie" (p. 11). His examples of "Vayne fantasie" include those of characters in classical drama—Ajax, Orestes, Pentheus (pp. 13, 17)—and of figures described by Galen and other authorities, but he also refers to his observations of the mad in Bedlam, deceived by their own visions. Distinguishing between what he considers to be "walking spirites" sent by the devil or by good or evil angels and fantasies that have no supernatural cause, Lavater is unusual for his time in his effort to record the inner experience of the emotionally disturbed, their obsessions, hallucinations, recurrent fears, and other suffering.

Also notable are the efforts of the Dutch physician Johann Weyer (Weir), whose *De Praestigiis Daemonum*[28] sought to explain witchcraft as an unfortunate effect of ignorance and mental disturbance, especially melancholy, on the imagination. Although recent revaluations[29] of Weyer suggest that his enlightened attitude toward witches must be viewed in relation to his extreme intolerance toward magicians, one should not underestimate the importance of his exposure of the fallacies of the *Malleus Maleficarum* and his observation that physical and mental illness are often the cause of the delusions of the professed witch. Referring to accusations by Sprenger and Krämer as "inappropriate, absurd, and often impious" (p. 13), Weyer describes the old women accused of witchcraft as victimized by senility or melancholy and thus accessible to the influence of the devil. Weyer himself ascribes great powers to the devil, but he is most concerned with his influence as the "pater tenebrarum, falsitatis, & confusionis," the cause of ignorance, "omnis mali origo & fons" (p. 561).

It is no doubt true, as Christopher Baxter points out, that Weyer is limited by his inconsistency of approach, his anti-Catholic bias, and by his own "simplistic theological commitment."[30] But these shortcomings should not obscure his contribution, if not to the cessation of witch-hunting, then certainly to the development of distinctions between psychopathology and spiritual corruption. In defending the witch and condemning the magician, Weyer has not "simply reversed back on the figure of the magician the late medieval transference of the image of the learned, demon-worshipping magician onto the popular image of the witch."[31] His distinction between the witch's ignorance and emotional instability and the magician's conscious and informed attempts to gain power over natural phenomena is an important one. However inconsistent he may be on the question of the witch's responsibility for her delusions, he treats them as symptoms of melancholia that, as a physician, he has observed and described. Weyer's contribution is not to the area of religious toleration but to the slow, irregular, and all too limited advancement of medical psychology. Both his insistence that the strange manifestations of melancholia or other illness must be treated by a physician, not attributed to witchcraft, and his admission that there are symptoms arising from natural causes that a physician cannot explain should not be underestimated in their influence on Reginald Scot and others who were to further explore the psychological bases of conduct generally assumed to be diabolic.

In England during the sixteenth century, physicians,[32] while generally assuming on biblical authority that possession by the devil caused insanity, often regarded this as but one of the many "kinds" of madness they classified according to manifest symptoms. Most of these classifications were derived from ancient sources. Thus, one finds frequent references to the Greek term *mania* and its Latin equivalents *insania* or *furor*, the victims of which are said to behave like wild animals. This and other types of madness, especially melancholy, are generally traced to humoral imbalance, with emphasis on physical rather than moral causes.

Two sixteenth-century works on madness particularly relevant to this study, since it is likely that Shakespeare was acquainted with them, are also impressive documents in their own right; Reginald Scot's *The Discoverie of Witchcraft* (1584) and Timothy Bright's *A Treatise of Melancholie* (1586) approach madness from different points of view, but both regard it primarily as a disease, and express a compassionate concern for alleviating the suffering the mad endure. Reginald Scot, who was not a physician but a justice of the peace and member of Parliament, is well known for his conclusion, based on both legal and medical evidence, that many of the old women accused of witchcraft were mentally incompetent or actually insane. Countering the sensational evidence of the *Malleus Maleficarum*, Scot's speculations on the psychology of the accused, whom he describes as afflicted with "melancholie,"[33] are sometimes remarkable for their insight into mental aberrations, and especially into the ease with which so-called witches could be persuaded that the most bizarre fantasies of their accusers were real. One of Scot's aims is to demonstrate that the "poore melancholike women, which are themselves deceived," are no more dangerous than others suffering the physical and mental effects of melancholia: "For as some of the melancholike persons imagine, they are witches and can work woonders, and doo what they list: so doo other, troubled with this disease, imagine manie strange incredible, and impossible things" (pp. 52-53). After listing various delusions of those afflicted with melancholia—that they are "monarchs" or "brute beasts, . . . urinals or earthen pots," Scot asks why the so-called witches' fantasies, induced by "weakness both of bodie and braine," should be taken any more seriously than these delusions (pp. 53-54). Indeed, those labeled witches are "destroiers of themselves" (p. 58), not of others.

In discrediting popular claims for witches' control over the elements, Scot bases his arguments on conventional Christian theology: it is God alone who has such powers. But, as Sidney Anglo points out,[34] Scot goes far beyond this assumption in proving "witchcraft impossible" (p. 112). In fact, Anglo argues convincingly that in *A Discourse upon divels and spirits*, the last section of the *Discoverie*, Scot "advances a metaphorical interpretation" of spirits and devils "which, in effect, approximates to a psychological theory, and which virtually reduces spirits to an operation of the human imagination. . . . To say that somebody is possessed of a devil is as much as to say that the person is a lunatic." Scot applies this method not only to biblical references to spirits and devils but to manifestations of witchcraft. Spirits and witches "are either purely metaphorical expressions of mysteries beyond human comprehension, or, more usually, of psychological disorders and physical disease perfectly susceptible to the ministrations of a skilled physician" (pp. 126-29).

Like Weyer, to whom he refers with admiration, Scot regards the "melancholike humor" that occasions countless delusions and the confessions of witchcraft as a physical illness: "Howbeit, these affections, though they appear in the mind of man, yet are they bred in the bodie, and proceed from this humor, which is the verie dregs of bloud, nourishing and feeding those places, from whence proceed feares, cogitations, superstitions, fastings, labours, and such like" (pp. 57-58). Recognizing that the psychological effects of this humor are expressed metaphorically, he dismisses these symbolic forms, as he does dreams, as having neither existence nor power. Scot's very concentration on disparaging the notion that such fantasies have supernatural powers no doubt prevented him from recognizing their importance as clues to the psychological roots of the disease he diagnosed as their origin.

Hardin Craig points out that Scot's contemporary, Timothy Bright, intended his *A Treatise of Melancholie* "to provide a ground for the operation of his theology" and "to show that, although Galenic therapeutics of melancholy was excellent and applicable, it might not be made to include contrition and those stings of conscience which God himself chooses to inflict on the sinner."[35] Nevertheless, Bright does make a distinction between moral and physical or humoral causes of madness. "Melancholie," he says, "signifieth in all, either a certayne fearefull disposition of the mind altered from reason, or else an humour of the body, comonly taken to be the only cause of reason by feare in such sort depraved."[36] Although Bright attributes the first to a guilty conscience, enduring the wrath of God and the pain of remorse, the remedy he prescribes, the acceptance of sincere counsel, indicates that he rejects the harsh punishment recommended by those of his contemporaries who equate madness with sin and believes instead in the efficacy of compassion for the relief of spiritual torment.

Bright views madness as essentially a disorder of the "braine," the "instrument of reason." When "vnconsiderate judgement, simplicitie, & foolishness make their seat" in the brain, "dispossessing reason of her watchtower," human life descends far below "the condition of the brute beasts." In treating melancholy and madness as assaults upon and dispossessions of reason, through which "the excellencie of man appeareth aboue all other creatures,"[37] Bright echoes a long tradition of commentaries on madness, classical, medieval, and contemporary. The suggestion that the very suffering of melancholy, a remnant of madness, could motivate an apprehension of reason as a formative principle of the self, which appears within the conventional motifs and images of Hoccleve's poetry, is but a mild deviation from the standard view. It remained for Shakespeare, who was obviously drawn to the subject of madness, an important one in many of his plays, to challenge the long-accepted compartmentalization of mental functioning.

There is no clear evidence that in his depictions of madness in *King Lear* Shakespeare was influenced by theoretical studies such as Scot's or Bright's; certainly, he does not echo them as he does Samuel Harsnett's *A Declaration of Egregious Popishe Impostures*. Still, one can assume that he was acquainted with the various approaches to madness mentioned above—as physical illness, spiritual penance, and psychological affliction—that are to be found throughout Renaissance technical and imaginative writing, where emphasis on one point of view does not necessarily exclude others. If in the vast literature dealing with madness in the late sixteenth and early seventeenth centuries it is easy to detect dependence on classical and medieval authorities, one also discovers fresh observation and an enlarged perspective, the implication that the "grounds and reasons of [the] passions"[38] elucidate essential characteristics of human consciousness. This emerging spirit of inquiry[39] is reflected in *King Lear* in the comprehensive portrayal of madness as both individual and general inner experience, with far-reaching personal, social, and political consequences. In dramatizing the very structure of Lear's emotions and thoughts, Shakespeare incorporates medieval assumptions about human nature and institutions as well as the current scientific skepticism which had begun to challenge them.[40] His portrayal of Lear's mind functioning on levels of consciousness and awareness previously unexplored in literature elucidates the process of discovery characteristic of the Renaissance and is one of its profoundest manifestations.

Having altered the essential framework of the legend[41] of Lear's grandeur and folly by introducing the theme of madness and creating a realistic depiction of its physiological and psychological manifestations, Shakespeare creates a new prototype: the mad king who naked confronts his own unconscious impulses and motives and the forces within nature and society that have determined both his power and his impotence. Lear's insanity has long been considered critical to the meaning of the play as a whole. Despite the variety of approaches to his madness—ranging from the judicatory to the diagnostic—most critics conclude that it is the avenue to Lear's self-discovery and his new awareness of suffering and injustice in society. Although it is undoubtedly true that his dissociative, obsessive, and hallucinatory states disclose to both Lear and the audience hitherto unknown aspects of his character as well as impulses generally hidden within the human mind itself, critical oversimplifications of the concept "reason in madness" and thus of self-discovery have done little to elucidate Lear's actual emotional and mental experience of insanity.

Robert Heilman's view that Lear employs his "immense imaginative resources" to achieve "insight" into "the moral reality of the world" and "himself"[42] suggests an intellectual or philosophical reassessment of his values rather than the extreme emotional upheaval that Lear undergoes. In approaching *King Lear* as "an almost schematic pattern of the relationships of minds to experience" (p. 181), Heilman clarifies the basic components of the dramatic conflict, but the rather old-fashioned dichotomy he sets up between the imaginative and rationalistic characters in the play and their opposing approaches to experience only equates and thus confuses the creative capacities of the human imagination with the processes of madness. Lear's "original failure," according to Heilman, "has an intellectual form. . . . Lear thinks badly, unimaginatively." Madness, somehow producing "a restored imagination," provides "a new uncompromisingness of insight" (pp. 217-19). Heilman's repeated use of the word "imagination" does not help to elucidate either the mental limitation or enlargement he seems to refer to, but one thing is clear: for him there is a rather simple relationship between Lear's madness and the growth of his imaginative and intellectual capacities. It is a point that Kenneth Muir makes more directly: Lear "acquires wisdom by going mad."[43]

Analyses of Lear's "reason in madness" as an acquisition of wisdom or an enlargement of imagination reduce the complexity of his experience, for these are functions of a mind essentially in control of itself and its environment—of sanity rather than madness. In his madness, Lear's visions of human life are made up of the fragmented, unintegrated, disconnected observations and insights of those who have lost intrapsychic controls. The most significant revelation that madness produces in *King Lear* is not of the horrors beneath the royal surface of life; it is their particular appearance and form in Lear's expression of "unconscious mechanisms in consciousness,"[44] his enactment of a level of inner reality hitherto unknown to both him and the audience. In following the clues Shakespeare has provided, my intention is to explore Lear's madness as a dramatic construct of processes of a mind enduring its own extremes of instinctual demand and deprivation and converting these into passions, suffering, distortions, and revelations, all these processes merging in an individual yet representative symbolic transformation of external circumstances and experiences.

Almost from the beginning of the play, Shakespeare makes us aware that it is Lear's emotional and mental condition that defines him. His descent into madness is gradual.[45] From his first rage at Cordelia to the obvious expression of his madness in iii, iv, he wavers between apprehensive observation of his own inner disturbance and a defiant and desperate effort to maintain his familiar image of himself as, layer by layer, his former physical and emotional security disintegrates.

Lear's immediate reaction to Cordelia's refusal to accede to his demand for limitless devotion is an expression of violent wrath. Having declared that he will henceforth welcome her as he would barbarians and cannibals[46] (with whom he obviously identifies her), he responds to Kent's effort to calm him with the warning: "Come not between the Dragon and his wrath" (i, i, 122). J. C. Maxwell's comment on the line suggests that the image of the dragon is for Lear a deeply personal one: "the notion conveyed appears to be that of Lear's wrath as an extension of his personality—a sort of anthropologist's 'mana'—his union with which must remain intact if he himself is to hold together. A dragon cannot *be* a dragon without his wrath."[47] Lear not only uses his wrath to assert his failing authority, he makes it clear that it fills the lacuna Cordelia's "Nothing" has left in the composite image of himself as king and father loved above all else to which he had expected that his daughters would respond on demand. If love cannot affirm his identity, then, at least for the present, wrath must replace it. Lear explains and defends his angry reaction in the next lines:

> I lov'd her most, and thought to set my rest
> On her kind nursery. Hence, and avoid my sight!

Although Lear's conduct, in the first act at least, confirms Regan's judgment that "he hath ever but slenderly known himself" (I, i, 293-94), he reacts to the unexpected results of his own crucial decision with observations and questions that indicate his apprehension of the disparity between his own and others' perception of reality and even of his own nature. His not entirely playful question directed at the Fool: "Dost thou call me fool, boy?" (I, iv, 154) is soon followed by his intense response to Goneril's scolding:

> Does any here know me? This is not Lear:
> Does Lear walk thus? speak thus? Where are his eyes?
> Either his notion weakens, his discernings
> Are lethargied—Ha! waking? 'tis not so.
> Who is it that can tell me who I am?
>
> (I, iv, 234-38)

No longer protected by the myth of his own omnipotence, Lear discovers qualities in his daughter that he could not earlier have imagined. The reversal of roles has so shaken his image of himself that for the moment he does not respond with his customary anger. Reality, as he has apprehended it through the narrow focus of his impulses and his power, is now disintegrating before his eyes and, since his familiar responses will not serve him in these new circumstances, he experiences a sense of dissociation from his own perceptions, and thus from his conception of himself as an autonomous being. His cry, "Who is it that can tell me who I am?" heralds the disintegration not only of his self-image but of the natural and political order[48] that he had envisioned as but an extension of his own attributes and powers.

Retreating from the threat of his own question, Lear again reverts to a more comfortable anger. He rages at Goneril, disowning her as his daughter and calling her a "Degenerate bastard" and a "Detested kite." As his recognition that he has never known Goneril's true nature leads to the acknowledgment that he judged Cordelia's "most small fault" all too harshly, he again becomes the observer of his own judgments. Striking his head as if to punish his failure of insight, he cries out:

> O Lear, Lear, Lear!
> Beat at this gate, that let thy folly in,
> And thy dear judgment out!
>
> (I, iv, 279-81)

The dramatic portrayal of Lear's self-chastisement makes it clear that this is not a recognition of an intellectual or moral error arrived at through any logical process; it is rather an expression of the shock of acknowledged self-betrayal and the consequent regret and despair. For this torment Lear now blames Goneril, for she has revealed to him the potential cruelty that can exist in an apparently obedient and loving daughter, and this assault, which threatens his very belief in his powers of reason and judgment, releases his own violence. The famous curse in which he calls upon the goddess Nature to punish Goneril with sterility or monstrous offspring is itself a revelation: Lear does not explore or comprehend, though he does experience, as does the audience vicariously, the extremes of hatred that parental love outraged can produce.

The anguish that reduces him to tears at this point results not only from Goneril's cruel treatment but from the endurance of his own rage and hatred. Again he feels he must retreat emotionally and physically. Declaring that he has yet "another daughter," his one hope in this crisis is to "resume the shape" which those who have hurt him think he has "cast off for ever" (i, iv, 314-19). The "shape" can only be the image of the proud ruler and the revered father to which Lear clings despite the evidence that his voluntary surrender of his kingdom has already deprived him of any basis for that role.

His actual emotional weakness and helplessness emerge in his self-deceptive fantasy that Regan will share his anger at Goneril, "will flay [her] wolvish visage" (i, iv, 316), and thus restore him to his former "shape." This fantasy is but a fragile defense against what Lear already knows but will not yet face and what the Fool dares to make explicit in his jests about Regan: "She will taste as like this as a crab does to a crab" (i, v, 18). As Lear half-heartedly responds to the Fool's gibes, he ruminates obsessively on his grievances and probes their surface for his own responsibility. Suddenly, "I did her wrong,—" (i, v, 24) emerges, the "her" ambiguous, probably referring to Cordelia or possibly to Goneril,[49] but in any case to the image of a daughter whom he has never understood. Then, typically another defense: "So kind a father!" (i, v, 33). Wavering between self-accusation—intensified by the Fool's jests—justifiable fear of the future, and a desperate effort to reestablish his former concept of himself, Lear feels himself overwhelmed by his own impulses and emotions. He struggles for psychic control, but his cry:

> O! let me not be mad, not mad, sweet heaven;
> Keep me in temper; I would not be mad!
>
> (i, v, 47-48)

is an acknowledgement of unknown forces within which have begun to undermine his customary defenses—the comfort of his narrow definition of his "nature" (i, v, 33) and the other protective assumptions built up over a lifetime of unchallenged authority.

Before he portrays Lear as utterly overwhelmed by madness, Shakespeare introduces a prototype of the madman in the figure of Edgar simulating the role of a Bedlam beggar. Although Edgar's exaggerated gestures and exclamations sometimes suggest the contrived roles and hidden purposes

of Harsnett's "bogus demoniacs,"[50] his performance recreates for the audience the actual madman's alienation and
his physical and emotional suffering. Furthermore, Edgar's
soliloquy from the "hollow of a tree," where he hides from
the "hunt" (II, iii, 2-3), like an animal fleeing its pursuers, is
an important commentary on the theme of madness in *King
Lear*. It introduces the concept of self-preservation in madness; it makes the familiar identification of the madman with
the beast; and it suggests the extreme poverty and humiliation to which the poor and the mad were subject in
Elizabethan society, all of which are important motifs in the
play:

> Whiles I may 'scape,
> I will preserve myself; and am bethought
> To take the basest and most poorest shape
> That ever penury, in contempt of man,
> Brought near to beast; my face I'll grime with filth,
> Blanket my loins, elf all my hairs in knots,
> And with presented nakedness outface
> The winds and persecutions of the sky.
> The country gives me proof and precedent
> Of Bedlam beggars, who, with roaring voices,
> Strike in their numb'd and mortified bare arms
> Pins, wooden pricks, nails, sprigs of rosemary;
> And with this horrible object, from low farms,
> Poor pelting villages, sheep-cotes, and mills,
> Sometime with lunatic bans, sometime with prayers,
> Enforce their charity.
>
> (II, iii, 5-20)

Edgar assumes the role of madman as a means to "preserve"
his life in a world that has suddenly and incomprehensibly
become hostile. This transformation into a state he describes
as primitive, indeed bestial, is at once a practical solution and
a deliberate choice of what in actual madness is an unconscious one, a retreat to archaic cognitive and behavioral patterns as an escape from an unendurable situation, and an ef-

fort to "preserve" some form in which survival is possible. Renouncing his name and all it signifies as "nothing" (II, iii, 21), Edgar assumes a disguise that would seem utterly alien to him, yet in the persona of poor Tom he is to emerge not only as a foil to Lear but as a sensitive recipient of and commentator on Lear's ambiguous communications of his inner turbulence.

When Edgar again appears, he is poor Tom, a madman pursued by the foul fiend, but for Lear the descent into madness is gradual and agonizing as his fearful observations of his own wild thoughts and emotions increase with each visible proof of his loss of his former identity and role. His efforts to calm his mounting hysteria at the spectacle of Kent in the stocks:

> O! how this mother swells up toward my heart;
> *Hysterica passio*! down, thou climbing sorrow!
> Thy element's below.
>
> 　　　　　　　　　　　　　(II, iv, 56-58)

and shortly afterward when Regan and Cornwall refuse to speak with him: "O me! my heart, my rising heart! but, down!" (II, iv, 121) now appear vain even to him. Lear's reference to *"Hysterica passio"* rising from below toward his heart obviously reflects the humoral theory of melancholy. But here and elsewhere in the play, Shakespeare uses the traditional physiological symptoms only as manifestations of madness fundamentally psychological in its genesis and effects. As Lear's desperate fantasy that he will find a haven with Regan is shattered by her friendly greeting to Goneril, he cries out:

> 　　　　　　　O sides! you are too tough;
> Will you yet hold?
>
> 　　　　　　　　　　　　　(II, iv, 198)

The struggle to maintain wholeness of being has become "too tough," and there is a regretful tone in this wonder at his own stubborn resistance. His farewell to Goneril is a plea for his own sanity:

I prithee, daughter, do not make me mad.
I will not trouble thee, my child; farewell.

(II, iv, 220-21)

But it is useless for him to try to persuade himself that his "farewell" rids him of his grief and anger. Beginning with the conventional, "But yet thou art my flesh, my blood, my daughter," he goes on to rage:

Or rather a disease that's in my flesh,
Which I must needs call mine: thou art a boil,
A plague-sore, or embossed carbuncle,
In my corrupted blood.

(II, iv, 223-27)

This is more than a harsh attack on Goneril. It is an expression of Lear's only partly conscious awareness that, wherever he may assign the cause, the "disease" lies within his own being, and he turns to Regan for assurance that he is not utterly abandoned to his own rage and terror. When she too insists on impossible conditions for his stay, he begs the heavens for a patience he knows he cannot attain. Then, as if for a moment's relief to impersonalize his pain, still addressing the gods, he considers the possibility that it is they who have turned his daughters against him, and asks to be touched with "noble anger," his familiar weapon. Paul Jorgensen suggests that in this passage Shakespeare may well have adapted the remarkably sound psychological insights of Bright and Charron, who, Jorgensen says, "anticipate modern conclusions, reached first by Freud and then at greater length by Karl Menninger, in proposing that pathological grief . . . may be merely a disguise for anger. As a remedy for grief" both Bright and Charron "cautiously prescribed that its concealed cause, anger, be given vent."[51] For Lear, as Shakespeare portrays him at the very beginning of the play, anger has long been a means of self-assertion, an expression of his role as omnipotent ruler. Thus, this plea has a special poignancy; it is a hope, which he knows is groundless, for control—at least over himself—that he has already lost. Indeed, a moment later, he acknowledges the only mental condition that can define his desperation: "O Fool! I shall go mad!" (ɪɪ, iv, 273-88).

The next time we see Lear, he is confronting the storm on the heath, urging it on to wreak vengeance on the world. The critical commonplace that the storm is merely a metaphorical expression of Lear's own tumultuous feelings misses its actual meaning for Lear. As Marvin Rosenberg indicates, "Shakespeare's text offers no such simple correlation between the passions of man and the universe."[52] Furthermore, the importance of the storm thematically is that it points up both the indifference of natural forces to human need and the refusal of human beings to accept this neutrality. His vulnerability intensified by exposure to its physical effects, Lear's projection of his inner turbulence—"this tempest in my mind" (ɪɪɪ, iv, 12)—on the storm discloses the very process of symbolic transformation of natural forces by a mind in conflict and distress.

Initially, Lear finds emotional relief in the storm (ɪɪɪ, ii, 1-66). In his impotence, he identifies with its violent energy; in his loneliness, he adopts it as a powerful ally, capable of releasing his own most dangerous impulses on a hostile world. He commands the "cheeks" of the wind to "crack" as they "rage" and "blow," projecting the intrinsic connection between his own disintegrating image and his uncontrollable anger on the winds themselves. The "thought-executing fires," his agents of destruction, must also "Singe" his own "white head." The sexual imagery,[53] which suggests a superhuman intensity and violence, further reveals Lear's inner disintegration as his aggressive impulses overwhelm his instincts of productivity and love. Eros, which Freud describes as the instinct "which seeks to force together and hold together the portions of living substance" (*SE*, xvɪɪɪ, 60), is to be utterly destroyed: "Nature's moulds" must "crack" and "all germenes spill at once," as Lear's own concept of love and its products, and with it his self-image, has been shattered, replaced by hatred and rage. Lear transforms external nature into a manifestation of his own unconscious fantasy,

in which self-destruction and violent aggression are one impulse: nature must destroy itself in destroying humankind.

Lear's address to the storm is interrupted by the Fool's
realistic, if cynical, comment on what he views as the only alternative available to them: "O Nuncle, court holy-water in a
dry house is better than this rain-water out o' door. Good
Nuncle, in, ask thy daughters blessing. . . ." Although Lear
ignores this advice, the words enter his consciousness, evoking further violent and obsessive transformations. Converting the "rain-water" from which the Fool would seek refuge
into his own instrument, Lear urges it on to greater fury:
"spout, rain!" For a brief time, Lear has used the storm as a
means of displacing his daughters with the universe as a
whole, redirecting his disillusionment and rage; now the
Fool's notion that he ask for his daughters' blessing brings
the original source of pain back into focus and his daughters
become part of the fantasy centered around the storm. First
he distinguishes between their violations and the indifferent
violence of the elements:

> Nor rain, wind, thunder, fire, are my daughters:
> I tax you not, you elements, with unkindness;
> I never gave you kingdom, call'd you children,
> You owe me no subscription. . . .

But then the suggestion that he accept "court holy-water"
conjures up an image of himself as a "slave, / a poor, infirm,
weak, and despis'd old man," and the rain, wind, thunder,
and lightning, his former allies in vengeance, now become
"servile ministers," conspiring with his "two pernicious
daughters" (iii, ii, 14-24). Lear's rapid shift from identification with the force and power of nature to admission of age
and infirmity is less the expression of "self-pity"[54] than of a
desperate inner quest for some self-image that can give him a
degree of comfort, some defense, however frail, against his
feeling that he—and with him his world—is disintegrating.

In his constant references to Lear's daughters, the Fool
seems to sense and make explicit their intrusion into every
defense that Lear erects in the fantasy world that gradually

becomes his only recourse. Lear, in his despair, can more readily accept the storm as an agent of his daughters than the reality that he has only them to protect him from "rainwater." His unconscious efforts at displacement for a measure of relief distort his view of reality, so that in his blunted fantasy of omnipotence he becomes a victim of the universe rather than merely an outraged father, but this process also opens his perspective in wild flashes of insight into social and natural forces which have determined his nature and condition.

When Kent appears, exclaiming at the terrifying intensity of the storm:

> man's nature cannot carry
> Th' affliction nor the fear
>
> (III, ii, 48-49)

Lear again ignores its actual dangers to him, continuing to dwell on its symbolic meaning; it will serve to expose "man's nature" in all its cruelty and hypocrisy:

> Let the great Gods,
> That keep this dreadful pudder o'er our heads,
> Find out their enemies now.
>
> (III, ii, 49-51)

His concern with justice here, and later in III, iv, vi, and IV, vi, when the concept becomes a rationalizing element of his hallucinations, is a continued displacement of his immediate concerns and grievances, the dramatization of an unconscious process which stirs up and releases fragmentary but significant details of social criminality and hypocrisy that Lear had apparently known for a long time, but that only now affect him personally. These memories reveal conflicts, long submerged, between instinct and conscience, power and integrity. The "wretch" he addresses who has "within" a variety of "undivulged crimes"—murderous assault, perjury, incest, insidious plots—is general enough to include the unconscious wishes of the human race as well as unpunished actual crimes. Certainly Lear's command:

> close pent-up guilts,
> Rive your concealing continents, and cry
> These dreadful summoners grace.

with its image of inner torments bursting through their covering reflects his own feelings of inner dissolution and disintegration. But Lear retreats from this perception of his own involvement in the general scheme of corruption:

> I am a man
> More sinn'd against than sinning.
>
> (III, ii, 51-60)

At this stage, his awareness of his psychic condition is almost entirely centered on his tenuous hold on sanity. Recalled by Kent to the specific reality of his abandonment by
his daughters, he cries out, "My wits begin to turn" (III, ii,
67). Only out of his concern for the Fool does he realize that
he too is cold and, as he goes toward the hovel for shelter, he
suggests that the "one part in [his] heart" that still responds
to the realistic demands of the present is "sorry yet for" the
Fool (III, ii, 68-73). In scene iv, as Kent urges him to enter the
hovel, Lear's resistance is at least in part self-protective: "Wilt
break my heart?" he asks, aware that he has hardly heeded
the physical dangers of the storm, but has used it as a distraction from the "tempest in [his] mind." Kent's emphasis on
his exposure brings to the forefront of his consciousness the
crucial fact that he can hardly assimilate: "In such a night / To
shut me out?" and again he turns from the extremity of his
psychic pain in terror: "O! that way madness lies; let me shun
that; / No more of that" (III, iv, 1-22). He urges Kent and the
Fool to enter the hovel, while he remains outside, seeking
further relief in the storm:

> This tempest will not give me leave to ponder
> On things would hurt me more.

and in a prayer on behalf of the "Poor naked wretches"
whose suffering his own desperate condition has for the first
time made real. Reflecting a momentary inner fusion of his

former exalted role with his present degradation, his exhortation to "Pomp" to "Expose thyself to feel what wretches feel" incorporates his own regret for his neglect as king of the defenseless victims with whom he now identifies himself (III, iv, 24-36).

As if to justify Lear's avoidance of the hovel as a symbolic focus of the anxiety, rage, and terror of abandonment, the Fool rushes out crying for help when he discovers Edgar within disguised as the madman, poor Tom. Yet, when Edgar emerges from the hovel, Lear welcomes him as an embodiment of these very feelings unchecked by any remnant of convention or rationality. His first words to Edgar: "Didst thou give all to thy daughters? / And art thou come to this?" express unquestioning identification with the madman (III, iv, 39-49). Lear's struggle to adapt his former concept of himself and the world to painful new external conditions and to only partly acknowledged internal demands is over, and he gives way to the madness he has feared and tried to submerge since the first act of the play. As Edgar continues to enact a fairly conventional Bedlam beggar, Lear ignores his frequent references to "the foul fiend." In *King Lear*, it is only feigned madness that the devil instigates. Edgar, in Lear's eyes, can have been driven mad only by the human cruelty with which he himself is obsessed: "What! has his daughters brought him to this pass?" He seems not to hear the Fool's effort at realistic, if bitter, wit: "Nay, he reserv'd a blanket, else we had been all sham'd," merely cursing the daughters of all men in reply. To Kent's blunt statement: "He hath no daughters, Sir," Lear responds with fury, ruling out factual reality as treasonous to the inner realm, with its own laws of perception and logic, that is now his only kingdom:

> Death, traitor! nothing could have subdu'd nature
> To such a lowness but his unkind daughters.
> Is it the fashion that discarded fathers
> Should have thus little mercy on their flesh?
> Judicious punishment! 'twas this flesh begot
> Those pelican daughters.
>
> (III, iv, 63-75)

Lear's concern with the generality of his own plight—the physical and emotional torment inflicted by "his unkind daughers"—reveals the guilt that lies beneath his obsessions. His judgment on "discarded fathers": " 'twas this flesh begot / Those pelican daughters" indicates that he is coming to grips with feelings deeper and more significant than remorse for his dependence on unreliable daughters; as his defenses break down, his words convey an awareness he has tried to avoid, that he and all fathers are implicated in the cruelty of their offspring. Like painful recurrent dreams, his hallucinatory obsessions increasingly express an overwhelming need to confront the elements of his own and human nature that, ignored in the past, have determined his present condition.[55]

Edgar, perhaps to comfort Lear, for a moment turns Fool, converting "pelican" into "Pillicock" in a mildly bawdy song. The Fool's comment, which follows, a seemingly off-hand remark, is actually an extremely important one: "This cold night," he says, "will turn us all to fools and madmen" (III, iv, 76-78), suggesting the potential folly and madness within all human beings, which extreme human or natural stimuli can release. It is a prelude to Edgar's anatomy of the servingman and to Lear's even more basic reduction of man in general. Edgar's choice of servingman ("either a fashionable lover or a servant"[56]) as the former occupation of poor Tom and his bitter description of his lust, greed, and deceitfulness suggest that, in speculating on the causes of his desperate condition, he has associated his own plight with episodes of betrayal that he witnessed in the past. The shock of his sudden fall from favor, the unwarranted antagonism of his father, and the effort to survive through pretended madness have forced Edgar to examine his society with a new sensitivity. His own assumed role has made him conscious of the deceits that had been an accepted part of his life at court. In pretending to have been a servingman, he imagines himself as participating in the corruption of the world he has fled for his life. It is perhaps no accident that the debauched and conniving servingman he describes could be the brother whose treachery he will soon discover and punish. His conventional association of various evils with animals: "hog in sloth, fox in stealth, wolf in greediness, dog in madness, lion in prey" (iv, iv, 93-95), is in marked contrast with his slightly later description to Gloucester of his own regression to the life and habits of an animal: "Poor Tom; that eats the swimming frog, the toad, the todpole, the wall-newt, and the water; that in the fury of his heart, when the foul fiend rages, eats cow-dung for sallets; swallows the old rat and the ditch dog . . ." (iii, iv, 132-36). The madman's undifferentiated incorporation of live creatures and their dung seems innocuous by comparison with the incorporation by the fashionable world of the most repellent and vicious characteristics of animals.

Lear's distinction between man's appearance falsified through his "sophisticated," or adulterated, use of the animal world and his essential nature as "a poor, bare, forked animal" is more explicit. Identifying with Tom, he enacts his compulsion to retreat to a different, more primitive, phase of his own and human existence (iii, iv, 105-11). Lear has been associated with ancient and medieval archetypes of the wild man—"animal and primordial infant," the "naked lunatics of the 'wild man' legends"[57]—and certainly his declaration, even before he realizes that he is utterly abandoned:

> I abjure all roofs, and choose
> To wage against the enmity o' th' air;
> To be a comrade with the wolf and owl,
>
> (ii, iv, 210-13)

and the more dramatic expression of his alienation from society in iii, iv, as he tears off his clothes, prepared for a naked confrontation with the elements, do recall these legendary figures. But Lear's reversion to infantile and archaic behavior conveys far more than the "libidinal impulses"[58] that the wild man principally and graphically symbolizes in a variety of bizarre forms, for Lear in his madness is an explorer of consciousness.

For Lear, reason in madness is not, I believe, the sporadic endurance of "excruciating lucidities when he looks out for a searing instant from his dark abyss, reflects on himself, knows what is happening in his mind, and flees back into the roaring gulf of his terrible madness."[59] Reason emerges obliquely in his very retreat from the unendurable suffering of the present and in his displacement of recent events with fragmentary and confused memories, associations, and fantasies that, ironically, enlarge the tragic meaning of his individual plight. It is through the very hallucinations formed out of this material, releasing unconscious emotions and conflicts into consciousness, that Lear painfully and deviously struggles to answer for himself the question that, with desperate clarity, he had put to others at the beginning of the play: "Who is it that can tell me who I am?" His obsessions and hallucinations reveal that, in his very retreat from the anguish of his present despair, he unconsciously strives toward a restitution of his own ego—a construction of a continuous, integrated sense of his real existence in relation to time, nature and society, cause and effect.

The following pages will explore the extent to which he succeeds in reconstituting feelings and inner knowledge of his own unified being through the expression of impulses long denied or disguised and the investment of feeling in social and moral issues formerly assigned to the periphery of his consciousness. As he gradually relinquishes his delusions and becomes aware of the actual familial and political conflicts he had so large a share in initiating, his new apprehension of his role as man and king is limited by so diminished a self-image as to suggest a relationship in its extreme opposition to his former imagined omnipotence. Still, in recreating his own character on stage—an act unique in drama—Lear is a heroic figure. Filled with hate; obscene, violent, even murderous, yet desperately longing for love and envisioning justice, Lear portrays the inner drama of human beings' struggle to define their nature within society, where organized deceptions reflect a lawless universe.

He interprets his own classic infantile act of tearing off his clothes as a return to the infancy of the race: he would start all over again as "unaccommodated man." Mad as the gesture may be, it is a symbolic expression of an unconscious wish that generally submits to censorship, even in dream and fantasy, once and for all to tear away the barriers civilization has placed in the way of discovery and renewal of submerged impulses and passions. The social denial of this urge is conveyed in the Fool's uncomprehending, though once again realistic, comment: "Prithee, Nuncle, be contented; 'tis a naughty night to swim in," and Edgar's conventional madman outbursts about "the foul Flibbertigibbet" (iii, iv, 109-22), apparently an effort to reinforce his disguise as Gloucester enters. For Lear at this moment, who experiences his own struggle to survive as an elemental anxiety of early man, Edgar is not poor Tom but a "Noble philosopher" who will explain "the cause of thunder"; he is a "learned Theban," a "good Athenian," a composite of ancient sources of scientific and ontological wisdom. Shortly afterward (iii, vi), in the farmhouse where Gloucester offers them shelter, Lear insists that Edgar take the role of "most learned justicer" in the trial of his daughters. Merging psychic levels are manifested in Lear's words in this scene. Asked by the Fool "whether a madman be a gentleman or a yeoman," he responds emphatically "A King, a King!" (ll. 9-11), an assertion of the only identity he can claim at this time—the mad king who is himself an indictment of kingship, yet who claims the prerogatives as madman of arraigning and punishing the guilty. As mad king, he will "have a thousand with red burning spits / Come hizzing in upon" his daughters (ll. 14-15), but suddenly the violent impulse is tempered by an equally intense craving for justice that Lear conveys in a variety of ways throughout the period of his extreme disturbance.

From the evidence of the mythical figures discussed in the previous chapter, it is clear that the mad protagonist's involvement with justice is an ancient and continuous one, which seems to portray symbolically a struggle within the recesses of the human psyche to resolve a conflict that is at once individual and social, an unconscious confrontation between impulse and conscience released into consciousness. Dedicated to ritual madness, the Bacchants announce that justice condemns Pentheus to death. In the *Oresteia*, trial by jury evolves within a context of violence and madness. The raving

Cassandra foresees an ironic justice in the anguish of the triumphant Greeks, and Ajax enacts in his delusions an ancient vision of justice dishonored by his peers. In Lear's demands for justice one can discern his confusion, guilt, grievances, and obsessions, but his hallucinations also disclose a struggle to exceed the limits of his present sense of injury, to formulate through the enactment of memories and conflicts a concept of justice out of his very being, based on the evidence of his own and his society's history, too long repressed or distorted. Out of this reason in madness, this unconscious impulse to revaluate a lifetime of unassimilated memories and experiences, he begins to construct an altered self-image.

In iii, vi, Lear moves from the concrete enactment of a hallucination that he conducts a trial of his daughters to the central question that underlies any concept of justice: "Is there any cause in nature that make these hard hearts?" (ll. 78-79). At first, like a child playing out his secret grievances and wishes, he becomes overseer and defendant at his daughters' trial. Declaring that he "will arraign them straight," he appoints his judges: Edgar, "most learned justicer," the Fool, "sapient sir," his partner, and Kent, also of "th' commission"; demands the "evidence," and cites his complaint against Goneril: "she kick'd the poor King her father" (ll. 20-49). The childishness of the accusation and the concrete representation of psychic assault portrays Lear's inner regression to the ego state[60] of an early stage of life, one that practically all children undergo, in which a sense of injustice is first experienced in reaction to an unwarranted physical blow.

Lear interprets his next hallucination—that Regan appears before the court but immediately escapes—with the exclamation: "Corruption in the place!" As he turns to Edgar, demanding, "False justicer, why hast thou let her 'scape?" (ll. 53-56), it seems evident that he has unconsciously structured this hallucination to convey another perennial quandary encountered and uncomprehended in the past: the widespread avoidance by authority, which certainly included himself, of corruption and injustice. The unsolved problem, eventually dismissed from conscious awareness, now emerges in its

immediate relevance to his own condition. Overwhelmed by
these painful associations of past and present, by his sense of
general and personal helplessness in the face of uncontrollable evil, Lear condenses his terror of a hostile and threatening
world into a child's cry of abandonment when his very pets
turn on him:

> The little dogs and all,
> Tray, Blanch, and Sweetheart, see, they bark at me.
>   (ll. 62-63)

After Edgar provides the comfort appropriate for a
frightened child, casting his spell on the imaginary dogs, Lear
turns again to his obsession with punishment. But his declaration "Then let them anatomize Regan, see what breeds
about her heart" (ll. 77-78) not only expresses the extremity of
his personal vindictiveness; it also indicates the more complicated feelings and attitudes that his obsession releases. The
question that follows does not refer only to his daughters.
When Lear asks "Is there any cause in nature that make these
hard hearts?" he suggests that even his own suffering must
be considered as a consequence of general human motivations he has never before acknowledged, and that these reflect natural forces which must be explored before cruelty and
injustice can be comprehended. He then retreats from the
very prospect he has opened into a new delusion and,
though he never again directly confronts this central issue, it
emerges obliquely in the various bizarre forms his madness
takes. If Lear never arrives at an answer to his own great
question, he himself exemplifies the causes in nature that he
seeks and the psychic battleground on which their effects are
endured.

Some of the strangest manifestations of Lear's madness are
those Cordelia learns of from people who have seen her
father, as she waits anxiously in the French camp at Dover for
her officers to find him:

> why, he was met even now
> As mad as the vex'd sea; singing aloud;

Crown'd with rank fumiter and furrow-weeds,
With hardocks, hemlock, nettles, cuckoo-flowers,
Darnel, and all the idle weeds that grow
In our sustaining corn.

(IV, iv, 1-6)

and when he next appears he is *"fantastically dressed with wild flowers"* (IV, vi, 81, stage directions). There is something Dionysiac in his appearance and in the manner in which he announces himself as beyond civil authority: "No, they cannot touch me for coining; I am the king himself"[61] (ll. 83-84). Lear's hallucination—that he is "coining" press-money—is in keeping with his general tone of command in this passage. The justification for his prerogative comes from nature itself: "Nature's above art in that respect" (l. 86); and nature has provided his accoutrements as well as his power. Muir points out that *"coining* often had a sexual significance,"[62] and, since Lear's primary obsession with vengeance against his daughters underlies his delusion of "coining" money to conscript an army, it is possible that the hallucination also transmits his conflicting feelings about his own responsibility for his plight, which emerged in his first encounter with Edgar: " 'twas this flesh begot / Those pelican daughters." Furthermore, Lear has not only "coined" or engendered pernicious offspring; he has also invented (another meaning of the term)[63] his ritualistic role as nature's king, deprived of his former authority only to assert deeper and more authentic claims. In this, the last and climactic portrayal of Lear's unrelieved insanity, he enacts in his hallucinations his intense preoccupation with kingship, justice, sex, and mortality. His diffuse and erratic thoughts on these apparently unconnected matters contain their own logic—reason in madness—which relates them by exposing the presence of unacknowledged drives and fears beneath the grandest disguises: virtue and law for lust and violence, the omnipotence of absolute monarchy for the insatiability of human desire and the terror of human frailty.

Lear seems to justify his own hallucinations, his bizarre

appearance, his strange demands, on the basis of nature's elemental revelations, of which he is the wild and compulsive interpreter in this scene. Among the very weeds and flowers he has chosen to adorn himself with are those believed to be nature's remedies for madness. On Lear's person, the fumiter, hemlock, and cuckoo-flowers[64] serve both to identify him as a madman and as talismans to protect him against his confusion and fear. Edgar, watching over the blinded Gloucester, is apparently struck by Lear's self-protective adornments. Asked by Lear for a password, he replies, "Sweet marjoram" (IV, vi, 94), ritualistically offering him another of nature's remedies for mental disease.[65] Although Lear insists on his prerogatives as king, his revaluations of his past in this scene indicate, as does his strange appearance, that he is struggling to grasp a new concept of authority as emerging from and subject to the power, irrationality, cruelty, and threat of nature itself. He now resents and mocks those who formerly hid this truth from him, and thus denied the very self that has emerged in madness.

Turning to the blind Gloucester, whom he apparently notices for the first time when Gloucester says that he knows Lear's voice, Lear exclaims: "Ha! Goneril, with a white beard!" The confusion of Gloucester with Goneril is actually a momentary projection of his own destitute state on her. Lear's exclamation is one of satisfaction in a wish fulfilled, that the wretched creature with a white beard—so like himself—is Goneril, punished at last as she deserves to be. His next remark clearly indicates that the white beard he is concerned with is actually his own: "They flattered me like a dog, and told me I had the white hairs in my beard ere the black ones were there." "They" includes all those who with flattery and other deceptions fostered the image of omnipotence he accepted as his due from his youth to old age. It was nature that taught him he had been deceived: "When the rain came to wet me once and the wind to make me chatter, when the thunder would not peace at my bidding, there I found 'em, there I smelt 'em out" (IV, vi, 97-105).

His ensuing outbursts convey a mixture of rage at his deprivation of his accustomed unchallenged, if fantasied, omnipotence and a wry satisfaction in the recognition of the conditions of mortality. Although Lear's tone and manner are accusatory and ironic, the nature of his memories and hallucinations at this point indicates that he is probing the limitations of kingship and justice, seeking himself: "Go to, they are not men o' their words: they told me I was every thing; 'tis a lie, I am not ague-proof" (ll. 105-107). Lear's ironic juxtaposition of "every thing" with "ague-proof" suggests that the personal and social structure of kingship is based on deception exposed by the most mundane of experiences. He continues in response to Gloucester's: "Is't not the King?" mocking the arrogant presence and awe-inspiring power of the role he now resumes:

> Ay, every inch a king:
> When I do stare, see how the subject quakes.
> (ll. 110-11)

Granville-Barker has observed that Gloucester's "dutiful" question "begins to transform him in those mad eyes. And madness sees a Gloucester there that sanity had known and ignored."[66] Gloucester's adultery, apparently taken for granted, at least on the surface of Lear's consciousness, as a courtier's right, had actually elicited much deeper but unacknowledged feelings that now emerge. The king Lear now portrays conducts the trial for adultery long suppressed in his own psyche, and it exposes his conflicting emotional responses to his own instinctual needs and deprivations in his judgment of the "subject." Issuing a pardon on the basis of natural instinct:

> The wren goes to 't, and the small gilded fly
> Does lecher in my sight.
> (ll. 115-16)

he bitterly equates human sexuality with mindless, loveless coupling. In his royal decree: "Let copulation thrive," the affirmation of lust and fertility is the ironic residue of disappointment in and contempt for the human beings subject, as he is, to nature itself.

Beneath this revaluation of human morality and behavior—partial and bitter yet ultimately enlarging—lies, as always, his personal grievance:

> for Gloucester's bastard son
> Was kinder to his father than my daughters
> Got 'tween the lawful sheets.
>
> (ll. 117-19)

Lear, of course, does not know that Edmund has been as heartless as his own daughters. His error intensifies the pathos of the blinded Gloucester, helpless before his deluded king, and adds to the evidence of the general unpredictability of human conduct, determined by irrational forces which, whether sanctioned by law or breaking its confines, can be equally destructive.

Releasing from all strictures human lust as it appears in his own most disturbing fantasies with the cry: "To 't, Luxury, pell-mell!" Lear makes a last excuse to his censor projected as the official power now denied him: "For I lack soldiers" (ll. 119-20), before launching forth on a diatribe against the corruption of women that discloses a history—of which his own is only a portion—of repressed hatred mingled with fear and desire. He is not unique in this play in conceiving of women as agents of the devil. Albany certainly has sufficient cause to be horrified at the inhumanity of Goneril, but the metaphor he uses to condemn her grows out of a broader context than the present conflict, reflecting as it does assumptions about women in general that the Renaissance inherited from the Middle Ages:

> See thyself, devil!
> Proper deformity shows not in the fiend
> So horrid as in woman.
>
> (IV, ii, 59-61)

and he goes on to equate her with the devil himself: "thou art a fiend, / A woman's shape doth shield thee" (ll. 66-67). Albany's and Lear's identification of woman with the devil echoes attitudes common enough in medieval religious and secular literature. Indeed, Lear's image of woman, insatiable in her sexual appetites, fiendish in her power to corrupt and destroy, is that of the *Malleus Maleficarum*:

> Down from the waist they are Centaurs,
> Though women all above:
> But to the girdle do the Gods inherit,
> Beneath is all the fiends'; there's hell, there's darkness,
> There is the sulphurous pit—burning scalding,
> Stench, consumption; fie, fie, fie! pah, pah!
> Give me an ounce of civet, good apothecary,
> To sweeten my imagination.
> There's money for thee.
>
> (IV, vi, 126-34)

In dramatizing Lear's symbolic transformation of his turbulent and conflicting feelings about women's sexual attributes into the pit of hell, Shakespeare elucidates a pervasive religious and social construct. Though by no means the only such vehicle, the image of woman, whether as idealized vessel of purity or as agent of devilish lust, served throughout the European Middle Ages and Renaissance as both denial and unconscious projection of the chaotic inner reality that threatened the emotional and intellectual repression enforced by the rigid hierarchy of church and court. The latent political implications of such a threat are indeed enacted in *King Lear*, where sexual and political aggression—the "infidelity, ambition, and lust" decried in the *Malleus Maleficarum*—unite in the persons of Goneril and Regan. They not only violate the hierarchy of family relationships and the sanctity of marriage, but finally destroy the personification of female purity and representative of established values—Cordelia.

In the breakdown of his customary compartmentalization of experience, Lear himself seems to press the connection between his obsession with sexuality, his recognition of the devious motivations of authority, and his acknowledgment of his own mortality. The "stench" of his own "imagination" suggests that the "sulphurous pit" projected on women lies within the souls of the monarchs and judges of society. The hand of the king, he tells Gloucester, "smells of mortality," the "great image of Authority" is but a "cur" that has usurped power, and the "rascal beadle . . . hotly lusts to use" the whore "in that kind" for which he has whipped her. Declaring that "Robes and furr'd gowns hide all," he repudiates the entire hierarchy of hypocrisy, salvaging nothing of its morality or law: "None doth offend, none, I say, none" (IV, vi, 135-70).

Lear's compulsion to divest himself of the paraphernalia that civilization has accumulated to obstruct human beings' apprehension of their own nature, which he first expressed as he attempted to tear off his clothes on the heath, has led to his repudiation of all authority and all established codes of conduct. Stripped of his own "Robes and furr'd gowns," abandoned to the loneliness and frailty they would deny and the instinctual demands they disguise, Lear has in madness released the elements of his being—the rage, lust, skepticism, and fear—that must enter into the construction of a new conception of reality. Reluctantly struggling against a political and social history of repression and denial, the mad old king rejects the last comforting assumptions of the medieval world that formed him and endures the chaos out of which the discoveries of the new age must ultimately emerge. In his despair, he cannot know that he is not entirely alone, that he has in fact reached another human being in his ravings. It is in an aside that Edgar utters his cryptic comment: "O! matter and impertinency mix'd; / Reason in madness"; although he cannot respond directly to Lear, Edgar has made the connections implicit in Lear's apparently bizarre and unrelated disclosures and, in the last speech of the play, he suggests that he has lived with and understood their meaning.

From Lear, as this scene closes, his own revelations elicit little but rage. Although he urges "patience" on Gloucester, his own fury is not yet spent. Its last extreme expression is heard just before Cordelia's attendants arrive to rescue him. Yet, as he cries out in the most direct release of the violence he has contained throughout his ordeal, imagining that he is overwhelming his "son-in-laws": "Then, kill, kill, kill, kill, kill!" (l. 189), one feels that the worst of his inner conflict is

over. He is ready to rally whatever resources remain to him in
a contest in which he is tragically limited. Reality for Lear offers only the threat of death from the daughters and the
kingdom he once believed he ruled with benevolence, and
the recognition that love, however pure, cannot withstand
the forces unleashed by hatred and cruelty.

To those who come to rescue him, Lear describes himself as
the "natural fool of Fortune," and asks: "Let me have sur-
geons; / I am cut to th' brains" (IV, vi, 193-95). The self that
Lear presents as he gradually emerges from madness is frail
and continually aware of his vulnerability to the exigencies of
nature and the effects of chance. To Cordelia he says: "I am a
very foolish fond old man," and, unsure of his ability to deal
with his changed circumstances, not quite believing that it is
really Cordelia who cares for him, not yet recognizing Kent,
he confesses: "I fear I am not in my perfect mind": (IV, vii, 60-
63). A little later on, he begs Cordelia:

> You must bear with me
> Pray you now, forget and forgive: I am old and foolish.
> (IV, vi, 83-84)

His one desire is to be allowed to remain with Cordelia, and
he is roused from his image of his own helplessness only in a
vain attempt to save her life. With Cordelia dead in his arms,
he describes his last efforts to prevent the final horror he
must face: "I kill'd the slave that was a-hanging thee" (v, iii,
274).

Lear's madness has not reconciled him to a world in which
corruption and lawlessness prevail. Nor does his conduct reflect moral or intellectual advancement resulting from his
madness. He achieves a brief interval of partial lucidity and
comfort with Cordelia; then, unable to control the forces that
have destroyed him, he dies. Yet Lear's madness is the crucial experience of his life and therefore of this play. His obsessions and delusions expose a chaotic realm within ruled by
instinct and passion, which extends far beyond the individual
psyche. He himself bares the processes by which it exerts its
influence over court and law, family and nation, and in so

doing he symbolizes the ancient concept of *anagnorisis*, discovery. Reason and madness in *King Lear* are removed from their theological base. Manifestations of human beings' engagement with their fellows and with external nature rather than of divine favor or punishment, their interaction reveals the torturous processes through which the mind discovers truth in its own distortions, and recognizes the limits of mortality in its own fantasies of omnipotence.

IV

The Spleen, the Vapors, and
the God Within

Madness as a popular theme and pervasive metaphor in English literature from the late seventeenth to the mid-eighteenth century conveys the obsessive concern of the age with formulating a theory of mental functioning. During this period, the term madness, at some times symbolizing political rebellion and religious nonconformity and, at others, describing individual aberration, is used to connect these disparate experiences. Furthermore, such manifestations of madness are generally defined in accordance with a mechanistic theory of mind, which employs physiological speculation to support religious and political repression. This dominant approach to the mind is opposed in a variety of forms that disclose important aspects of the intellectual and emotional history of the period absent from or distorted in most of its major literary works. In 1679 the Earl of Rochester defends "certain instinct" against the simplistic concept of man as a "reas'ning Engine," and sneers at the moralistic and inhibitory interpretations of reason that were becoming increasingly popular.[1] Moreover, in medical and pseudo-medical writing, and in imaginative literature, ranging from personal outcries in verse against the humiliations of Bedlam and conventional descriptions of the vapors and the spleen to the direct communication of emotional withdrawal and thought disturbance in Christopher Smart's *Jubilate Agno*, one finds a struggle to confront the idiosyncratic transformations of experience that create the confusion and terror of madness. The emphasis of this chapter is on such forms of resistance to the prevailing approach to madness, which will also be discussed, since it enters in both gross and subtle forms into the very modes of opposition that it inspires.

Neither the compassion for mental suffering expressed in the most enlightened of Renaissance commentaries on madness nor the insistence on the generality—indeed, the universality—of this condition in a book as popular as Robert Burton's *The Anatomy of Melancholy* seem to bear much relation to official judgments on or treatment of the insane in England or on the Continent during the seventeenth and eighteenth centuries. Whereas Burton, or Democritus Junior, quotes widely from ancients and moderns to prove that "we are *ad unum omnes*, all mad, *semel insanivimus omnes*, not once, but always so, *et semel, et simul, et semper*, ever and altogether as bad as he,"[2] the insane during these centuries were generally treated not as alternate selves of the sane, but as their "Antipodes,"[3] whose cure could be effected, if at all, only through some form of prescribed punishment. Commentators[4] have remarked on the disparity between Thomas Willis' sophistication as a physician and "clinical observer" and his primitive responses to the problem of madness, his advocacy of "threatenings, bonds, or strokes, as well as *Physick*," as cures for the insane. Such "punishments," he suggested, were more efficacious than "*Physick* or Medicines."[5]

Willis, an important figure in medical history, celebrated for his work on the anatomy of the central nervous system and "as the discoverer of the eleventh pair of cranial nerves,"[6] is one of the most illustrious examples of the period's general ignorance, indeed avoidance, of the complicated psychological factors that enter into mental functioning. His explanations of the causes of madness range from daemonic possession to the most mechanistic notions regarding humors (which he later discarded), body fluids, nerve tissue, animal spirits, and "depraved" blood, "either hereditary or acquired" (p. 204).

Willis' discussion of madness arising from the "depravation of the Animal Spirits" reduces psychology to moralistic physiology. Even when "a violent Passion" initiates the onset of madness, the condition itself develops "because the Animal Spirits are too much overthrown, and hurried into confusion; or because they are elevated above measure, and endeavour to stretch themselves forth beyond their sphere." When "Animal Spirits" are "driven beyond their orders and wonted passages," they behave like revolutionary forces, causing "confusion," invading the blood and the brain, and disrupting the orderly arrangement of the systems of the body. The analogy is not only implicit in Willis' language; it leads him to the conclusion that "Ambition, Pride, and Emulation, have made some mad." His explanation, which follows, describes the "Corporeal Soul swelling up with an opinion and pride of its own excellency," endeavoring "to expand or stretch it self forth most amply, beyond the border or sphere of its body, the Animal Spirits being tumultuarily called into the Head" (p. 203). Willis thus constructs imaginary physiological processes based upon traditional injunctions against ambition and pride that would disrupt the established, political, economic, and religious order.

Both Willis' achievements and his limitations profoundly influenced later developments in the investigation of mental pathology. As Zilboorg and Henry point out, he, along with "Theophile Bonet and [Giorgio] Baglivi . . . laid the foundation of a psychiatry without psychology which took root in medical science and which, while rendering inestimable service to neuroanatomy, neurophysiology, and neuropathology, almost totally disregarded the study of the very psychological phenomena which these men seem to have set out to study."[7] Seeking the roots of emotional disturbance in the soul, Willis, Thomas Wright,[8] and Everard Maynwaring,[9] who were among the most distinguished seventeenth-century investigators of the mind and its "passions," built upon a base that medieval and Renaissance theologians and physicians had inherited from the ancients, particularly Aristotle. Despite the remarkable advances in clinical observation in England, France, Italy, and Germany during this time, the

Aristotelian concept of the soul, defined by its faculties of nutrition, perception, understanding, and movement, persisted.[10]

Throughout the seventeenth and eighteenth centuries, various adaptations of ancient theories appear in medical writings and, especially as popularized by the all-inclusive Burton, in imaginative literature as well. In the *Anatomy*, Burton lists and describes the traditional Hippocratic humors, referring to minor differences among later commentators. He defines spirit as "a most subtile vapour, which is expressed from the blood, and the instrument of the soul, to perform all his actions," thus, "a common tie or medium between the body and the soul." Then, he summarizes one of the widely accepted Renaissance classifications of the faculties of which, he says, there are "three kinds, according to the three principal parts, brain, heart, liver. . . ." Natural spirits "are begotten in the liver, and thence dispersed through the veins, to perform those natural actions. The vital spirits are made in the heart of the natural, which by the arteries are transported to all the other parts. . . . The animal spirits [are] formed of the vital, brought up to the brain, and diffused by the nerves. . . ."

In anatomizing the soul, Burton begins by quoting from Aristotle's *De Anima*: the soul is "the perfection or first act of an organical body having power of life," a definition, he indicates, "which most philosophers approve." Questions arise, however, concerning "the essence, subject, seat, distinction, and subordinate faculties" of the soul, and Burton proceeds to quote and summarize the theories of ancient and Renaissance authorities on these matters. The "common division of the soul" that Burton here summarizes, which was as popular during the Renaissance[11] as the categorization of spirits by their physiological location, is "into three principal faculties—vegetal, sensitive, and rational." Burton's lengthy discussion of these three "distinct faculties" points up their traditional Aristotelian functions. The vegetative is concerned with "retention," "digestion," "maturation," and other such physical processes. The sensible soul, whose "general organ is the brain," has the powers of both apprehension and movement. The "apprehensive faculty" is composed of both the "outward" senses of "touching, hearing, seeing, smelling, tasting" and the "inward" senses: "common sense, fantasy, memory," which exist within "the brain-pan." It is fantasy or imagination that in dreams, sickness, and melancholy produces "absurd shapes" or "monstrous and prodigious things," and that "forcibly works" in "poets and painters." Pleasure and pain lie within the province of the "moving faculty" of the sensible soul, which controls "affections and perturbations," feelings and passions. The rational soul, which "includes the powers, and performs the duties of the other two, which are contained in it," is made up of the "understanding," that is, "the rational soul apprehending," and "the will, which is the rational power moving; to which two, all the other rational powers are subject and reduced" (ɪ, 169-92).

Echoes of Aristotle's concept of the faculties of the soul from the Middle Ages to the eighteenth century reiterate his emphasis on the soul's inherent capacity for rationality. The function of man in Aristotle's view, is the exercise of the faculties of the soul κατὰ λόγον, in accordance with reason, or at least "not without reason" (*Nic. Ethics*, 1098A). The curious conjunction of age-old topographical classification and moralistic assumptions regarding will and rationality with a growing awareness of the importance of anatomical research and clinical observation creates far less consistency in both professional and popular approaches to mental disorder in the eighteenth century than is generally recognized. Furthermore, the traditional inconsistency in the determination of the causes of mental disturbance, the wavering between the religious and the organic—spiritual corruption and physiological malfunction—recorded by Burton continues to appear in medical accounts and in literary descriptions and symbols.

Incorporating these inconsistencies, philosophical and medical theories on mental disorder in this period, and the literary works that echo them, nonetheless convey a dominant attitude toward madness: it is to be classified in relation to the various ways in which it prevents the individual from executing his proper role in society, and it should be treated as physiological malfunctioning. The widespread preoccupation with the subject of madness in medical, philosophical, and literary works generally reveals one primary concern: suppression of its symptoms and effects. The metaphors of madness so pervasive in Pope and Swift reflect the prevailing avoidance of any empathic exploration of the mind designated as mad.

In surveying the medical and philosophical approaches to madness of the Restoration and eighteenth century, Michael De Porte[12] has emphasized the general distrust of the imagination and of individuality. As De Porte and others have observed, suspicion of fantasy and its idiosyncratic manifestations certainly does not appear for the first time at the end of the seventeenth century. Like so many of the attitudes toward the mind that persist in the modern world, its roots are in ancient Greek philosophy—particularly Plato. This fear was reinforced by the Stoic contempt for passion and belief in the primacy of reason and by Neo-Platonic rationalistic mysticism, both of which were influential during the Middle Ages and the Renaissance. Fear of the imagination is evident in the traditional and persistent faculty psychology, which assumes that failure to control the "passions of the heart" or the "passions of the mind" leaves them prey to the imagination, which distorts reality to comply with their demands.

Late seventeenth- and early eighteenth-century philosophical and medical authorities assumed the validity of such fears. Thus, Hobbes turned the traditional conception of creative madness into a warning: "without steadiness, and direction to some end, a great Fancy is one kind of madness."[13] Physicians cautioned against excessive imagination as they did against the passions. Philosophers, medical and other self-proclaimed authorities on madness, including the major imaginative writers of the period, however different their positions and their tone, whether serious, comic, or satiric, all seemed to have one end in view: inhibition of the personal feelings and the individual transformations of experience that were manifested in what they deemed anti-social conduct. Thus, it is not to the major figures, either in medicine or literature, of the period from the late seventeenth to the mid-eighteenth century, that one must look for exploration of madness as an encounter with an asocial self, the idiosyncratic adaptations of impulses and desires that the age shunned in the "human nature" it was so eager to fix in a permanent definition.

A compelling and sympathetic interest in the irrational does exist even in conjunction with the mechanistic notions and moralistic attitudes that dominate the period. Thomas Tryon, whose *Discourse of the Causes, Natures and Cure of Phrensie, Madness or Distraction*[14] is generally regarded as extraordinarily "modern" for its period,[15] is probably more representative of individual curiosity, insight, and compassion at odds with the medical and philosophical dogma of the time than would appear from an examination of most contemporary commentaries on madness. To be sure, Tryon is in many respects an eminent example of the values of the Enlightenment. A retired businessman, who had risen from poverty to wealth by self-education and industry, he often reflects the religious and political assumptions of the period in his very language. Thus, he begins by accepting the current view that *"Madness and Phrensie* do generally, and for the most part . . . arise and proceed from various Passions and extream Inclinations, as *Love, Hate, Grief, Covetousness, Dispair,* and the like." These, he goes on to say, "stir up the *Central Fires,"* a process which eventually causes "the *Imaginative property* and *Soul's Power"* to become "rampant, unbounded, or as it were without a Guide" (pp. 251-52). The terms Tryon uses to describe this state are those of political revolution: *"Saturnine* and *Martial* Poysonous Fires" cause "Hurley-burley, Confusion, Strife and Inequality between the properties in the *Seven-fold Wheel of Nature"* which "subvert the government of the inward Senses and Spirit of Wisdom, and puts Reason under Hatches" (pp. 253-54). He sees this condition as one of "War" (p. 254), indeed "intestine Civil War" (p. 255), and, true to the spirit of the Restoration, he finds the ultimate cause of such rebellion in pride: "The truth is, *Pride* may justly be said to be the chief *Procatarick*, or remote original cause of *Madness*" (p. 256).

But, if Tryon uses the conventional political and religious image of rebellion against reason and order to describe madness, he goes far beyond such clichés in his effort to understand what actually takes place in the minds of the mad. Tryon's view of the "Affinity or Analogy between *Dreams* and *Madness*" (p. 249) is, as has been indicated above,[16] hardly new, but it is instrumental in leading him to an acceptance of the irrational as an essential and valuable constituent of human nature. Convinced that the "Soul and Spirit" continue to function in sleep and that, although we may not remember "particulars" of our dreams, "yet when ever we sleep we *dream*" (pp. 31-32), he regarded the imagination as the creative faculty continually operating in all human beings, when they are asleep and awake (pp. 259-60).

In madness, as in dreams, says Tryon, the imagination is "unbounded" (p. 252); thus the insane, like "innocent Children, do speak forth whatever ariseth in their Phantasies" (p. 258). Madness is not a symptom of physiological imbalance but a manifestation of uncontrolled imagination. Indeed, what separates the mad from the sane is that their imaginations are not sufficiently controlled by judgment: "For what wild, incoherent, absurd, ridiculous notions should we hear from the most serious people, if they should continually Speak, and form into words the various Imaginations, and Conceptions that do continually arise . . ." (p. 259). The imagination, moreover, derives from the "generative" powers of God; "for all Material and Immaterial were and are brought into Manifestation first by Imagination, Desire, and Motion." Were imagination, along with desire, not "captivated, darkned, and as it were chained in the Clouds of gross flesh, and dark Powers of the outward and corporeal Nature, it would do wonders" (pp. 259-61). Because in madness, some of the marvelous powers of the imagination are freed, "it is not perhaps always so very deplorable an estate," says Tryon. He then goes on to describe the "naked" innocence of the mad, who "appear even as they are," and the hypocrisy of the so-called sane, in whose deceit and cruelty there is "far greater *Madness* and Evil" than in the conduct of those "deprived of their Sences" (pp. 261-63).

The climax of this section is Tryon's declaration that "the World is but a great *Bedlam*, where those that are *more mad*, lock up those that are *less*" (p. 266). Tryon's description of the symptoms and uninhibited expression of the insane is, of course, limited to those that support his moralistic view that theirs is the innocence of the true Christian. But he is interested in more than their moral purity. It is finally the truth that reason hides and madness reveals that concerns him, and this truth consists of what he calls the "natural Inclinations," the "inward Properties" of the soul. Madness, for Tryon, is a revelation of mental functioning; it is a "real turning of the inside of all the natural Properties and Faculties of the Soul outward" and thus offers insight into the "thoughts and Imaginations" normally repressed or disguised by reason and custom (pp. 276-78). Tryon was not the first to recognize the similarity between the bizarre fantasies expressed by the mad and those suppressed by the sane, but his interest in this mental phenomenon and his respect and compassion for the aberrant expression of the passions and the imagination make his work remarkable for its time. Still, even his speculation on madness as a revelation of what today would be called unconscious processes leads him to no new discovery regarding the thoughts and feelings of the insane.

It is poets of this period—deranged or sane, with only minimal talent or highly gifted, even some whose conception of insanity is largely determined by the very clichés of the age—who begin to shed doubt on the mechanistic view of the mind, out of a compulsion to divulge qualities of the self that such a structure cannot contain or define. One type of verse, generally sub-literary but extremely interesting, that appears from the late seventeenth century through the eighteenth, is the account of one's own or a generalized patient's experience in Bedlam. The most moving of these, a collection entitled *Lucida Intervalla*[17] by James Carkesse, appeared in 1679, before the rather rigid pattern of conventional description of and moralizing on lunatics had become popular.[18] Carkesse, who had been a clerk in the office of Samuel Pepys (to whom he refers, p. 5) during Pepys's first appointment as secretary to the Admiralty, produced the poems of this volume while he was a patient at Finsbury and later at Bedlam under the care of Dr. Thomas Allen. What makes Carkesse's doggerel extraordinarily interesting and at times affecting is his capacity to reveal the psychic means he devises to maintain some consistent sense of his own identity and some hope of survival within the asylum that he depicts as Hades.

Carkesse's is indeed a personal struggle to resist the authorities by valuing the excessive feelings and wild imaginings that Tryon was to defend in the mad. For Carkesse, as for Tryon, these are signs of creative power, and the society, personified in his doctor, that condemned him to Finsbury and Bedlam is itself mad. The epigraph of his book, "semel insanivimus omnes," which he quotes from Burton, signifies his acceptance of his own aberration as universal.

Among Carkesse's favorite themes is the physician as antagonist: "Quack" or "Mad-Quack," whose misfortune it is to be mad without wit (p. 31). Throughout his poems, the doctor is associated with the humiliating and ineffectual treatment to which the poet is subjected: the darkness, beatings, and chains, the purges, bleeding, and forced vomiting. But in Carkesse's view, the physician's greatest inadequacy emerges in his advice that the poet stop writing. In "The Doctors Advice" (p. 27), Carkesse is urged to "leave off the *Poet* and *Lampoon*," on the basis that "*Apollo* never singly made a *Poet*," without assistance from "the *Moon*." Implicit in the Doctor's final argument is Carkesse's defense:

> Then *Wit forswear*, and like me prove but *Dunce*;
> The *Sun* and *Moon* will quit you both at once.

The second section of the poem, entitled *"The Patient Replies,"* apparently an acceptance of the Doctor's direction, actually turns his own remedies against him:

But if 't be thus, your Phys: I'le spill o' the' *ground*,
Vomit up *Helicon*, and then I'm *sound*.

In his case, the despised vomiting will bring forth what Carkesse regards as his essential nature: the Helicon within,
which must find expression if he is to be "sound."

A similar metaphor serves as a defense against the discom-
fort and humiliation of this treatment in another poem: "To
Mr. Doctor, on his giving him A VOMIT":

What *Homer* our Great *Grandfather* did *Vomit*,
We licking up, turn sucking *Poets* from it:
Doctor, if this be my Fate, when I *Spue*;
That Lapping Curs rise, all *Lampooning* you;
Your *Physick* you must save, and past all hope,
With *Crocus Metallorum* buy a *Rope*.

(p. 37)

The doctor is defeated in this poem by his own prescription,
as the poet converts his disgust and anger at a physiological
insult into a fantasy of poetic conquest. Furthermore, in ad-
vising the physician to use the emetic he had prescribed for
the poet, *Crocus Metallorum*, a powder made from calcinated
metals,[19] to buy the means of committing suicide, Carkesse
indicates what he regards as the proper function of the popular remedies for madness of the period. Frightened on
another occasion when forced vomiting is again prescribed,
he reassures himself:

But thanks to *Apollo*, who is on my side,
And hath with *Antidote* me fortify'd

that he will "elude" the "ill effect" of such "needless" treatment. "*Purges* and *Vomits*," he declares, "*Helicon* shall correct" (p. 30). Incarcerated, subjected to harsh, debilitating
measures for emotional as well as physical repression, he establishes his own empathic entities in Apollo and Helicon,
symbols of the creative and restorative powers of his own
imagination.

Throughout *Lucida Intervalla*, Carkesse wavers between the

claim that his madness is only a masquerade and the proud declaration that he, like all inspired wits and poets, is indeed mad. But the most prevalent and consistent theme of the volume is that his emotional responses to his environment, however aberrant, are valid, and that these, conveyed through the agency of Apollo, and thus of poetry, are his most potent defense against madness, therefore his only means of survival. This theme appears in a variety of forms, and, if Carkesse is in no sense a gifted poet, he reveals a remarkable capacity to communicate his feelings, especially anger in lampoon, and to disclose the ways in which the "Self-curing Poet" (p. 36) maintains an image of himself that defies official judgment.

"The Poetical History of Finnesbury Mad-house" (pp. 9-15) is an account of the consignment to the asylum of a "parson," who is probably Carkesse himself, for he so describes himself in a dedicatory poem, "To His Royal Highness" (p. 5) and elsewhere in the volume. In "The Poetical History . . . ," as in other poems, Carkesse expresses resistance to the diagnosis of madness, the treatment, and the atmosphere of the asylum by using them as the subject of irony or by countering them with mythical omnipotence. The Doctor's diagnosis "That *Learning* had made the Man *Mad*" is for Carkesse only evidence of "How little the *Doctor* had." Continually, he emphasizes the superficial bases of the Doctor's judgments and his mechanistic and thus ineffectual treatment. After expressing wonder that "neither *Vomits* nor *Purges*" have any effect, the Doctor describes his patient's reaction to chains:

> My *Fetters* they were but *Straw*
> 　To the Sinews of His Armes
> And he burst Bars and Doors, as I saw,
> 　By I know not what mighty *Charmes*.

Carkesse depicts the "parson's" powerful emotions breaking through the constraints of the asylum as he identifies him with Dionysus, the mad god, destroying the prison to which Pentheus had consigned him. His "Charmes" are both pagan and Christian, poetic and religious. The Doctor continues:

> Moreover I him in the *Hole*,
>   As under a Bushel, confin'd;
> Lest God's Word, the Light of the Soul,
>   In my Mad-house should have Shin'd:
> Ne're the less into the *Dungeon*,
>   He let in the Rayes of the *Sun*,
> And i' th' Pit, where him I did plunge in,
>   Made Night and Day meet in one.

Carkesse draws on familiar religious allusions or actual experience, such as a visit to the asylum by a beautiful woman (pp. 42, 43), to create for himself a conception of light in the darkness of the madhouse. More powerful, however, than the Christian God as an antidote to the darkness, the vermin, the chains, and the other indignities, is the image of Apollo, inspiring the release of his most intense feelings in verse. In "His Apology" (p. 16), Carkesse concedes to the doctor the privilege of ascribing his rage, in the jargon of the day, to "Gall," but to him it is "Poetic Fury," attributed in the Latin version of the same poem to the influence of Apollo. He also invokes the spirit of Dionysus in this poem, as he makes a pseudo-apology for engaging "Among your *Rats* and *Mice*" in "my *Satyre Dance*."

Carkesse's psychic defenses and efforts at "self-curing" are primarily defiance, anger, mockery (including self-mockery), and adherence to a belief in the efficacy of self-expression that opposes the code of the asylum. All these emotions and attitudes he projects on Apollo and the Muses. Defending his self-image with the conviction that "By *Muses* he's [the doctor's] defy'd" (p. 28), he continually observes the physical and psychic effects of the asylum on himself, and counters them with the powers he invests in poetry. Admitting "My joynts are stiff, and I'm opprest with cold," he consoles himself in the lines that follow:

> But influence of *Apollo* still is strong,
> My *Satyr* brisk, lively my *Muse* and *Song*.
>
> (p. 28)

Carkesse takes literally Juvenal's "facit indignatio versum," which he quotes as an epigraph (p. 31); the madman's "indignatio" is acceptable to Apollo, who presides over both medicine and poetry and thus is viewed as intrinsic to his cure. In fact, not only is the doctor defeated by the poet's capacity to endure the horrors or overcome the effects of his treatment through self-expression in verse, but the poet can actually cure himself in this way:

> Physitian, *heal thy self*, we say; but know it,
> In earnest said to the Self-curing Poet.
>
> (p. 36)

Inherent in Carkesse's concept of self-cure is his resolution of the conflict between his psychological need to express "Poetick Rage" and "Gall in Ink" (p. 39) and the prevailing medical principle of suppression. Since Apollo is god "Of *Poetry* and *Medicine* too" (p. 40), the anger and yearning Carkesse feels he must convey in poetry are acceptable modes of cure. The impossibility of Apollo's being "At War . . . with himself" (p. 40) in his two functions as god of poetry and of medicine allows Carkesse to maintain his unorthodox position in the repressive environment in which he must survive; in this symbol of the ancient god, he thus creates his own medical sanction for the acceptance of his emotions. With this support he has himself created, his adherence to his role of poet also allows him to acknowledge his own madness and to adapt his bizarre associations to his struggle for survival. In *"To a Friend, upon his sending him* Venison *to* BEDLAM" (p. 58), Carkesse describes himself in the conventional animal images used for the mad:

> If like be fed by like, what better meat
> Can *Horn Mad*, wild as *Buck*, then *Venison* eat?

He develops the idea of feeding madness and intensifying it with salt and pepper, all of which encourage wit. But the associations that emerge in connection with his identification with animal metaphors also reveal his fears; in the asylum, like so many of the madmen described in literature, he is the hunted, in this case by his keepers:

> Now *Doc* and *Pot*, those *whiffling Curs*, in couple
> That always *Hunt*, I'le keep at *bay* and *bubble*; . . . .

Finally, receiving the venison, like almost all the many experiences in the asylum, painful or comforting, that he describes, becomes a basis for the creation of his verses, and thus a means to survival:

> For *Goat* and *Venison* differ so small a matter,
> That *Buck* will lusty make my *Bedlam Satyre;*
> And (*when with Rope Sir Quack has cur'd the smart*)
> My *Brisk Lampoon*, survive the long-liv'd *Hart*.

Carkesse's poetic aspirations are only slightly less grandiose than his fantasies of being an imprisoned emperor (p. 22) or a fallen prince (p. 44), but they have some basis in reality. If Carkesse was at best a mediocre poet, his volume does communicate the loneliness as well as the private heroism of an actual psychological struggle against the mechanistic medical treatment of his time. His ingenuous revelations of the psychic defenses he constructs from the most sordid details of his dehumanizing environment elicit from the reader both recognition and dread. In his very naiveté, moreover, Carkesse confronts directly, if primitively, what is to be one of the most subtle aesthetic problems of eighteenth-century literature: the simultaneous fascination with and distrust of the irrational.

In the work of the greatest writers of the period, Swift and Pope, this conflict is brilliantly resolved in monumental metaphors of madness as folly and pride, which actually reflect their age's avoidance of the complex psychic deprivations and defenses of the insane. Both Swift and Pope accept the traditional view that excessive imagination or fancy overwhelming reason creates madness; this condition, moreover, results from willful aggrandizement of the self, the sin of pride. What is most striking in all Swift's metaphors of

madness and in those of Pope's *Dunciad* is their reflection of
the common assumption that the symptoms resulting from
this imbalance of mental faculties reduce their victims to a
subhuman state. The animal associations observed so frequently in literature in connection with madness seem to
have been taken literally in the eighteenth century, both by
physicians treating the mad and those who went to observe
them in Bedlam as an afternoon's amusement. With few ex-
ceptions, such as Thomas Tryon or Sir Richard Blackmore,[20]
commentators on madness seem incapable of making any
connection between the symptoms of insanity and human
guilt, panic, overwhelming rage, or other forms of psychic
anguish. Instead, regressive acts such as urination or defeca-
tion in the presence of visitors, hallucinations, or threats of
violence, were cited to characterize the mad as monstrous. It
was believed, moreover, that the insane could endure extremes of cold and pain without suffering, a notion that
seems calculated to separate further the mad from the sane
and to justify the inhumane conditions in which they were
kept and the cruelty of the treatment prescribed. Again and
again in eighteenth-century descriptions of inhabitants of
Bedlam one is struck by an attitude of detached amusement,
which is actually an evasion of the very revelations of the
inner sources of the conflict and suffering that the strange
conduct enacts. Ned Ward, for example, describes a Bedla-
mite "as hard at work as if he'd been treading mortar. 'What
is it, friend,' said I, 'thou art taking all these pains about?' He
answered me thus, still continuing in action: 'I am trampling
down conscience under my feet, lest he should rise up and fly
in my face. Have a care he does not fright thee, for he looks
like the devil and is as fierce as a lion, but that I keep him
muzzled. Therefore get thee gone, or I will set him upon
thee.' Then he fell aclapping his hands, and cried, 'Halloo,
halloo, halloo, halloo, halloo,' and thus we left him raving."[21]
The poignancy of a human being projecting his own guilt on
the devil and struggling with it in symbolic physical combat is
lost on Ward; he is not even curious about this bizarre manifestation of what is, after all, not an unusual human preoc-

cupation. Ward, however, like most of his contemporaries, sees only the symptoms.

This emphasis on symptoms underlies some of Swift's most brilliant rhetorical effects. His depictions and imitations of the thought processes of the mad convey no effort to probe beyond the current mechanistic platitudes. Even as he mocks these as pretentious evasions, he himself evades madness as a psychic condition by viewing it as willful ignorance, self-deception, and moral corruption. The mind behind the symptoms of Swift's madmen is confused only by arrogance and evil.

The most perceptive of the recent commentators on madness in *A Tale of A Tub*, Michael De Porte,[22] argues convincingly that the narrator is a madman (p. 69 ff.). "There are suggestions," says De Porte, "that he left Bedlam before he was fully cured and that the *Tale* itself is written as a kind of therapy, as a diversion to turn his thoughts away from dangerous things." De Porte goes on to demonstrate how the uncurbed imagination of the narrator is manifested not only in his grandiose conception of himself and his purpose but in the very structure of the *Tale*. Acknowledging that the digressions are, "to be sure, part of Swift's plan for alternately satirizing the corruption of religion and learning," De Porte shows that they also "underscore the fragmentation and incoherence" of the narrator's thinking. Within the digressions themselves, De Porte points out, there are abrupt shifts in subject, topics mentioned but never treated, and other evidence of disordered thinking. But even these brilliant effects are, as De Porte suggests, no more than a rhetorical adaptation of the Hobbesian view of "how fancy could lead a man into mad and impertinent detours of thought" (pp. 74-75).

Swift's satirical depiction of the inexplicable corruption inherent in human nature, unrestrained and actually fostered by the self-indulgent moderns and emerging in the thought processes of a madman, reveals the contempt and loathing he shared with his contemporaries for madness itself. To call Swift's interpretation of the prototypical modern "the result of a perceptive study of a schizophrenic mind"[23] is to accept his notion that pride and ignorance of the history, the ethical values, and the great art of the past constitute insanity.

No reader of *A Tale of A Tub* can resist Swift's most effective evidence of the modern's mental deficiency—his absence of memory. Yet Swift's conception of memory is as conventional as his view of madness. One could hardly expect him to consider the operation of memories repressed by the unconscious mind, but an eighteenth-century man could have been aware of the vast range of his own memory and its individuality: its fusion of the personal and the historical, the vague and the precise; its emotional as well as its intellectual functions; its inexplicable lapses and recoveries. But Swift, at least in *A Tale of A Tub*, avoids such complications, accepting the Hobbesian view of memory as a repository of long established truths and values, an agent of reason and thus of suppression: "Man excelleth beasts only in making rules to himself, that is to say, in remembering, and in reasoning aright upon that which he remembereth."[24] The personal and historical memories that haunt the insane have no place in Swift's caricature of the mind of the modern as madman. Swift's modern has no memory, and thus is guided by no rules based upon the wisdom of the past, restrained by no inherited codes of morality.

Ironically, Swift's very lack of interest in exploring the cognitive and emotional components of madness and the absence of compassion, at least in his work, for its victims make his metaphors of social madness such a powerful weapon. Using the most mechanistic of traditional physiological explanations for mental aberration—the vapors "issuing up from the lower faculties"[25] to invade and disturb the brain— Swift plays with every conceivable biological and scatological association of this concept, especially the notion popularized by Renaissance literature and, of course, by Burton, that the humors create the "spirits" or vapors as links between man's body and his soul. When the humors are diseased, the spirits or vapors upset the mechanism of the brain, and madness ensues.

All Swift's madmen—rulers, philosophers, poets, scholars,

critics—are characterized by symptoms of the vapors, but none so variously and ingeniously as the religious enthusiast. That Swift is hardly unusual in his distrust of religious enthusiasm is well known; the cultural milieu in which his religious convictions were formed has been described in detail in C. M. Webster's considerations of earlier satirists of the Puritans[26] and more recently by Philip Harth in *Swift and Anglican Rationalism.*[27] Harth and De Porte have demonstrated that Swift was familiar with Henry More's *Enthusiasmus Triumphatus* (1656), in which he treats enthusiasm as a form of delusion caused by melancholy in contrast with authentic religious experience which issues from "a Principle of the *purest Reason* that is communicable to humane Nature."[28] By the time Swift wrote *A Tale of A Tub* the equation of madness with religious fanaticism was a commonplace in attacks on dissenters, as was the metaphor of Bedlam as their suitable habitat. The brilliance of Swift's use of this common metaphor in connection with religious enthusiasm lies in his adaptation of the theory of the vapors to express his hatred of the fanatical presumption that would impose an individual vision of religious experience on mankind.

Beginning with the Aeolists (section VIII), who "maintain the original cause of all things to be wind," Swift develops a fantastic pseudo-logical argument to establish a connection between the traditional description of the soul as spirit— "spiritus, animus, afflatus, or anima"—and various physiological effects of the vapors, especially their release in belching and breaking wind. The reception of belches as "sacred," the worship of the "gods of the four winds," especially "the chief of these," to whom his adherents "performed the adoration of *latria*," and the various "mysteries and rites" Swift describes all lead to his ultimate argument: for the enthusiast, the vapors, the commonly accepted physiological sign of madness, have replaced God as the origin of religion; it is the vapors that are the God within, the "inspiration" of the private vision.

In the "Digression on Madness," the narrator's persistent explanation of all human functioning—indeed, all human achievement—on the basis of the vapors extends this religious vision into secular life for the purpose of converting society itself into a great Bedlam. The spokesman for modernity has attempted to understand and interpret what Swift himself suggests could only be regarded as the disgusting and ridiculous behavior of the inhabitants of Bedlam. The narrator, confident of his intuitive responses to his fellow Bedlamites, has concluded that the madman "tearing his straw in piecemeal, swearing and blaspheming, biting his grate, foaming at the mouth, and emptying his piss-pot in the spectators' faces" is only revealing "talents" that might be adapted for military purposes: "give him a regiment of dragoons, and send him into Flanders. . . ." Other bizarre symptoms are interpreted as signs of various other "talents" useful to the state. Implicit in these wild speculations is Swift's response to those who, like Thomas Tryon, sought clues to hidden facets of human nature and repressed human conflict in the expression and conduct of the mad.

As the narrator recommends the conversion of symptoms into social occupations, he discloses the madness already current in society: the ignorance, stupidity, pretentiousness, and, most significantly, the pride of military and political leaders, lawyers, businessmen, physicians, and poets, whose power he would extend infinitely. But he also unwittingly reveals Swift's own judgment on madness: it is moral depravity in the form of pride, which must be suppressed by the harshest measures necessary. This is, of course, the traditional theological view, which continued to influence popular thinking and medical theory regarding madness. In fact, the attribution of madness to pride enters into the very mechanistic theories that Swift satirizes.

A Tale of A Tub offers no insight into the mind of the madman. Swift would have laughed with scorn at such an intention, which only his mad narrator could envision. In Swift's works, madmen are hardly human and certainly not individuals. They are all alike, metaphors of the social evil resulting from the unrepressed fantasies and impulses that would extend the narrow borders of the self properly confined in its place on the great religious, economic, and social chain of being. His use of madness as a satiric weapon discloses how profoundly he incorporates many of the assumptions and values of the very society he attacks so savagely.

Like Swift, Pope juxtaposes the threat of chaos against rule by order, a motif that reaches a crescendo in the dissolution of "*Art* after *Art*," truth, religion, philosophy, and morality under the influence of the "great Anarch" of madness in the fourth book of *The Dunciad*[29] (ll. 640-55). Although he alludes to madness often in his poetry as the extremity of a distorted perception of the self, he is not concerned with the inner world of desires and terrors that constitutes madness but with irrationality as a social and moral evil. There is no need to dwell on Pope's extensive use of madness as a metaphor for disruptive folly and pride, a subject that has received a good deal of attention in recent criticism.[30] It has, however, never been observed that these metaphors are, for the most part, vehicles for avoiding the very roots from which they spring: the unconscious conflicts that produce individual and societal madness.

This is not to say that Pope is unaware of the irrational constituents of human impulse and motivation. Indeed, he can and sometimes does accept these as part of the normal human condition. In a brilliant passage in the "Epistle to Cobham," the first of the *Moral Essays*, Pope seems to glimpse the unconscious sources of human conduct:

> Oft in the Passions' wild rotation tost,
> Our spring of action to ourselves is lost:
> Tir'd, not determin'd, to the last we yield,
> And what comes then is master of the field.
> As the last image of that troubled heap,
> When Sense subsides, and Fancy sports in sleep,
> (Tho' past the recollection of the thought)
> Becomes the stuff of which our dream is wrought:
> Something as dim to our internal view,
> Is thus, perhaps, the cause of most we do.
>
> (ll. 41-50)

But even in the *Moral Essays*, it is not in Pope's poetic character to explore what is "dim," the realm of "dream" and fantasy. He soon announces his "clue" to human nature, the "Ruling Passion," which, "once found, unravels all the rest" (ll. 174-78), a notion as mechanical as the humors or the "Passions of the Heart," to both of which it is surely related. Furthermore, in most of Pope's poetry, and certainly in *The Dunciad*, the products of "Fancy" and of "dream" are hardly treated with the sympathetic acceptance of the lines quoted from the "Epistle to Cobham." Pope generally assumes that if human motivation originates in such unconscious sources, it can only produce arrogance and thus evil. The irrational is finally indistinguishable from the mad.

The most justly celebrated of Pope's depictions of madness are products of the satiric genius that exposes the manifestations of human self-deception and pride but avoids revelation of their roots in psychic conflict for which there is no implicit moral resolution. The Cave of Spleen in *The Rape of the Lock* is often cited as evidence of Pope's interest in libidinous drives and blind compulsions, but it should be observed that this is a special kind of interest. The melancholy attitudes and bizarre conduct of the inhabitants of the Cave reveal as little regarding psychic reality as do contemporary medical descriptions to which they bear a strong resemblance. The proponent of one of the most mechanistic theories of the period, Nicholas Robinson,[31] who concluded that all mental illness was determined by the improper elasticity of the nerve fibers, describes the symptoms of the spleen in language similar to Pope's. He emphasizes its melancholy and "pensive" phases (p. 171), and in analyzing the role of the "Fancy," says that "under a Fit of the Spleen," this faculty can no longer "see thro' all these Mists that . . . cloud her Actions, and would persuade us, that these Bodies of ours are chang'd into Tea Pots, Glasses, Goose Pyes, and the like odd and ridiculous Transformations" (p. 190). Robinson's *A New System of the Spleen, Vapours, and Hypochondriack Melancholy* appeared in 1729, some years after *The Rape of the Lock*, but the closeness of his description to Pope's suggests not that the physician echoes the poet, but that both report the symptoms of psychopathology common to medical literature and drawing-room gossip of the day. Pope's note to IV, 52, in fact, informs us that the "Goose-pye" that "talks" in the Cave "Alludes to a real fact, a Lady of distinction imagin'd herself in this condition."

In the famous passage immediately preceding this one:

> A constant *Vapour* o'er the Palace flies;
> Strange Phantoms rising as the Mists arise;
> Dreadful, as Hermit's Dreams in haunted Shades,
> Or bright as Visions of expiring Maids.
> Now glaring Fiends, and Snakes on rolling Spires,
> Pales Spectres, gaping Tombs, and Purple Fires:
> Now Lakes of liquid Gold, *Elysian* Scenes,
> And Crystal Domes, and Angels in Machines.
>
> (IV, 39-46)

Pope dramatizes the hallucinations commonly accepted as symptoms of the spleen in "a satiric catalogue of the scenic effects of contemporary opera and pantomime."[32] To refer to this passage as a description of "the id," as a recent critic[33] has done, is to read into it scientific and imaginative orginality for which there is no evidence. These nightmare images and the other fantasies of wild disorder in the Cave of Spleen are conventional ones, all depicting mere symptoms, passions and vanities that must be controlled by the rules of social order. Within the satiric framework of *The Rape of the Lock*, they are to be regarded no more seriously than are the victims of the spleen. Pope mocks the very disease he describes not as a manifestation of aberrant mental functioning but as mere self-indulgence. In stylized and graceful nightmares, in affected griefs and passions, the spleen is exposed as willful self-dramatization which, prettily employed, can even have a social function.

As Sir Richard Blackmore pointed out, among the symptoms of what was called the spleen were hysteria, hypochondria, melancholy, great agitation, and bodily pain. Despite the obvious suffering of its victims, mockery of the illness was common. In fact, Blackmore suggests that one reason patients enduring its effects "are unwilling their Dis-

ease should go by its right Name" may be "that the Spleen
and Vapours are, by those that never felt their Symptoms,
looked upon as imaginary and fantastick Sickness of the
Brain. . . ." Because the illness "by a great Mistake" has become "an Object of Derision and Contempt," people who
suffer it will not acknowledge it. In his effort to counteract
this general denial of the seriousness of such symptoms, by
both patients and observers, Blackmore explains that psychic
illness can cause physical suffering:

> It is certain, that Hypocondriacal Men, as well as Hys-
> terick Women, are often afflicted with various Pains and
> great Disorders; and could it be supposed that this was
> nothing but the Effect of Fancy, and a delusive imagina-
> tion, yet it must be allowed, that let the Cause of such
> symptoms be never so chimerical and fantastick, the
> consequent Sufferings are without doubt real and un-
> feigned. Terrible ideas, formed only in the Imagination,
> will affect the Brain and the Body with painful Sensa-
> tions. . . .[34]

The mental and physical anguish that the disease called the
spleen entails, which Blackmore insists is real, is implicitly
denied in *The Rape of the Lock*. Belinda, with her artfulness,
converts even the spleen into a social grace; she suffers
neither alienation nor despair, but instead makes the spleen
part of the elegant realm that she inhabits and controls. Um-
briel himself is aware of her power:

> Hear me, and touch *Belinda* with Chagrin;
> That single Act gives half the World the Spleen.
>
> (IV, 77-78)

In the miniature world of *The Rape of the Lock*, madness itself
is reduced to a fashionable malady, which has its own rules
and conventions within the social order.

Neither beauty nor charm mitigates the social madness
satirized in *The Dunciad*; the folly and pride exhibited by its
protagonists cannot be incorporated into the traditional social
framework, but threaten its very bases. In this poem, the

popular metaphor of Bedlam as a representation of society as a whole is employed not only, as is common in the age, to mock the irrationality of greed, ambition, and self-deception, but to presage the dissolution of high culture and with it civilization itself. The metaphor of madness that pervades *The Dunciad* is not a vehicle for probing the psychological roots of social disorder. Actually, the poem reflects its age in its evasion of such exploration and in its focus on the symptoms of intellectual and moral derangement. Those concerned with what is "dim to our external view" in *The Dunciad* are abhorrent, surrounded by mists and clouds which carry the medical connotations of vapors produced by the "Mists" of uncontrolled fancy. The dreams and fantasies are not those that emerge from the elegant theatrical underworld of the belle whose name the loving poet will inscribe "mid'st the Stars"; they escape from "The Cave of Poverty and Poetry" (i, 34) to make their unwholesome way into "Journals, Medleys, Merc'ries, Magazines" (i, 42). On the last of these Pope comments: "These were thrown out weekly and monthly by every miserable scribler; or picked up piece-meal and stolen from any body, under the title of Papers, Essays, Queries, Verses, Epigrams, Riddles &c. equally the disgrace of human Wit, Morality, and Decency."

In its closeness to Bedlam, the Cave of Poverty and Poetry is, of course, implicated in madness, and all three, madness, poverty, and bad writing are from Pope's point of view the products of pride and willful self-deception. Pope had long perceived an intrinsic satiric connnection in these three evils. In *The Narrative of Dr. Robert Norris, Concerning the strange and deplorable FRENZY of Mr. John Denn– –*,[35] published in 1713, lack of literary talent and discrimination combined with an inability to accept such limitations produce the conventional symptoms of madness—paranoiac fear, "fiery" eyes, raving and violence. Dennis himself ascribes his "Distemper" to a "Criticism" (p. 160). The doctor, who declares that the "Symptoms of His Madness seem to be desperate," explains "that if Learning be mix'd with a Brain that is not of a Contexture fit to receive it, the Brain ferments till it be totally exhausted," and concludes that the only cure for Dennis is to "eradicate these undigested Ideas out of the *Perecranium*, and reduce the Patient to a competent Knowledge of himself" (pp. 163-64). The filth of Dennis' person, the disorder and ugliness of his surroundings, and his madness itself are all evidence of his pride.

Although Dennis is hardly the most important of the Dunces, Pope refers to him explicitly as a symbol in *The Dunciad*: "And all the Mighty Mad in Dennis rage" (*Dunc. Var.* I, 104; *Dunc.*, 1743, I, 106). In his note to this line in *The Dunciad Variorum*, Pope is intentionally ambiguous about his allusion to madness: "This is by no means to be understood literally, as if Mr. D. were really mad. . . ." He then refers to evidence of Dennis' actual madness in his own *Narrative of Dr. Robert Norris*, but dismisses it along with satires on himself as "idle Trash." What he actually means, Pope says, is "that *Excellent and Divine Madness*, so often mentioned by *Plato*, that poetical rage and enthusiasm, with which no doubt Mr. *D*. hath, in his time, been highly possessed. . . ." In this note Pope parodies his own tendency—common in the satirist—to disclose and defend the very satiric techniques he uses.[36] One of the most brilliant of these in *The Dunciad* is his mockery of the commonly accepted symptoms of madness even as he employs them to signify moral and intellectual deficiency. Tony Tanner has suggested that "one of the more disturbing effects of *The Dunciad* is the fantastic unawareness of the participants: they tumble into pools of excrement, they compete in urinating competitions, they dive happily into deep mud, without ever giving any sign that they are aware of anything odd about their behaviour." Tanner goes on to comment on the "inhuman" quality of Pope's dunces.[37] Pope's frame of reference for such conduct may well have been the reports of visitors to Bedlam, describing with what seems a strange detachment and often with hilarity the conduct of the madmen they observed.

The separation of the symptom from the human being manifesting it, typical of medical treatment of the period and of popular response conditioned by medical and social authority, is an essential feature of Pope's metaphors of madness, which dehumanize religious enthusiasts, poets who rely on divine inspiration, the ignorant who claim wisdom, all those whose pride leads them to "See all in *Self*" (IV, 480). In dehumanizing such solipsism, Pope's metaphors of madness powerfully convey what he regards as a threat of anarchy, the destruction of the traditional social stratifications in which the self must adapt to its assigned role. Ultimately the purpose of the dunces is "To blot out Order, and extinguish Light" (IV, 14). The note to this line is explicit: "*Order* here is to be understood extensively, both as Civil and Moral, the distinctions between high and low in Society, and true and false in individuals: *Light* as Intellectual only, Wit, Science, Arts." The separation of the fragmented thought and violent emotions manifested in madness from the human beings suffering the effects of such symptoms parallels the rigid distinctions Pope sees as essential for the maintenance of an unchanging order. Such distinctions deny that disorder is inevitable in all societies as in all individual human life, inherent in the very dynamics of social change. The increasing economic strength of the middle class, the growth of popular literature, the spread of dissenting sects, all the evidence of energy and power where it had not previously been felt spell anarchy in *The Dunciad*, the "low" impinging on the "high," fantasy and distortion claiming their own view of truth. Pope's denial that there is any validity in this claim is most intensely expressed in his association of the poor, the "low," the visionary with the madman who, from the darkness to which he is consigned, would challenge the very distinction between the "true and the false in Individuals" and society that is the basis of Pope's brilliant satirical effects.

Most eighteenth-century poetic depictions of mental aberration beyond its obvious symptoms seem tentative and generally ineffectual compared to the brilliant caricatures of madness created by Swift and Pope. Poets such as Anne Finch, Matthew Green, and William Cowper often seem to subvert their own efforts to break through medical or religious formulae. Yet in poems by Finch and Cowper the very ambivalence discloses an individual experience of and response to mental states heavily charged with official designations.

Anne Finch's choice of the Pindaric ode as the genre for "The Spleen"[38] indicates her assumption that the emotional and stylistic intensity associated with the Pindaric are appropriate to her subject and implies a hope that the genre itself will release insight normally prohibited by stock responses of shame or contempt for psychic disorder. Her awareness that the "real cause" of the spleen has not been found, and that the disease manifests itself differently in each of its victims seems to promise a departure from conventional terminology and mechanistic explanations. But such expectations are disappointed by her generalized depiction of mental suffering as a "Dead" or stormy sea, as "fond delusions" and "airy phantoms" and by her echo of the all too familiar notion that the spleen results from the "vapours" rising from "o'erheated passions" to the brain. Yet there are passages—both mildly satiric and discreetly confessional—in which "The Spleen" reveals an awareness rare for its time of the complex relationship between social determinants and individual experience of psychological disturbance, especially in its interpretation of the spleen as a defense against aggression or alienation.

One of her examples is the wife struggling against her subservient role in marriage. Confronting her "lordly" husband, "born to imperial sway," she is "arm'd with spleen," converting weakness into a weapon which he feels compelled to "servilely obey." Fools pretend to be suffering from the spleen only to "imitate the wits" and to find an excuse for their "dullness," but it is actually the gifted who, in their loneliness, their disappointment in the "slow returns where they so much dispense," who are "inclin'd" to the melancholia of the spleen. Finch gently satirizes the fool, and, more than a decade before Pope, whom she probably influenced, the belle for whom the symptoms of the spleen have a social usefulness, but even these are depicted as efforts to exert control through the affectation of sickness and despair.

Her revelation of her own struggle with the effects of the

spleen conveys her deepest apprehension of its symptoms as a manifestation of conflict between the expectations of society and personal commitment. She portrays herself as attacked by the spleen at the very time that she "rail[s]" against it in her poetry; the disease, moreover, manifests itself chiefly in the "decay" of her "verse," rendering ineffective the talent by which she defines herself:

> My lines decried, and my employment thought
> An useless folly, or presumptuous fault.

The spleen diminishes her confidence in her art and discloses her psychological vulnerability in daring to conceive of herself as different from most women of her time and class. Returning to her image of herself as poet, she describes her delight in original creation:

> Whilst in the Muses' paths I stray,
> Whilst in their groves and by their secret springs
> My hand delights to trace unusual things,
> And deviates from the known and common way;

and goes on to contrast her own deviation from the "common way" with the conventional occupations of women—embroidery or painting "on glass / The sov'reign's blurred and undistinguished face, / The threat'ning angel, and the speaking ass." The spleen is thus a psychological threat to the assertion of her talent against a conventional and useless social role she sees as her only alternative to self-fulfillment as a poet. In her brief and restrained confession of despair, Anne Finch approaches the spleen as an antithetical force within herself, the antagonist of the very impulse to apprehend it in poetry. She ends her poem declaring that no cause for the spleen has been found by physicians in "the well-dissected body" and acknowledging that its "secret, . . . mysterious ways" yield to no known treatment.

Anne Finch's attitude toward the spleen in this poem retains something of the metaphysical ambiguity of mood, a fusion of the objective composure of observation with the intensity of personal response, wit with a suggestion of mystery and dread of the unknown. Matthew Green's poem on the same subject with the same title, which appeared thirty-one years later, is typically Augustan in the self-assurance of its tone and its explicatory method. Although in "An Epistle to Mr. Cuthbert Jackson," with which "The Spleen"[39] begins, Green declares that he plans to write of his own experience, he actually is not concerned with his own or anyone else's mental conflict or melancholy; his aim is to describe his method of combating such symptoms. The body of the poem is a compendium of popular medical explanations of the physical causes of the spleen and prescriptions for its avoidance or cure. In his own case, he says, "Reason" initially quieted the "frightful figures" produced by the spleen (ll. 43-47), and the rest of the cure consists in the main of a cheerful reliance on a simple diet, exercise, humor, entertainment at the theater or concert hall, conversation, and nature.

Behind the wit and light-hearted assurance that mental disorder can be conquered by reason lies a rigid prohibition against the private vision or any other intensely personal feeling or expression:

> I never am at meeting seen,
> Meeting, that region of the Spleen;
> The broken heart, the busy fiend,
> The inward call, on Spleen depend.
>
> (ll. 282-85)

Obviously reacting against his own upbringing as a Quaker, Green warns against the dissenters' "meeting," but avoids any personal reference to its dangers. His admonitions against passion and fancy are equally generalized. Inevitably, he adds the writing of poetry to the list of prohibitions. It is interesting to notice that in this respect his approach to the spleen is the direct opposite of Anne Finch's, for whom the disease is the antagonist of the poet and of poetry itself. In Green's view, the "Muses' revelations" will "find men cracked, or make them so" (ll. 500-501).

In its equation of religious or poetic inspiration with the

spleen, Matthew Green's poem would seem to be merely a
gentle reduction of general attitudes far more effectively conveyed in the satires of Swift and Pope. What is interesting
about Green's poem in the context of the age is his repeated
assertion that he writes about his own experience. Whether
this is true or merely a rhetorical pose, it is significant that the
assertion is contradicted by his highly conventionalized descriptions of the effects of the spleen and the means of avoiding it. If there is any personal revelation in this poem, it is of a
deliberate suppression of troublesome feeling:

> At helm I make my reason sit,
> My crew of passions all submit.
>
> (ll. 816-17)

denial of the very personal nature of the mental illness he
writes of and a rejection of poetry itself. How effectively such
denial operates is indicated in the fact that a poem entitled
"The Spleen" should communicate no sign of conflict or suffering.

However differently Finch and Green portray mental illness, in approaching it under the designation of the spleen,
they deal with symptoms of limited extent and duration, classified among the inevitable disorders that are contained
within an essentially ordered cosmic and social framework.
For William Cowper, mental disorder is madness, the central
and overwhelming experience of a lifetime. Its ramifications
are boundless. In his letters, autobiography, and poetry,
Cowper seems compelled to portray the grand assumptions—life and death, God and the devil, good and evil—and
the basic emotional responses of love, hate, fear, and joy as
these are symbolically transformed by the irrational thought
processes, the delusions, and the pain of insanity. Yet it is
not a madman who speaks from Cowper's writings, but a rational being who has repeatedly endured, remembers all too
well, and lives in continual dread of, psychic dissolution.
Biographers of Cowper and commentators on his work have
attempted to explain the genesis of his mental illness and
have traced his references to it, both direct and oblique, in his

poetry.[40] These studies are no doubt useful for understanding both the man and his work, but it seems to me that in relation to the theme of madness in literature what is most interesting is Cowper's use of irrational terror, confusion, nightmares, visual and auditory hallucinations, and the loss of self-control to disclose the interplay of unconscious and conscious processes of mind manifested in both the commonplace activities the poet shares with most human beings and in his unique personal experience.

Cowper's *Memoir*[41] reveals extraordinary insight into such intrapsychic processes. Describing the circumstances leading to his emotional breakdown of 1763, he tells of "the horrors of [his] fears and perplexities" (p. 52) in having to face a public examination before the bar of the House of Lords for the position of the Clerkship of the Journals. The very thought of a public examination[42] was so terrifying to Cowper that the requirement seemed to him an inevitable exclusion from the post. Yet he could not simply withdraw from competition for fear of injuring the reputation of the cousin who had recommended him. Their very plan to secure the post for Cowper now inspired guilt, since they had "both expressed an earnest wish for [the] death" of the former Clerk of the Journals in order that Cowper "might be provided for." When the man actually did die, Cowper saw himself "involved in still deeper guilt" (p. 46), as if the wish itself had caused the clerk's death. Attempting to prepare for the examination and certain he could never face it, he saw madness as the only way out of his painful conflict:

I now began to look upon madness as the only chance remaining. I had a strong foreboding that so it would fare with me; and I wished for it earnestly, and looked forward to it with impatient expectation. My chief fear was, that my senses would not fail me time enough to excuse my appearance at the Bar of the House of Lords, which was the only purpose I wanted it to answer.

(pp. 60-61)

But he soon realized that he could not retreat into madness by conscious choice, and thus decided on suicide as another way to "dissolution" (p. 62). He goes on to describe his growing irrationality as he plotted three attempts at suicide—which proved unsuccessful. He records his gradual loss of rational control over his fantasies and impulses both before and after these attempts: his use of the arguments of casual acquaintances supporting suicide as "a satisfactory decision" (pp. 65-66), his interpretation of a letter in a newspaper as "a libel or satire" on him and as an effort by its author "to secure and hasten the execution" of his "self-destruction" (pp. 67-68), and his assumption that a ballad he heard on the street was about him (p. 94). In depicting his agonizing confict regarding suicide, Cowper reveals that the madness he consciously sought as an escape from the dreaded examination was also an unconscious choice, a retreat from the repressed guilt and fear a public interrogation evoked and from absolute "dissolution" in death, which he desired and feared.

Cowper describes in some detail the psychic and physical manifestations of his gradual retreat into madness: attempting to commit suicide by drinking laudanum, he experienced a "conflict that shook me to pieces suddenly. . . , not properly a trembling, but a convulsive agitation, which deprived me in a manner of the use of my limbs" (p. 72). In a second attempt his hands became "dead and lifeless" (p. 75). Yet he is aware that these temporary disabilities did not prevent his committing suicide but rather were symptoms of his struggle "between the desire of death and the dread of it" (pp. 72-73). Writing retrospectively, from an Evangelical point of view, he attributes his inability to destroy himself to God's intervention, and there is no doubt that he held deeply to this belief. Yet in his *Memoir*, his letters, and his poetry, he also discloses his lifelong ambivalence toward his savior, his unconscious doubt, rage, and fear of abandonment (to which he periodically regressed in madness) converted into dependence, at once hostile and worshipful.

The circumstances leading to Cowper's conversion, as it is

recounted in his *Memoir*, include his conviction of total sinfulness and his utter despair; his grateful acceptance of his cousin, Martin Madan's assurance that in this respect he is no different from other human beings, since all partake of original sin, "the corruption of everyman born into the world"; his recognition that his "case required" the "remedy" of a belief in "the all-atoning blood of Jesus, and his righteousness for our justification" (pp. 102-103); a period of increased nightmares and terror, "a stronger alienation from God than ever" (p. 105); and finally a descent into madness, "that distemper of mind which I had so ardently wished for" (p. 106). At the asylum at St. Albans, under the care of Dr. Nathaniel Cotton, a convert to Methodism, Cowper, after months of "self-loathing and abhorrence," "conviction of sin, and expectation of instant judgment" (p. 109), slowly began to entertain the possibility that he was not utterly doomed to damnation. He describes his actual conversion as taking place on his picking up the Bible and reading Romans 3:25: "Whom God hath set forth to be a propitiation through faith in his blood, to declare his righteousness for the remission of sins that are past, through the forebearance of God" (p. 119). His ability at this point to believe that his own "pardon" was "sealed in" the blood of Christ made possible Cowper's conversion. This was indeed the "remedy" he had foreseen for his derangement. With his conversion came a period of joyous relief from the anguish of madness and despair. But even in the *Memoir*, written soon after his conversion, Cowper makes it clear that the peacefulness he then enjoyed was not to be a consistent frame of mind: "O that the ardour of my first love had continued! But I have known many a lifeless and unhallowed hour since, long intervals of darkness, interrupted by short returns of peace and joy in believing." And now he acknowledges an "anger" of which he had not been aware before his conversion. It is "that passion . . . which *now* gives me the most disturbance, and occasions the sharpest conflict" (pp. 119-23).

Cowper's evangelical interpretation of his irrational terrors and nightmares, his longing for insanity and death, does not diminish his extraordinary ability to convey unconscious conflict and motivation manifested in conscious decision, action, and expression. Hoosag K. Gregory has observed the significance of a childhood episode that Cowper recalled as his fears of the examination led to thoughts of suicide. When Cowper was about eleven years old, his father asked him to read and give his opinion of a "vindication of self-murder," only to remain silent when the boy argued against it. In his *Memoir*, he recalls his childhood inference that his father "sided with the author against me," and confesses that "the circumstances now weighed mightily with me" (pp. 63-64). Gregory interprets the adult man's preoccupation with this incident in a time of great conflict as evidence that "Unconsciously, Cowper believed that his father wanted him to die."[43] Cowper's concern with this episode, though obviously revealing, in itself seems insufficient evidence for so precise a formulation of his unconscious response to his father's silence. He himself provides evidence in the very next paragraph of his more complicated reaction to this incident as it continued to affect his adult life, when he goes on to recount his quest for justification for suicide from strangers. He describes himself engaging in a discussion on the general question of "self-murder" with "an elderly well-looking gentleman" in a chop-house (p. 64) and with another person in a tavern (p. 65), all the while seeking valid reasons for his own suicide. In his present distress, he has obviously recreated the circumstances of the childhood incident, posing to casual acquaintances the question that his father had once asked him. This time, however, he identifies himself with his image of his father in agreeing that suicide can be justifiable when life becomes unendurable. It can express the "indignant fortitude of spirit" of those who "despise life" (p. 65). The circumstances of his repetition of the childhood episode suggest not so much that the boy believed his father "wanted him to die" as that he felt his father placed little value on life, that he saw human existence—and thus the boy himself—as worthless. His silence, moreover, must surely have seemed a denial of the boy's "reasons" for opposing suicide, his assertion of whatever frail belief in himself he retained. His rage at his father's remoteness could not be expressed; it could only be turned on himself, intensifying a sense of alienation and worthlessness by then well established. Cowper's account suggests at least a preconscious awareness of the connection between the boy's interpretation of a painful incident and the man's compulsion to justify the emotional desolation associated with it. Furthermore, his view of his madness as an escape, his delineation of its stages, and his perception of his conversion as a "remedy" indicate the conflict between self-awareness and denial that is to characterize his later work.

In the *Memoir*, his letters, and his poetry, Cowper views his mental breakdowns, his nightmares, and his phobias as daemonically instigated or as a sure sign of his eternal damnation by God. But his portrayal, especially in his poetry, of his confrontation with the powers of heaven and hell manifested in daily life discloses his own psychological transformation of such conceptions. It is his capacity to apprehend the subtle connections between the apparently innocuous and the deeply painful, between nightmare and commonplace reality, the boundless emptiness of madness and the narrow limits of rationality that creates the unique quality of many of his poems.

Cowper used the period of insanity he recounts in his *Memoir* and the breakdowns he was to endure throughout his life as the emotional sources of a poetry fundamentally neoclassical in its subject matter, in the didacticism of its tone, and in its versification. Apart from an occasional somewhat stylized reference to the spleen, he ignores the mechanistic reduction of madness characteristic of his time; even his acceptance of the notion that imagination is a threat to mental stability is transformed by his individual view of its operation. The irrational terrors, the sense of alienation, helplessness, and abandonment, the self-loathing, and the loss of control over himself and his surroundings that he experienced in madness reappear in his poetry. His psychic pain and conflict are revealed in their very conversion to Evangelical religious fervor and in his personal conception of God, heaven, and hell; in the didacticism of his portrayal of daily, commonplace experience; and in his evocation of the chaos and emptiness ever threatening not only his own reclusive life but the lives of those apparently secure, the leaders of society and the makers of history.

"A Song of Mercy and Judgment,"[44] written a year or two after his recovery from the breakdown of 1763 described in his *Memoir*, contrasts his present state of grace, and thus rationality, to his former spiritual damnation in madness. One of the most striking features of this poem celebrating the effects of his conversion is its concentration on the physical and psychological manifestations of madness. These—the "waves of deep affliction," the sadness, the inability to eat, the loss of bodily strength, the fear of God, the guilt, the visual and auditory hallucinations of "scenes and voices" from hell—and the image of the poet, "Bound and watch'd" to prevent his attempting suicide, are clearly a record of personal experience. Contrasted with them the voice of God, "well tim'd and suited," seems conventional and pale. The "wond'rous story" the poet tells conveys the anguish of madness far more vividly than it does the joy of conversion. Its joys were indeed to be short-lived. The emotional drama of Cowper's relationship to God, as he recreates it in his poetry, contains far more anguish than pleasure.

Early in 1773, during his third breakdown, he had a dream that profoundly affected him for the remainder of his life. As Thomas Wright recounts it, in this dream Cowper "heard a 'word' which caused him to cross the line that divided a life of hope from a life of despair. The 'word,' no doubt, was '*Actum est de te, periisti*'—'It is all over with thee, thou hast perished.' Henceforth Cowper was a doomed man. God had forsaken him for ever."[45] Cowper refers to this dream several times in his letters, but it is his poem, "Lines Written During a Period of Insanity" that expresses the rage and guilt that determined his conviction of damnation.

The poem, probably written around 1774, is a startling revelation of the way in which Cowper converted his own aggression and anger—the "passion" he had described in the

Memoir as giving him "the most disturbance and occasions for the sharpest conflicts"—into symbolic action by ascribing motivations he himself could not accept to God. The ambiguity of the source of the "Hatred and vengeance" he is destined to endure is evident in the first stanza:

> Hatred and vengeance, my eternal portion,
> Scarce can endure delay of execution,
> Wait, with impatient readiness, to seize my
> Soul in a moment.

The "eternal portion" of his soul in life and in the hereafter is determined by his own nature and the judgment of God. "Hatred and vengeance" in this stanza seem to have a life of their own, as, unable to bear delay, they wait impatiently, urgent feelings and abstract forces plotting further psychic destruction and punishment. No doubt Cowper projected on God the rage he could never allow himself to feel at the mother who died when he was six and the father who in his eyes scorned his own pleasure in his youthful existence, but God has now become more than a composite of such feelings; He is the central psychological principle by which Cowper experiences his own relation to the world. God's law, as Cowper interprets it, establishes the harsh axioms by which he unconsciously transforms reality.

In the self-contempt his guilt demands, the only identity the poet can maintain is as the worst of sinners. "Damn'd below Judas: more abhorr'd than he was," threatened with a sentence "Worse than Abiram's," his very corruption defends him against total psychic dissolution:

> Man disavows, and Deity disowns me:
> Hell might afford my miseries a shelter;
> Therefore hell keeps her ever hungry mouths all
> Bolted against me.

Ironically, it is his very sense of depravity that keeps him from death, from the "shelter" of hell. It is not the eternal damnation of the afterlife that Cowper writes of in this poem, but the concept of God and of hell within his own soul. This very distinction is implicit in his contrast of his lot with Abiram's:

> *Him* the vindictive rod of angry justice
> Sent quick and howling to the centre headlong;
> *I*, fed with judgment, in a fleshly tomb, am
> Buried above ground.

Echoing the words of the vengeful God of the Old Testament, who promises, "I will destroy the fat and the strong; I will feed them with judgment" (Ezekiel 34:16), Cowper conveys God's anger and his own as one. His own irony is added to God's, as he interprets his "Hard lot," the "thousand dangers," and "thousand terrors" he must live with as the way in which he is "fed" by God. Dependent on God for life, the only sustenance he receives from Him is the "judgment" that makes his life a "fleshly tomb," his own mind a hell beyond any threatened in Christian theology. His rage at this judgment, his guilt in feeling it, and the judgment itself are indistinguishable, as are his belief in God and the conviction of his own damnation.

The hostile dependency that motivates Cowper's construction of his image of God and his response to that image emerge in other poems in various forms, such as a plea for release from his own anger in "Prayer for Patience" or, more obliquely, in his portraits of man as "a worm" or a "felon" living in terror or at best in hope under the awful power of God ("Hope," ll. 711-35). But it is God as the cause of and the only possible cure for his madness who most clearly externalizes the conflicting aims of aggression, love, and dependence unresolved even in the august heroic couplets on the classical theme of "Retirement." Inviting the reader to observe the "symptoms" of the "patient" suffering from melancholy, to

> see a statue move:
> Lips busy, and eyes fixt, foot falling slow,
> Arms hanging idly down, hands clasp'd below
>   (ll. 284-86),

he asks for a "sympathy" that will "contract a kindred pain" (l. 199). No such compassion can be expected of the "frowning God" who aimed his "barb'd arrows" at Job (l. 304), alone, like the melancholic, in his suffering. The anguish of madness is indeed "God's severest stroke" (l. 314). With no apparent cause He reverses the "screws" of the "harp" that is man, "in a moment . . . with ease" inflicting the alienation, the "wounds," the pain of madness. The "sad suff'rer" has no recourse other than acceptance; he must "understand / A father's frown, and kiss the chast'ning hand," for the very source of his madness is its only "cure" (ll. 327-46). Dependence on such power at least partly displaces the implicit rage at its arbitrary execution, but resentment and fear remain among the chief components of Cowper's tortured love for a God whose "curse" ("Table Talk," l. 467), "frown" ("Expostulation," l. 249), and "wrath" ("Hope," l. 609) continually threaten his own creation.

As victim and observer of madness, Cowper also conveys a unique perception of himself through his symbolic transformation of external reality in his identification with animals and in the image of psychic disaster that every commentator on his work has noticed, a stormy and destructive sea. According to Gregory, Cowper's identification with "scenic and animal nature," as reflected in his writing, expresses "an escape from . . . conflicts" and "a retreat from complexity and thus a lessening of terror."[46] On these matters, as in his discussion of Cowper's objections to hunting because of his identification with animals as victims, Gregory is convincing. But, in his emphasis on Cowper's use of this material as a means of controlling his impulses, Gregory ignores less obvious and, it seems to me, more important elements of this identification, especially with animals.

In the most famous passage of *The Task*, Cowper's overt identification with a "stricken deer" is also clearly an identification with Christ, the gentle aspect of God who "heal'd" him and "bade" him "live." Accepting this mercy, at least temporarily, the poet sees his own aberrations as exemplifying the condition of humankind:

> I see that all are wand'rers, gone astray
> Each in his own delusions. . . .

The apparently rational preoccupations of men and women are mere deceits, their "seeming wisdom" actually "So hollow and so false." The stricken deer's own suffering has taught him to pity their "frantic" avoidance of the

> pow'r who swears
> That he will judge the earth, and call the fool
> To a sharp reck'ning that has liv'd in vain. . . .
> (iii, 108-90)

In this passage Cowper's alienation from worldly concerns colors but does not alter a basically Evangelical judgment on the vanity of any pursuits uninspired by Christian piety.

But there is another passage in *The Task* (vi, 321-411) in which Cowper reveals a very different type of identification with animals—at once more basic and more complex. In "The Winter Walk at Noon," it is not the suffering but the pleasure of animals that involves him: the "sight of animals enjoying life," he says, can only "augment" his own happiness. His description begins with the conventional "bounding fawn" and "wanton" horse, but he soon moves on to a remarkable portrayal of the "total herd," engaging in a type of ritual dance:

> The total herd receiving first from one
> That leads the dance a summons to be gay,
> Though wild their strange vagaries, and uncouth
> Their efforts, yet resolv'd with one consent
> To give such act and utt'rance as they may
> To ecstasy too big to be suppress'd—

Three years before writing *The Task*, Cowper had described himself as a person "whose feelings are always of an intense kind. I never received a *little* pleasure from any thing in life; if I am delighted it is in the extreme." The very intensity of his feelings, he says, affects "the nerve of [his] imagination" so that it "twangs under the energy of the pressure with so much vehemence, that it soon becomes sensible of weariness and fatigue."[47] Although his particular reference is to the difficulties he experienced in writing, the letter indicates the emotional intensity that could not find release in the pious, secluded, sexually repressed existence he chose as a defense against madness. Even more revealing than this letter is his identification, in the lines quoted above, with the instinctual movements of the herd, which he views as a kind of Dionysiac rite, an ecstatic release of the pleasure inherent in the natural. In these animals he sees "a thousand images of bliss" unsuppressed.

Contrasted with the "frenzy" of the men who exploit them, the wildness of the animals is innocent and even their rage is justified. Far from an "aversion to wild nature,"[48] Cowper here discloses a kind of ungrudging envy for animals enjoying the wilderness within and without, free of human tyranny:

> The wilderness is their's, with all its caves,
> Its hollow glens, its thickets, and its plains,
> Unvisited by man. There they are free,
> And howl and roar as likes them, uncontrolled;
> Nor ask his leave to slumber or to play.

The animals can enjoy not only "uncontrolled" pleasure, but the role of "monarch," as the lion spares his "victim," man, "trembling at his foot." The vicarious delight Cowper expresses in the animals' instinctual freedom and power has a curious place in the long tradition of mythological, social, and literary identification of aberrant human behavior with the animal's uninhibited manifestations of its appetites and desires. The melancholy poet, repressed, withdrawn, continually recalling and dreading the terrors of madness, represents his own unconscious wishes in the "wanton" horse, the ecstatic herd, all the howling, roaring beasts enjoying sensuality, expressing yet in command of aggression, satisfactions permitted only to these creatures, with whom he can identify himself because they are also victims of arbitrary and remorseless powers.

Instinctual release for human beings—and especially for Cowper himself—is an ever-present danger. In the image of a storm at sea, as has often been observed,[49] he repeatedly portrays the turbulence of his own emotions, especially when he feels threatened by or recalls a period of insanity. But storms and shipwrecks also symbolize God's wrath and the dangers of the unknown in the universe. In his most effective use of this image, Cowper's own anxiety is projected on the world, where he sees the small portion of order and rationality mankind has achieved—and survival itself—continually threatened by chaos, by the destructiveness inherent in external and human nature, as God has created them and invests them with his presence.

The sea, which is "the most magnificent object under heaven," in "all its various forms, . . . an object of all others the most suited to affect us with lasting impressions of the awful Power that created and controls it,"[50] betrays human beings, becoming symbolically the source of error, confusion, and self-destruction:

> Man, on the dubious waves of error toss'd,
> His ship half founder'd, and his compass lost,
> Sees, far as human optics may command,
> A sleeping fog, and fancies it dry land. . . .

Human "schemes," "systems, philosophic dreams" are the mere delusions of man, who will learn the meaning of his voyage when he "reads his sentence at the flames of hell" ("Truth," ll. 1-10).

This theme is present in much of Cowper's poetry, but it is most powerfully realized in his last two poems: "On the Ice Islands Seen Floating in the German Ocean" and "The Castaway." Speaking from what he regarded as the unique position of a man who once glimpsed salvation only to discover his eternal damnation, he discloses to those trusting in religion, civilization, art, or their own skills how flimsy are these protections against chaos. "On the Ice Islands," Cowper's translation of his own Latin poem, "Montes Glaciales in Oceano Germanico Natantes," is based on a newspaper article about icebergs observed floating in the German sea. He begins by asking "What portents" these icebergs are, and associates them with the long history of "human woes" and "calamitous" times, extending into the present. Shining like "burnish'd brass," yet stark and "uncouth," the ice mountains could not be moved by "skill / Or force of man." They have come from the Arctic, "Self-launched," and, "As if instinct with strong desire to lave," have moved south to unwelcoming seas. Like Delos, they are floating islands, but they remain its opposite, for Delos, "fav'rite isle" of Apollo, was a productive land of "Herb, fruit and flow'r," but these are merely ice.

Addressing the ice islands, Cowper tells them that Apollo scorns them, regarding them as fit only for the "Cimmerian darkness" from which they emerged. The ocean produces not only violent waves and storms but mountains of ice, "instinct" with hidden desires portending disaster. Warning them that if they do not return to their native shore, they will be "for ever lost," Cowper projects his own identification with the dark and the chaotic on them, his feeling that he has never belonged to the civilized, ordered world in which his struggle to create was a hold on rationality. Delos, the Aegean, Apollo, and all the symbols of light and art to which he consciously committed himself have never protected him against his knowledge of the "horrid wand'rers of the deep" threatening creation, natural and aesthetic, yet inherent in it.

In this poem Cowper's persistent fears of psychic dissolution are suggested through a symbol of the malign forces in nature; in "The Castaway" the symbolic reference is explicit. Yet "The Castaway" should not be read merely as a personal statement. The last two lines, of course, reveal that the poet's encounter with symbols of abandonment and dissolution has been more terrible than any actual drowning, yet the poem itself deals with the illusion of control in a chaotic and hostile universe. Love, friendship, loyalty, courage, and skill are all vulnerable and finally useless before the "furious" power of nature and in the apparently willful absence of God.

The drowned sailor has engaged in an actual contest with

the sea, but his struggle is also symbolic. Not cruelty but necessity has determined the "flight" of his comrades, their only possibility of "rescue." In a pitiless universe, they are "pitiless perforce." Even those who are saved must accept the harsh conditions of survival, the renunciation of heroism, the denial even of fellowship. For the drowning sailor, as for the poet, "No voice divine the storm allay'd / No light propitious shone." God withholds his presence from both the sailor who struggles for a brief time, "self-upheld," and from the poet "whelm'd in" the "deeper gulphs" of madness that is a conviction of damnation. Yet the circumstances in which both "perish'd, each alone," are not so different. Cowper sees his own terror of emptiness and dissolution in every human being's fate. Salvation in this poem is only temporary rescue in a universe antagonistic to human values and desires; death is abandonment not only by one's fellow men but by God.

In his last years, Cowper experienced God as a "perpetual irresistible influence" that he felt controlled his "volitions" and "actions."[51] The letters of these years are explicit in their bitterness toward the Being who, Cowper was convinced, regretted having "made" him and whom he increasingly held accountable for his frustration, rage, and despair.[52] Although he did not question the certainty of his damnation, his psychic pain finally drove him to reject the terms by which it was decreed: "This doctrine I once denied, and even now assert the truth of it respecting myself only. There can be no peace where there is no freedom; and he is a wretch indeed who is a necessitarian by experience."[53] In "The Castaway," as in his last letters, the poet, long abandoned by God, abandons Him. Here, Cowper's depiction of human isolation in a hostile universe portrays his last and bitterest psychic defense.

Like Cowper, Christopher Smart emerged from one of his earliest mental breakdowns with the conviction that God had rescued him, that his life from that time on must be dedicated to the service of his savior. There, for the most part, the similarity between the two men ends; their mental illness, their conception of themselves as poets, and their vision of God's determining role in their lives are very different. Whereas Cowper spent the rest of his life wrestling with a judgmental deity, ever threatening destruction, Smart conceived of God as the creative force of the universe, whose demand for continual prayer was but an inspiration to praise, his own form of creation.

All recent commentators on Smart's poetry have in one way or another developed the point made by W. H. Bond that the "poet who went into the madhouse in 1756 was very different from the poet who emerged seven years later, and *Jubilate Agno* is the crucial document for an understanding of his transformation."[54] Although *Jubilate Agno* has yielded biographical, cultural, and religious material about the nature of this transformation, no one has shown how its structure and language convey Smart's madness as a dialectic in which the self is continually surrendered and reconstituted through symbolic recreations of reality that reflect its own struggles, defenses, assertions, defeats, and compromises.

The key to this process has been provided by Bond's discovery that in *Jubilate Agno* Smart adapted the "antiphonal or responsive" structure of Hebrew poetry to his own purposes, intending "a line-for-line correspondence between the *Let* and *For* verses" (pp. 18-20). Bond further points out that, in parts of the poem, the contents of the *Let* lines are impersonal, those of the *For* lines personal, and suggests the possibility that Smart intended to read the *For* lines himself in public performance (pp. 20-22). Portions of the manuscript are missing; thus, even if Smart followed this plan throughout his writing of *Jubilate Agno*, as Bond believes he did, there are long *Let* and *For* passages without their expected correspondences. Furthermore, even when both sections do exist, the separation between the impersonal contents of the *Let* and the personal ones of the *For* lines breaks down for a good part of the second third of the poem.

Both Smart's adherence to his original structural principle and his deviations from it are crucial personal expressions, more basic revelations of the course of his psychic experience than are his actual references to his madness in the poem.

The long sections in which *Let* and *For* passages correspond express a unity beyond that of the particular contents of each pair of lines. In the *Let* lines, Smart reconstructs in idealized terms the world from which he was banished, and in the *For* lines he creates a symbolic role for himself within it. In the breakdown of this correspondence, the symbolic unity Smart struggled to establish within himself and to impose on creation dissolves in chaotic associations that seem to mock his original aim.

For seven years, from 1756 to 1763, with only brief intermissions, Smart was confined to either a private or a public institution for the insane. It is known that in May 1757 he entered St. Luke's and was discharged the next year as "incurable"; shortly after he was admitted to Potter's private madhouse at Bethnal Green, where from 1759 to 1763 he wrote *Jubilate Agno.*[55] In the circumscribed atmosphere of a madhouse, in which he felt imprisoned, he conceived of a universe in which he could function in harmony with nature and human beings by literally investing the word with the presence of God. The ways in which this conception of creation manifests itself in the language of *Jubilate Agno* will be discussed a little later; it is important at this point to recognize its connection with his larger view of himself as a messianic voice, a David who was destined to reveal the essential structure of the universe in accordance with God's original plan.

A. D. Hope[56] argues convincingly that Smart's "system" of the universe, although "thoroughly eclectic" (p. 277), is based on the "Covenant Theology and theories concerning the millennium" (p. 273) popular in the late seventeenth and early eighteenth centuries. These Smart discovered during his student days at Cambridge in the work of such writers as Sir Isaac Newton, Edward Stillingfleet, Richard Kidder, Thomas Burnet, William Whiston, J. Keill, and Richard Burthogge.[57] As Hope describes it, the essence of Smart's "system" is that the "universe as created by God is both a spiritual and a corporeal hierarchy of beings." Thus, heavenly bodies, plants, stones, earth, fire, and air are also spirits. "God is immanent in his creation" in every physical and spiritual aspect of motion, attraction, and recurrence (pp. 274-75). In addition, "spiritual vision" reveals "a series of mysterious correspondences between creatures," however different they may appear. Hope suggests that the "series on the mystical significance of the bull, who is an animal and also 'the word of Almighty God' " (B2, l. 678), further indicates this mysterious series of verbal, physical, and spiritual correspondences (pp. 278-79). The most important quality of these correspondences is their reflection of the nature of God, who, as Hope says, "is primarily the great artist and creator." Furthermore, creation, in continually praising its creator, will eventually undo the effects of the fall, this "work of regeneration" culminating in "the second coming of Christ" (p. 280). Hope goes on to describe Smart's role in "this millennial scheme" as that of "the new David of the new order" who will establish the Anglican as the universal church (p. 281). Many commentators have remarked on Smart's view of himself as David, but Hope indicates the important relationship between Smart's "conception of the universe" as "created by a musician-artist-Creator" and of himself as representing in the new David "the messianic and redemptive function of music and poetry" (pp. 283-84).

Hope's delineation of Smart's millennial vision and his own imagined role in its realization summarizes the major thematic structure of *Jubilate Agno*. But, as any reader of the poem knows, within this grand structure philosophical and religious speculations are merged with chaotic associations, personal memories and grievances, mechanical repetitions, and other signs of psychic confusion and despair.

The sections in which the *Let* and *For* lines correspond (especially the first half of B1) reveal most clearly the relationship between Smart's psychic disintegration and his apocalyptic vision of the world and himself. Yet these lines do not convey apathy or acute disturbance. In fact, they depict a struggle to reconstitute a shattered self by creating a universe in which his own repressed anger, guilt, conflict, insecurity, and grandiose aspirations are not only acceptable but fruitful elements of a harmonious whole.

The *Let* lines of B1 continue, in the manner of those of A, to exhort all corresponding elements of creation to praise God. Smart has projected his own compulsion to pray continuously on all constituents of the universe, which rejoice in prayers of praise. The guilt, anxiety, and defensive grandiosity that, at least in part, motivate this compulsion, thus enter into the very restoration of creation itself, whose state, like his own, is fallen. His own conviction of sin, merged with the decline of all created life after the fall, is converted into prayer, the agent of regeneration. The corresponding *Let* and *For* lines contain many similar conversions. In this respect, the first few pairs of B1 are particularly interesting:

Let Elizur rejoice with the Partridge, who is a prisoner of state and is proud of his keepers.
For I am not without authority in my jeopardy, which I derive inevitably from the glory of the name of the Lord.

Typically, the Biblical reference of the *Let* line establishes an aspect of essential order. Elizur, whose name means "God is my rock," was the census-taker who determined which men of Reuben were fit for battle. He was also a leader of the host. Thus, he is a figure representing control over himself and his tribe. As Elizur rejoices with the "Partridge," the "prisoner of state," imprisonment is converted into a condition of pride; the stony walls of the prison take on the associations connected with God as the "rock." In the corresponding *For* line, the poet partakes of this general conversion, insisting that his "jeopardy"—his feelings of abandonment and resentment at being imprisoned in a madhouse—cannot deny the "authority" he derives from "the glory of the name of the Lord," which he has evoked in the name "Elizur" and which he will use to invest creation with moral order.

In the next pair, Elizur's father, Shedeur, whose name means "God is my light," is to rejoice with Pyrausta, an insect, "who dwelleth in a medium of fire, which God hath adapted for him." God himself is involved in the process of adaptation within the great realm of creation which extends into the personal *Let* line in "a zeal to deliver us from everlasting burnings." The sense of sin implied in "burnings" is thus "adapted" to function as an avenue to the "light" of God.

B1 continues to reflect Smart's struggle for psychic adaptation in relation to his view of divine order. Corresponding to "Let Zurishaddai with the Polish Cock rejoice—The Lord restore peace to Europe" (in which the meaning of the Hebrew name, "my rock is the Almightly," is associated by rhyme with the "Polish Cock") is a line that conveys the poet's effort to view his personal problems within the larger perspective of history under the rule of God: "For I meditate the peace of Europe amongst family bickerings and domestic jars" (l. 7). And a little later on (l. 11), he makes explicit the psychic defense adapted to poetic method in this section of B1. Corresponding to "Let Libni rejoice with the Redshank, who migrates not but is translated to the upper regions," in which the bird passively receives eternal life, is a line that describes the poet's active role in such transcendence: "For I have translated in the charity, which makes things better & I shall be translated myself at the last."

As B1 proceeds, Smart uses the *Let* lines as the context for increasingly personal references to his own life:

> Let Eli rejoice with Leucon—he is an honest fellow, which is a rarity.
> For I have seen the White Raven & Thomas Hall of Willingham & am myself a greater curiosity than both.
>
> (l. 25)

This admission and acceptance of his own strangeness occur in the context of the high priest Eli (the "uplifted") rejoicing over the oddity of a white heron (Leucon); this "rarity," moreover, is equated with honesty, of which Smart's own strangeness partakes by association. And in relation to the "King's Fisher, who is of royal beauty, tho' plebian size," Smart, in one of the loveliest lines of his poetry, writes of his discovery that his talent demands more than his natural desire for beauty: "For in my nature I quested for beauty, but God, God hath sent me to the sea for pearls" (l. 30). Merging the small bird with its crested head and the sea-diver, the metaphor conveys his effort to recreate his own identity as a poet and as a human being in harmony with the universe, which in *Jubilate Agno* are one.

According to Bond, in the passage starting at line 46 of B1, Smart's "great bitterness towards his family . . . reaches a climax. . . . This passage also illustrates how both halves of the composition gain in meaning and strength by being placed together. The *Let* verses taken alone do not appear to differ in tone from others around them; the *For* verses give the impression that Smart entertained towards his mother only the kindliest of feelings. Put them together, and symbols of cuckoldry, stupidity, and greed are suddenly combined with Smart's renunciation of his birthright" (p. 22). In his notes to ll. 46-51, Bond further points out that references to the stag, associated with horns, the kite, the wittal, the locust, the woodcock, and the gull reflect Smart's bitterness. His interpretation of these lines is no doubt correct, as far as it goes, but the passage reveals more than Smart's animosity. The *Let* lines, after all, continue to exhort rejoicing, and the very creatures that represent cuckoldry, greed, and cruelty are actually praised.

In this passage Smart commends platycerotes, stags with broad horns, for their "weapons of defence" that "keep them innocent" (l. 46); the kite, "who is of more value than many sparrows" (l. 47); and the wittal as "a silly bird . . . wise unto his own preservation" (l. 48). Onto the first and third creatures Smart unconsciously projects his own struggle for psychic defenses, which explains and even justifies the apparent harm they do. In this light, even the predatory kite can be viewed as more valuable than the harmless sparrow. The corresponding lines,

> For I this day made over my inheritance to my mother in consideration of her infirmities.
> For I this day made over my inheritance to my mother in consideration of her age.
> For I this day made over my inheritance to my mother in consideration of her poverty . . .

in their repetition suggest his rumination on the meaning of his surrender to the demands of the rapacious, and his effort to justify this on the basis of real need. But the *For* lines that follow also indicate that his apparent surrender has been a way of freeing himself from a bond of guilt:

> For I bless the thirteenth of August, in which I had the grace to obey the voice of Christ in my conscience.
> For I bless the thirteenth of August, in which I was willing to run all hazards for the sake of the name of the Lord.
> For I bless the thirteenth of August, in which I was willing to be called a fool for the sake of Christ.

He has found his own "defence" and his own means of "preservation" in obeying "the voice of God in my conscience." In the interplay of the *Let* and *For* lines in this passage, Smart both releases and controls his resentment. Viewing himself in the tradition of the "fool for the sake of Christ," he admits and accepts his suspicions of his family's deceitfulness and contempt for him and his rage at their selfishness, at the same time perceiving their motivations, as he glimpses his own, as forms of self-preservation, which, like the stag's, the kite's, and the wittal's, must somehow be used as agents of regeneration.

There are, however, other passages in which Smart's feelings of abandonment and betrayal expressed in the *For* lines have only a peripheral or no connection with the *Let* lines. Biblical figures rejoice with a horned dragon (l. 58) or a horned beetle (l. 115), as the corresponding lines reveal the poet's suspicions of cuckoldry, but the relationship between the universal realm and the personal one is merely mechanical. The same is true of the lines in which Smart tells of the humiliations of being observed by visitors to the madhouse as an object of curiosity and of being subjected to physical abuse. The complicated relationship between *Let* and *For* lines with which B1 begins breaks down and is restored only intermittently even in this Fragment as the poem increasingly reveals Smart's confusion of thought and identity, his alternation between grandiosity and almost total self-abnegation.

In B1, 144, for example, he identifies himself totally with God: "For I bless the Lord JESUS for his very seed, which is

in my body," and eleven lines later his aspirations are reduced to a plea for acceptance for the most passive and abject
of attitudes toward his own identity: "For I pray to be accepted as a dog without offense, which is best of all." Yet in
the *Let* and *For* passages of B1 and in the *For* passages, which
are all that remain of B2, although the psychological correspondence of recreated world and self breaks down, there are
remarkable and moving depictions of efforts to reconstitute
the self within sections that chiefly convey emotional withdrawal and intellectual confusion.

Such efforts are expressed in the three alphabet sequences
in B2 and C, which, far from being a "ridiculous exercise," as
Bond considers them (p. 23), are a way Smart has devised to
return to a childlike apprehension of reality, as if to begin his
life all over again. As Smart himself says: "For I have had the
grace to GO BACK, which is my blessing unto prosperity"
(B1, 135), and again: "Let Elizabeth rejoice with the Crab—it
is good, at times, to go back" (B1, 171). In so doing, he uses
the alphabet to reeducate himself to experience reality sensu-
ously and conceptually. His attribution of meanings to the
letters of the alphabet of the English language was no doubt
influenced, as W. F. Stead has suggested, by the fact that
"profound meanings" were "attached to the Hebrew characters by occult writers,"[58] but the nouns and adjectives Smart
assigns to the letters have nothing to do with occult thought;
they generally signify either persons or concepts common in
everyday usage, even when they express spiritual values.

Smart's first alphabetical sequence (B2, 513-36) begins, as
might a moralistic children's book, with "For A is the beginning of learning and the door of heaven," but for him this is a
literal statement of God's immanence in the word. The
childlike description of B, "For B is a creature busy and bus-
tling," indicates that Smart is using letters, as he often uses
words, as substitutes for reality; the letter, like the word, is
reified and itself becomes the object it signifies. Other letters
evoke perception: "For C is a sense quick and penetrating";
"For D is depth . . ."; "For N is new . . ."; "For O is open.
. . ." The most touching and revealing letter in this sequence
is I: "For I is identity," the elusive goal of this primitive

means of regaining contact with the world outside the asylum and with the self who first perceived its relation to the word.

Upon completion of this first sequence, Smart begins the next one (B2, 537-61), which is to describe pronunciation, with a direct reference to its usefulness in "the education of children," explaining that "it is necessary to watch the words, which they pronounce with difficulty, for such are against them in their consequences." Although he does indicate the pronunciation of the first few letters, he soon reverts to explaining them, less as signifiers than as receptors of or active participants in external reality. Here "I is the organ of vision"; like many of Smart's puns, it seems obvious, but actually it is a rather complicated transmission of his means of reestablishing confidence in his particular perception of the world and himself. Thus, in describing E, Smart visually creates an eye: "For E is east particularly when formed with little e with his eye." In this alphabet, as in the first one, letters and words are charged with feelings that the poet has withdrawn from the real world ("For W is world") and even, temporarily, from the self-created universe that had sustained him in the composition of large sections of B1. At the end of this sequence, he makes his approach to the word explicit: "For Action & Speaking are one according to God and the Ancients" (l. 562).

The third alphabetical sequence (C1-17), which is fragmentary, starts with H and consists of a series of words for each letter, all of which are equated with God, from the most concrete association of the release of breath in H, "a spirit and therefore he is God," to the all-encompassing I, "a person and therefore he is God." This alphabet, through sound and sign, merges all creation, including the self, with God: "For Christ being A and Ω is all the intermediate letters without doubt" (l. 18).

This conception of God as the most elemental of the processes of speech and thought helps to explain the formative principle of some of Smart's most chaotic associations, in which sound and sense, private and general meanings are merged. One may not accept the premise of his pun in "For being desert-ed is to have desert in the eyes of God and inti-

tles one to the Lord's merit" (B2, 333), but one must acknowledge his transformation of his sense of abandonment, the
amorphous feelings of disconnection with people and objects, into a merging with God's power to regenerate language, his means of survival. His punning in several
languages—English, Greek, Latin, Hebrew—with names of
people, animals, and places, sometimes conveys personal information and at others seems merely mechanical, based entirely on sound, but it is always in some way connected to his
conviction that the word creates relationship, control, the
meaning of existence. In B2, using the bull as the essence of
physical and generative potency, he regards it not as a symbol but as a word with the attributes of a living being: "For
BULL in the first place is the word of Almighty God" (l. 676).
His many associations with Bull are themselves words that
take on actual existence, through oblique or direct relation to
the ultimate Creator:

> For there are many words under Bull.
> For Bul the Month is under it.
> For Sea is under Bull.
> For Brook is under Bull. God be gracious to Lord
> Bolingbroke.
> For Rock is under Bull.
> For Bullfinch is under Bull. God be gracious to the Duke
> of Cleveland.
> For God, which always keeps his work in view has
> painted a Bullfinch in the heart of a stone. God be gra-
> cious to Gosling and Canterbury.
>
> (ll. 680-86)

The list continues with associations of sound and other associations with no apparent connection except as they convey
Smart's unconscious struggle for psychic integration by
merging his fragmented and confused thoughts and images
with what he conceives as the ordered vitality of God's creation fixed in lexical signs.

In Fragment C, there is a long passage (ll. 118-61) on the
"horn" which serves a similar function. Mingling Smart's
suspicions of cuckoldry with his repressed sexual desires and

his identification with animal potency, the horn is finally the power of the word which at once acknowledges and controls such feelings, making them acceptable by assuming their functions:

> For Christ Jesus has exalted my voice to his own glory.
> For he has answered me in the air as with a horn from
> Heaven to the ears of many people.
>
> (ll. 151-52)

Jubilate Agno is essentially a poem about language and mind. More than any other work of its time, it reveals the capacity of words to communicate the mind's defenses against its own obsessions, confusions, despair, and dissociation, its use of emotional isolation for the construction of its own reality. Sometimes Smart's condensations and displacements result in the obscurity of sentences in dreams, but these very processes conveyed in puns, multi-level associations, and grandiose fantasies disclose the ways in which the mind creates its own history. Most of the poem can be understood as a personal account of Smart's investment of the word with infinite capacities to open new avenues of love between the world and the self. Viewing himself as a spokesman of God, in madness he prepares the way for his greatest achievement, *A Song to David*. Here he develops the theme of perpetual praise, employing some of the very techniques he had used in *Jubilate Agno* with a coherence and order suggesting that, at least for Smart, the word did indeed have restorative powers.

Considered "incurable" by the famous Dr. William Battie, Smart, like Carkesse, became a "self-curing poet." The two men were utterly unlike in their capacities, their interests, or, apart from their madness, their experience. But in their approach to their experience of psychosis they, along with Cowper, have an important place in the psychological history of the period. Rejecting or simply ignoring the current mechanistic conclusions about mental aberration, they explored their own delusions and used their isolation for unique perspectives on the religious, social, and cultural assumptions implicit in the grand metaphors of madness that Pope and Swift erected as barriers to the private vision.

$$\mathbf{V}$$

Madness as a Goal

Representations of madness in myth and the continuous development of the theme in literature indicate that the rational ideal of Western civilization has always existed in combat—more or less open—with its instinctual source and opposition. Even at the height of the Enlightenment, from madhouse to salon, the intellectual and psychic constraints inherent in this ideal were exposed and challenged. But, from the nineteenth century to the present, aesthetic anti-rationalism, in various forms and even with contradictory purposes, has taken a new direction in questioning and sometimes assaulting the traditional concept and signifiers of the self.

Among the discussions of this development in recent literary criticism, the most perceptive seems to me Leo Bersani's *A Future for Astyanax*,[1] in which he traces the "stages" in what he calls the *"deconstruction of the self"* from Racine to contemporary literature. Bersani's principle of organization is "a polarity between structured desires and fragmented desires." The first he defines as "desiring impulses sublimated into emotional 'faculties' or passions and thereby providing the basis for the notion of a distinct and coherently unified personality. . . . The disguised repetitions of inhibited desires constitute the coherent self" (pp. 5-6). Fragmented desires, as he views them, are "desublimated"; the "deconstruction of the self" involves the restoration of a pre-Oedipal "heterogeneity of . . . desiring impulses" (pp. 6-7). Although Bersani's and other treatments of this subject, which I shall mention later on, are pertinent to my consideration of modern portrayals of madness as a psychic and aesthetic goal, their perspectives and points of view are different from mine. Bersani, for example, treats many works that do not explicitly deal with madness as a theme, and his concept of desire, while it has the virtue of a single standard, is sometimes too restrictive to disclose the complexity of the experience of psychic dissolution.

In using the term dissolution of the self, I wish to emphasize the psychological ambiguity of what is experienced and represented as compulsive choice, both individually and socially. I have divided this chapter into two sections, the first tracing the renewal and reinterpretation of the ancient myth of Dionysus deliberately employed to symbolize unconscious drives, from its Romantic culmination in Nietzsche to the present, and the second considering certain characteristics of the modern aesthetic vogue of madness and suicide, which first appear in the writings of two anomalous Romantics, Gérard de Nerval and Lautréamont.

1. THE RETURN OF THE DIONYSIAC

The Nietzschean Dionysus, as a symbol of psychic renewal through the dissolution of the self, is the climactic expression of the instinctual yearnings of European Romanticism and the prophet of their social and aesthetic development in the twentieth century. Nietzsche, of course, was hardly "the first," as he alleged,[2] "to take seriously, for the understanding of the older, the still rich and even overflowing Hellenic instinct, that wonderful phenomenon which bears the name of Dionysus." As Max Baeumer[3] points out, "Winckelmann, Hamann, and Herder had already discovered, comprehended, and formulated the concept of the Dionysian long before him." Baeumer shows how pervasive the symbol of Dionysus was in German Romantic poetry and fiction, and documents a fact well known at least to classicists: "in the research of the German Romantics in the areas of mythology and classical antiquity the antithesis Apollonian-Dionysian had been employed for decades" (p. 166). Furthermore, Baeumer demonstrates that Friedrich Schelling, long before Nietzsche, formulated an aesthetic theory of the "Dionysian, in contrast to the Apollonian, as an unrestrained, intoxicated

power of creation in the artist and the poetic genius" (p. 166);
others, such as Johann Georg Hamann and Johann Gottfried
Herder, further developed theories of ecstatic creation (p.
169). Still, it seems impossible to accept Baeumer's major
point: "One can grant Nietzsche the primacy he asserts for
himself only with relation to his 'transformation' of the
Dionysian into a 'philosophical pathos,' that is, into a rhetorical cliché" (p. 166). No matter how closely Nietzsche's
Dionysus may resemble earlier German Romantic interpretations of the god as a symbol of emotional and sexual release,
of poetic inspiration, and political revolution, there are crucial
differences from them in his conception of the Dionysiac.
What finally separates Nietzsche from his predecessors in interpreting the Dionysiac for the modern world is his formulation of an aesthetic psychology that challenges traditional
Western philosophical and semantic concepts of perception,
representation, in fact, of "the ego as being."[4]

It has often been remarked and is no doubt to some extent
true that the Dionysus of *The Birth of Tragedy* is a deification of
Schopenhauer's idea of "will," but even in this early work
the god has ambiguous functions that presage Nietzsche's
later renunciation of Schopenhauer. Nietzsche's Dionysus
heralds not only the central role of unconscious impulses and
motivations in twentieth-century theories regarding mental
processes, but the contradictory views of the function of such
forces in individual and social life. The "line" that Thomas
Mann conceived as running from Schopenhauer through
Nietzsche to Freud[5] is more often a divider than a connection.
Influenced by Freud and his various interpreters, many
European and American writers assimilated the conceptual
framework and the symbolic language Freud used to describe
the psychic struggle for the integration of unconscious and
conscious processes. But both the immediate and continuous
effects of Nietzsche's psychology were quite different. His
adherence to the Dionysiac in its unresolved conflict with the
Apollonian and his vision of ecstatic "primordial unity,"[6]
which appear throughout his writings, have been crucial influences on modern and contemporary anti-rationalism.

Their effects appear not only in direct allusion but in mystical distortions of basic Freudian principles.

What Mann has called Nietzsche's "one single omni-present thought" which "throughout his life he really only variated, extended, [and] impressed upon his readers"[7] is too familiar by now to require lengthy review. Complicated and often contradictory as Nietzsche's thought may be, it is surely not an oversimplification to say that in essence it is based on his conception of a grand conflict between instinct and con-sciousness, feeling and rationality, art and systems of moral-ity. In *The Birth of Tragedy*, Dionysus symbolizes the ecstatic release of the instincts in primordial ritual, which was to de-velop into ancient tragic drama. This first work of Nietzsche's celebrates not only the origins of the most authentic dramatic expression of the Dionysiac spirit but the possibility of the re-surgence of this spirit in psychic harmony and national pride in Germany in the last quarter of the nineteenth century.

But Nietzsche's "single omni-present thought" and the god he resurrected to convey the instinctual expression for which he sought "initiates" are more complex than they seem. Even in *The Birth of Tragedy*, his extended answer to his own question, "what is Dionysian?" (p. 20) contains basic contradictions regarding the nature and function of release in frenzy. Such contradictions at the heart of Nietzsche's psy-chology account at least in part for the paradox that the pro-ponent of the soul's freedom in *The Birth of Tragedy* should have conveyed in "that Dionysian monster who bears the name of Zarathustra"[8] inspiration for the Nazi superman.

In the self-critical and explanatory preface that he added to the 1886 edition of *The Birth of Tragedy*, Nietzsche approaches Dionysiac frenzy in a series of rhetorical questions that are crucial to an understanding of one aspect of his conception. Raising the possibility that the "origin of tragedy" lay in *"joy, strength, overflowing health, overgreat fullness,"* Nietzsche goes on to ask:

And what, then, is the significance, physiologically speaking, of that madness out of which tragic and comic

art developed—the Dionysian madness? . . . Is madness
perhaps not necessarily the symptom of degeneration,
decline, and the final stage of culture? Are there perhaps—a question for psychiatrists—neuroses of *health*?
of the youth and youthfulness of a people? Where does
that synthesis of god and billy goat in the satyr point?
What experience of himself, what urge compelled the
Greek to conceive the Dionysian enthusiast and primeval
man as a satyr? And regarding the origin of the tragic
chorus: did those centuries when the Greek body
flourished and the Greek soul foamed over with health
perhaps know endemic ecstasies? Visions and hallucinations shared by entire communities or assemblies as a
cult?

(p. 21)

The answers implicit in these questions assume that ritual
madness both expresses and channels instinctual impulses,
and thus fosters psychological health and communal unity.
The "neuroses of health" are the instinctual drives demanding release in communion with external nature and fellow
human beings. Recognition of such forces was encouraged in
ancient Greek Dionysiac festivals, says Nietzsche, as shared
experiences of the self, a celebration of the ecstatic as valuable
psychologically and socially. Intrinsic to this conception are
social acceptance and aesthetic control of frenzy, whether in
religious cult or tragic festival.

The "collapse of the *principium individuationis*" by which
human beings could achieve "self-forgetfulness" is described
as having a communal function: "In song and in dance man
expresses himself as a member of a higher community," and
thus joins with nature as it reveals its "artistic power . . . to
the highest gratification of the primordial unity" (pp. 36-37).
Paradoxically, in Dionysiac dithyramb, being is revealed and
fulfilled in its very loss of autonomy; the realization of the
deepest and most powerful emotions and impulses occurs in
a state of "self-abnegation" (pp. 40-41).

A fundamental contradiction in Nietzsche's psychology lies

in his conception of this psychic state, the breakdown of individuation. On the one hand, Apollo, "the glorious divine image of the *principium individuationis*" (p. 36), symbolizes the very principle which must "collapse" if human beings are to reach a state of ecstatic harmony with nature. On the other hand, this undifferentiated state, without the intervention of the Apollonian, is a hazardous one, leading only to barbaric "sensuality and cruelty." Nietzsche makes a clear distinction between the "*Dionysian Greek*" and the "Dionysian barbarian," between the "collective release" of the Greek worshipers' ecstatic identification with the deity and the "horrible mixture of sensuality and cruelty" which was encouraged in the name of Dionysus in the non-Greek world. Still, the Greeks, at first "insulated" from such barbarities by Apollo, who "held out the Gorgon's head to this grotesquely uncouth Dionysian power," were themselves subject to "similar impulses," which "finally burst forth from the deepest roots of the Hellenic nature and made a path for themselves." Such destructive drives were controlled by a reconciliation between the Apollonian and the Dionysiac, which Nietzsche calls "the most important moment in the history of the Greek cult" and was felt in the very "blending and duality in the emotions of the Dionysian revelers." It is at this point that nature "attains her artistic jubilee . . . and the destruction of the *principium individuationis* for the first time becomes an artistic phenomenon." Thus, the ecstatic Greek cults express their yearning for "primordial unity" with the earth and its creatures and achieve this state through the "symbolic faculties": the symbolism of words, dance, and especially the "rhythmics, dynamics, and harmony" of music. Such symbolic means, moreover, can be used only by the initiated: "To grasp this collective release of all the symbolic powers, man must have already attained that height of self-abnegation which seeks to express itself symbolically through all these powers—and so the dithyrambic votary of Dionysus is understood only by his peers." The "Apollinian Greek," says Nietzsche, must have responded to this votary with "astonishment" mixed with the "suspicion" that he was deprived of such an experience only by "his Apollinian consciousness" (pp. 39-41).

Yet, one may well ask, has Nietzsche himself not described the very Apollonian intervention which has channeled primitive impulses into such exalted and artful symbolic expression? In fact, his very recreation of Dionysiac ritual describes a control of impulses by releasing them symbolically into consciousness. The very words, dance, and music of ritual observance channel instinctual aims into harmonious social rather than highly individual and anarchic expression. Nietzsche admits again and again that the Dionysiac and the Apollonian cannot be separated, yet he persists in his compulsion to exalt the one by comparison with the other. Implicit in his conception of ancient Greek culture and art as the products of "the Dionysian and the Apollinian, in new births ever following and mutually augmenting one another," is a beneficent union of "these two hostile principles" (p. 47). But his suspicion of consciousness, of rationality, of the subjective, the "ego" (p. 48), always accompanies his acknowledgment of the necessity of Apollonian intervention.

Nietzsche's devotion to the Dionysiac is unqualified; his acceptance of the Apollonian generally ambivalent. But it is the "new opposition" (p. 82) that emerges at the end of the fifth century b.c. between the "Dionysian and the Socratic" that evokes his hatred for reason, control, and science. To Nietzsche, the "newborn demon, called *Socrates*" (p. 82) is the very embodiment of the *"theoretical man"* (p. 94), the very antithesis of "unconscious Dionysian wisdom" (p. 104). The spirit of Socrates, the "archetype and progenitor" (p. 110) of scientific rationalism, has dominated Western life and art until Nietzsche's own time. It is in opposition to what he names "Socratic" or "Alexandrian" culture that he calls upon his own age to restore "Dionysian magic" (p. 123).

Inviting his readers to participate with him in the reawakening of the Dionysiac spirit, Nietzsche again acknowledges the necessity for the reappearance of "Apollinian *illusion* whose influence aims to deliver us from the Dionysian flood and excess" (p. 129). But the Apollonian is in turn to be inspired by the Dionysiac so that it exceeds its own control and is itself forced into this very excess (p. 131). Together Dionysiac release and Apollonian illusion will restore to the German people "primordial power" (p. 136) and creativity long repressed. Nietzsche insists that Dionysiac wisdom is to enter consciousness strictly controlled by the "Apollinian power of transfiguration" (p. 143), but it must be remembered that for him the Apollonian even at its most beautiful and most essential is mere illusion. Preventing human beings from engaging in "orgiastic self-annihilation," it "blinds" them to the "universality of the Dionysian process" (p. 128). What is real is undifferentiated instinctual impulse, free of the consciousness of individuality, reason, and choice. Merging with primordial powers of creation and destruction, the initiate transcends his own mortality.

Nietzsche ends the critical preface he added to the 1886 edition of *The Birth of Tragedy* with a quotation from Zarathustra, whom he identifies as his more recent development of the Dionysiac. Early in *Thus Spake Zarathustra*[9] he momentarily considers the possibility of the ego's learning to value the "body and earth" (p. 144). But this soon seems impossible. Beyond the ego is the self, "a mighty ruler, an unknown sage" who "dwells" within and is the body. The "self laughs at [the] ego," contemptuous of its efforts at thought, and the ego is finally subservient to the self and the body, which are one (pp. 146-47). What begins as a remarkable conception of the ego originating in unconscious processes as a dynamic part of the self ends in contempt for consciousness. Nietzsche takes the unpopular side in the dualistic notion of mind and body that he ostensibly despises. In opposition to the ego, the Dionysiac "Will to Power" creates the superman, who is emancipated from the limits of self and time.

Nietzsche's later comments on *Zarathustra* reveal that in this work at least the Dionysiac is unqualified will, the omnipotence of the soul that perceives and controls eternity:

My concept of the "Dionysian" here becomes a *supreme deed*; measured against that, all the rest of human activity seems poor and relative. That a Goethe, a Shakespeare, would be unable to breathe even for a moment in this tremendous passion and height, that Dante is, compared with Zarathustra, merely a believer and not one who first *creates* truth, a *world-governing* spirit, a destiny—that the poets of the Veda are priests, and not even worthy of tying the shoelaces of a Zarathustra—that is the least thing and gives no idea of the distance, of the *azure* solitude in which this work lives.[10]

The Dionysiac has become the concept of the Ubermensch, the extreme union of all possibilities, limitless gratification, power, wisdom, love: *"that is the concept of Dionysus himself."* Repeatedly, Nietzsche invokes Dionysus as the spirit of almost unimaginable boundlessness: in "all abysses" the "eternal Yes"; the conversion of melancholy to dithyramb; *"joy even in destroying."* Dionysus and Zarathustra are one in "the tremendous, unbounded saying Yes and Amen."[11]

Yet in the same year in which these passages were written, Nietzsche with only slightly less fervor admits the possibility of "bounds" to the Dionysiac. In the section of *The Will to Power* dedicated to Dionysus, again defining his adherence to the god as an "affirmation of the world as it is," an *amor fati*,[12] he nonetheless returns to a qualified acceptance of the Apollonian as a necessary element in the development of the arts. As in *The Birth of Tragedy*, the Apollonian here is curiously ambiguous. On the one hand, it breaks the "will to the terrible, multifarious, uncertain, frightful," which is Dionysiac, upon its own "will to measure, to simplicity, to submission to rule and concept," from Nietzsche's point of view, the sad products of individuation. On the other hand, it is salutary in overcoming the "immoderate, disorderly Asiatic" at the roots of the Greek soul (p. 540). The immoderate for Nietzsche is admirable only when it leads to "a passionate-painful overflowing into darker, fuller, more floating states" (p. 539): a psychic merging with both "eternal fruitfulness and recurrence" and "the will to annihilation" (p. 543).

Antagonistic to Apollonian measure, detesting Socratic rationalism, scorning Christian martyrdom, the Dionysiac adherent is finally alone. Nietzsche describes himself, in *Beyond Good and Evil*, as "the last disciple and initiate of the god Dionysus,"[13] and in *Twilight of the Idols* as "the last disciple of the philosopher Dionysus."[14] In *Ecce Homo*, where he is no longer a mere disciple but is one with Dionysus / Zarathustra, he reveals his remarkable perception of the condition of narcissistic solitude and grandiosity to which the extremity of his philosophical position, especially the abnegation of the ego, has inevitably led. The "tremendous passion" of Zarathustra, unattainable by a Goethe, a Shakespeare, or a Dante, exists in an *"azure* solitude." Zarathustra, who "experiences himself as the *supreme type of all beings,"* is the "soul that loves itself most" (p. 305), that "speaks to himself" (p. 306), that is both "light" itself in his "loneliness" and filled with "revenge" and "spite" because of it (p. 307). The composite Dionysus/ Zarathustra finally regards and worships only himself. His grand vision of identification with and control of the principles of creation and annihilation is but a reflection of his own yearning for an "eternal return" to infantile omnipotence and omniscience. Commenting on his essay, *Wagner in Bayreuth*, Nietzsche explains that "in all psychologically decisive places, I alone am discussed." Furthermore, one could, he says, substitute the name Zarathustra for Wagner. The "Wagnerian reality" had ceased to exist (p. 274). It and Bayreuth had become only the primary material for the narcissistic vision that was progressively to displace reality itself.

The dissolution of boundaries between the self and symbols, representations, actual persons, places, and events, which Nietzsche identifies as the "Dionysian state" in *Twilight of the Idols* and compares with that of "certain hysterical types who also, upon any suggestion, enter into *any* role" (p. 519), has lately been admired as a "nomadism" that goes beyond "signifiers" and "signified" to "designations of intensity inscribed upon a body that could be the earth or a book, but could also be the suffering body of Nietzsche himself: *I am all the names of history.* . . ."[15] One can sympathize with this and other efforts to rescue the brilliance of

Nietzsche's revelations of dream and instinct as vital elements "of the total economy of [the] soul"[16] and thus of language and symbol, from his own limitations, his loss of control over his own material and method of probing the appearance of reality. But justification of Nietzsche for "confounding all codes"[17] cannot ignore the fact that the psychic "ease of metamorphosis"[18] Nietzsche values so highly produces shoddiness as well as illumination, and ultimately, megalomaniacal visions as solutions to social hypocrisy. The most subtle and perhaps the most accurate interpretations of Nietzsche's Dionysus/Zarathustra are the literary and philosophical descendants of these symbolic figures. Among the many twentieth-century works in which they reappear Thomas Mann's *Death in Venice*, first published in 1912, remains the greatest, not only because of the precision with which Mann depicts a human being's gradual recognition of unconscious determinants of his feelings and conduct, but because of Mann's very transmission of his own ambivalence toward this experience. Many years later, moreover, he was to incorporate Nietzsche's version of the Dionysiac into another legendary form of omnipotence in *Dr. Faustus*. In portraying the emotional and moral conflict of his protagonists, driven by ambiguous impulses toward consummation and destruction, Mann does not merely create an individual experience; he adapts an ancient myth to symbolize a conflict that is central to twentieth-century social and cultural life.

As Gustav von Aschenbach, the hero of *Death in Venice*,[19] gradually surrenders to Dionysiac frenzy, he carries with him centuries of cultural accretion to the myth he is driven to enact. In the process, Aschenbach, the very exemplum of accomplished modernity, himself becomes a mythical figure, a reluctant participant in the primordial struggle between the forces that Mann calls "life and mind." The "tension" between these, says Mann, is that of "two worlds whose relation is erotic *without clarification of the sexual polarity*."[20] In *Death in Venice* this basic tension is that of a mind in conflict with its own adaptations to history and culture.

At first the only mythical adventure that the detached and proper Aschenbach seems likely to encounter is one diluted by a literary consciousness, and indeed that is one level of his experience. But, ironically, it is the very nature of the art he admires and practices that the psychic processes that create its order and beauty should lead him back to its sources in narcissism, violence, lust, and death, the perennial constituents of personal and social history.

Aschenbach's psychic disintegration no doubt reflects Schopenhauer's concept of will as destiny, and, as Mann was later to describe it, his view of "sex" as "the focal point of the will."[21] Many commentators, including Mann himself, have remarked on the presence of the Nietzschean Apollonian/Dionysiac dichotomy in *Death in Venice*. Besides these omnipresent influences, the allusions to philosophy and literature, ancient and modern, are manifold: Homer, Plato, Goethe, Lessing, Platen; even the climactic Dionysiac dream is largely taken from Erwin Rohde's *Psyche*. These sources and others have been thoroughly documented[22] and discussed in relation to Mann's development as a novelist and his conception of myth as an expression of "the typical,"[23] but his use of them, especially of myth, as an avenue of psychological revelation has largely been ignored or treated superficially. André von Gronicka's analysis of the role of myth in *Death in Venice*, for example, is based on his view of "an unceasing tension between the poles of psychological realism and the symbolism of myth" (p. 48). The "realm of myth and legend" (p. 48) in the novella, as he sees it, is antithetical to the "sordid" reality of Aschenbach's actual experiences, but finally links even these to its timeless pattern of transcendence (pp. 60-61). Such a reading, it seems to me, avoids some of the most critical revelations of the myths that operate in the novella. Myth, far from opposing "psychological realism," is Mann's most pervasive clue to this psychological reality. In fact, his complex allusiveness creates Aschenbach's psychic transformation of experience through mythical and literary symbols that convey the very stages of the gradual disintegration of his ego.

Mann refers to the allusiveness of his style in this novella as an "art of mimicry" that "I love and instinctively use." In the next sentence, he elucidates this phrase by explaining that once, in seeking a "definition of this style," he said that it was a "mysterious adaptation of the personal to the objective."[24] The narrator's depiction of Aschenbach and Aschenbach's conception—actually, his creation—of Tadzio are products of this method. The "adaptation" of myth and literature by the author and his protagonist to their "personal" transformations of reality expresses their psychic ambivalence and portrays the dramatic conflict of "life and mind" in this novella, *"an eternal tension without resolution."*[25]

The narrator's attitude toward his protagonist in *Death in Venice* seems, at least on the surface, inconsistent. Burton Pike convincingly demonstrates that the "usual assumption" that Aschenbach is "Mann's representation of 'the' artist" is but "one perspective in the story." The other is that Aschenbach "is not a symbol for the artist in general," but rather "a flawed artist in a flawed society," a writer who, in denying his instinctual needs and powers, has compromised his talent to the popular ideal of heroism through repression (pp. 128-33). There is certainly enough evidence to support Pike's position in Mann's description of Aschenbach's work and the bases of his popularity; there is also, of course, the absolute mark of his conformity in the parenthetic clause that follows his name at the very beginning of the novella: "—or von Aschenbach, as he had been known officially since his fiftieth birthday—." But it is also undeniable that, despite the narrator's reservations, Aschenbach's story depicts crucial stages in the struggle for authentic creation. As Pike himself says: "Aschenbach is endowed with sufficient talent to aim for the pinnacle of art, and in his artistic intentions as in his life he is certainly one of Mann's serious artists" (p. 136). In explaining Aschenbach's failure to create the highest art, however, Pike views him too narrowly as an individual failure rather than as a construct of the dynamics of creation itself, which Aschenbach enacts. Thus, to describe Aschenbach as "a businessman among artists" (p. 136) is to oversimplify even the highly

Madness in Literature

disciplined life he had led before the events of the novella. Aschenbach's dedication to his art, as the narrator tells us, has molded his very features; the "adventures of the spirit" are reflected in his eyes and in every expression of his face (p. 15). Furthermore, the narrator speaks of Aschenbach's feelings for the ocean most sympathetically as "the hard-worked artist's longing for rest, his yearning to seek refuge from the thronging manifold shapes of his fancy in the bosom of the simple and vast," and then of "another yearning, opposed to his art and perhaps for that very reason a lure, for the unorganized, the immeasurable, the eternal—in short, for nothingness" (p. 31). Neither his impulse to create nor his need to escape the demands of his art are depicted in mundane terms. In connection with his role as writer, moreover, Mann elsewhere refers to Aschenbach's story as a "tragedy of supreme achievement."[26]

Both Thomas and Katia Mann have said that the experience Mann narrates in *Death in Venice*, "down even to the details,"[27] is autobiographical. Nonetheless, it is obvious that the factual material—the trip to Venice, the young boy, the threat of cholera, and much else—is far less important than Mann's ambivalent feelings about his protagonist. In *Confessions of an Unpolitical Man* (1918) Mann, denying that the life of a writer can be a "dignified" one, says that in a story (clearly *Death in Venice*) he questioned whether "wisdom and true manliness" can be achieved by the writer, whose "path" to "spiritual" beauty is only through sensual experience. He goes on to say that he made his protagonist, "who had become respectable," realize that someone like him "necessarily remains dissolute and an adventurer of feelings," that "his attitude of honor is a farce." In so doing and in exposing the folly of popular confidence in the artist as educator, Mann says, "I remained true to myself."[28] Elsewhere, some years later, he describes Thomas Buddenbrook and Aschenbach as "dying men, escapists from the discipline and morality of life, Dionysiacs of death."[29]

These and other harsh judgments on Aschenbach as a writer must be judged in relation to others far more sympathetic for, taken together, they disclose how complex is the "truth" to himself that Mann sought in this figure. Mann's very ambivalence toward Aschenbach, toward Dionysiac frenzy, and toward death are important clues to the novella that Mann himself considered "thoroughly ambiguous."[30] In the letter of 1920 referred to above, devoted almost entirely to *Death in Venice,* Mann seems to contradict his own judgment of two years earlier regarding the role of the sensual in the artist's life. Here in referring to homoerotic feelings, Mann describes them as existing "in a realm that in spite of its sensuality has very little to do with nature, far more to do with mind." The sensual is here not merely a disreputable path to intellectual and spiritual achievement but one with it. Mann is careful to distinguish such experience from "bourgeois," or family, love, however. For him "eroticism, of unbourgeois intellectually sensual adventures," is inextricably related to "the problem of beauty." If, admittedly, *Death in Venice* expresses something of his own bourgeois repressive attitudes toward passion, it "is at its core . . . hymnic." In this letter, Mann seems to accept the fact that in *Death in Venice* he did not entirely succeed in his effort to impose "Apollonian, objectively controlled, morally and socially responsible epic" values upon the "Dionysian spirit of lyricism." Although somewhat ruefully he admits that he felt compelled to objectify Aschenbach's story, and thus *"the intoxicate song turned into a moral fable,"* he nonetheless refuses to disavow or to denounce the Dionysiac insight to which his protagonist's excesses lead.[31] Perhaps because Aschenbach finally goes so far as to experience to its very limit the essential "tension of life and mind" resolved only in the "seductive antimoral power" of "death,"[32] Mann could not deny the necessity, indeed the value, of his struggle.

To approach *Death in Venice,* as Heinz Kohut[33] does, mainly "as an attempt by the author to communicate threatening personal conflicts" (p. 292) is merely to repeat in technical language what Mann in letters, diaries, and an autobiography had already disclosed more directly. When Kohut attempts to explain the psychological origins of the autobiographical information Mann has supplied, he superimposes meanings on events in the novella that, in the long run, reduce rather than add to its psychological revelations. Equating Mann with Aschenbach in a simplistic relationship between author and character, he creates a past for Aschenbach for which there is no intrinsic evidence. This method is especially unconvincing in Kohut's interpretation of Aschenbach's reluctant acknowledgement of his homoerotic desires and the climactic Dionysiac dream in which he experiences their most powerful expression. Apparently unaware of Mann's actual source for the dream in Erwin Rohde's *Psyche*, Kohut conceives of its "sources" as purely psychological. He posits three such sources: the first, "remnants of sublimatory ego activity; they account for the formal aspects of the dream which retains something artistic and impersonal, as if it were a beautiful fable from classical mythology," the second, the "disintegration of Aschenbach's personality" revealed in his "now unconcealed sexual desire for Tadzio," and third, "the undisguised emergence of a primal scene experience" (p. 297).

One of Kohut's most serious misjudgments is his treatment of the myth and ritual on which this dream is based—which were of far-reaching importance in the pre- and recorded social history of Asia Minor, Thrace, and the areas of Greece and Crete—merely as the individual "remnants" of Aschenbach's "sublimatory ego activity." His further comment, "as if it were a beautiful fable from classical mythology" seems to indicate that Kohut believes it to be Aschenbach's invention. Moreover, the violent expression of sexuality and the dismemberment and cannibalism practiced in such rites reappearing in Aschenbach's dream hardly seem to be evidence of sublimation in the form of "a beautiful fable." Kohut interprets the dream as a representation of Aschenbach's homosexual "fears and desires" resulting from childhood partial identification with his mother and desire for "the sexual love" of his father during a "primal scene experience" (p. 297). Needless to say, there is no evidence in the novella to support such a supposition regarding Aschenbach's or, for that matter, Mann's childhood experience, however reasonable such an explanation may seem as a general theory. Certainly, the dream, which recreates some of the most specific details of ancient Dionysiac rites, cannot without distortion be reduced merely to a representation of the trauma ensuing from a primal scene encounter.

Such so-called sources of Mann's or Aschenbach's conflicts are irrelevant to the main character and action of *Death in Venice*, and serve no purpose in analyzing its structure and theme. Furthermore, in treating Aschenbach as if he were an actual person, whose emotional history Kohut himself supplies, rather than a literary construct, with its own limitations and possibilities, he misses the subtle psychological meanings of this important dream, which must be explored within the context of its mythical and cultic background. In returning to this dream, I shall try to demonstrate that Mann uses this background to depict Aschenbach's psychological disintegration, with its homoerotic manifestations, as a regression to the primitive roots of civilization and the unconscious sources of art, which in this dream are one.

Much more convincing is Kohut's suggestion that Aschenbach's longing for the boundlessness of the sea, for nothingness, even for death, reflects Mann's own wish to restore the original oneness with mother (p. 299). But in this novella Mann is not concerned merely with the individual or "personal" origins of the yearning for primal union. He depicts the emergence of this yearning in amorphous sensations and its symbolic transformation into fantasies of sensuous release as the compulsion of the creator to return to an erotic source of art, which is also its opposition, threatening the extinction of the boundaries of the self and with them the capacity to construct a unique conception of reality.

Kohut attributes the origins of Aschenbach's "artistic attitude" of detachment to the crucial event of the "primal scene experience" that Kohut himself has constructed for Aschenbach as a fictive portrayal of the author (p. 297). Although he makes some perceptive comments on Mann's depiction of artistic sublimation and its disintegration, his view of these processes is limited by this superimposed construction of their genesis. The figure of Aschenbach does not encompass the entire being or experience of *the* artist, but it is through his point of view that we glimpse something of the psychic struggle that enters into creation: the drive to impose the evanescent self in enduring form upon the transience of reality, the self-imposed discipline, with its defenses against instinctual and narcissistic demands that lead to only partial and ever-threatening resolutions, and finally the confrontation with the nourishing and destructive "abyss" of the unconscious that is the artist's most enduring bond to history and society. This theme preoccupied Mann throughout his life, but in no other work, not even in *Dr. Faustus*, where the Dionysiac composer becomes a comprehensive symbol of the daemonic released in society, does Mann disclose so precisely the gratifications and repugnance of the mind abandoning its own controls and observing the very processes of the disintegration of the self.

The breakdown of Aschenbach's defenses against his unconscious drives begins with his inability to "check the onward sweep of the productive mechanism within him" (p. 3); ironically, it is the creative impulse that leads him to frenzy and to the final dissolution of the self in death. Consistently, he experiences his own fear, yearning, passion, frenzy, and his surrender of self-control through mythical and literary associations transformed to his own psychic requirements. Such associations, which release thoughts and emotions long repressed, transform five strangers he encounters in the external world into participants in the stages of his inner drama, as emissaries of death. These men—the first, apparently a visitor to the funeral hall in Munich; the second, the official who writes out his ticket to Venice on the ship from Pola; the third, the aged fop on this ship; the fourth, the gondolier in Venice; and the last, the Neapolitan jester—although they share certain characteristics that suggest death, are also different from each other, each functioning in a particular way in Aschenbach's fantasies. Several, but not all, have the snub nose and prominent teeth that are obvious suggestions of the grinning skeleton, along with the Devilish Adam's apple and "colourless, red-lashed eyes" (pp. 4-5). But, though the snub nose and bold manner of the first stranger are also satyric, it is the second, the one who issues his ticket to Venice, who has "a beard like a goat's" (p. 16), conveying even more specifically the lascivious characteristics of the followers of Dionysus.

Aschenbach is aware that his reaction to the man at the North Cemetery may be due to something about the stranger that "kindled his fantasy" or may involve "some other physical or psychical influence." In any case, this is his first "consciousness of a widening of inward barriers," which, characteristically, he attributes to "no more than a longing to travel." But his habitual psychic defense, denial, has begun to be overwhelmed by the strength of his desires, which appear like "a seizure," producing "almost a hallucination," a visual image of a "primeval wilderness-world of islands, morasses, and alluvial channels." The "hairy palm-trunks" and the lush vegetation emerge as out of a "dream." The landscape with its "crouching tiger" terrifies him, yet he acknowledges his "longing" for it. At this point, the vision is "inexplicable" to him; all he can do is to shake his head (pp. 5-6) in an ineffectual gesture of dismissal of his own elemental passions, which emerge as archetypal images of unrestrained natural productivity and aggression.

This generalized and fairly conventional vision of a primitive world, which seems dreamlike, is a momentary foreshadowing of the later dream of Dionysiac frenzy in which he is to confront the extremity of his own instinctual lust and violence. The sexuality here displaced on the "hairy" trunks of trees is later explicit in the "hairy pelts" of the maenads and the "horned and hairy men." The "tropical marshland" has associations of lushness and beauty, but in the Dionysiac dream he is to be overwhelmed by "the odour as of stagnant waters" (pp. 67-68). Aschenbach is able to rationalize his first experience of "Desire projected . . . visually" (p. 5) as a rather extraordinary expression of a need to find some respite from work, and thus to reduce even its mythical associations to the most innocuous of meanings: what he requires, he tells himself, is "three or four weeks of lotus-eating at some one of the gay world's playgrounds in the lovely south" (p. 8). The archetypal images are adapted to the insipid language of travel brochures. Despite such efforts to restore the stock responses of a lifetime of conditioning in repression, however, Aschenbach can no longer avoid his own impulses, try though he may to deny their meaning. Determined to find "a fresh scene, without associations" (p. 15), in which to rest, he first chooses an Adriatic island but, driven by an "inner impulse" (p. 16), he soon leaves it and heads for Venice, for centuries associated in European art with decay, disease, beauty, and creation.

On the voyage there, he begins to feel overwhelmed by "a dreamlike distortion of perspective," which he projects on the world he tries to shut out, but the "goat-bearded man" and the "elderly coxcomb" enter his consciousness as his "time sense falters and grows dim" (pp. 17-18). Incidents or experiences that could easily be regarded as no more than slightly unusual now release associations of unrestrained sexuality and of death, which converge to express a yearning for the dissolution of the conscious, rational self. The Venetian gondola evokes both these images—"of lawless, silent adventures in the plashing night; or even more, what visions of death itself," as if "death itself" were the culmination of "lawless" sensuality. Resembling a "coffin," the gondola seems to Aschenbach to have "the softest, most luxurious, most relaxing seat in the world," and he wishes that the trip "might last forever." The gondolier, with his "snub nose" and white teeth "bared . . . to the gums," resembles the earlier figures who presage death, but he is more explicitly mythical. Aschenbach, addressing him in his mind as Charon, pays this man who he thinks may be a criminal the respect owed to an uncontrollable force: "even if you hit me in the back with your oar and send me down to the kingdom of Hades, even then you will have rowed me well" (pp. 21-23). The ancient mythical symbols that enter his consciousness lend meaning and form to his sensuous indolence, both releasing and controlling long repressed feelings; he experiences no conscious desire to express them at this point, only a vague yearning, at least partly satisfied by an atmosphere congenial to the projection of disquieting emotions.

For a brief period, myth, art, and literature continue to function in this way in Aschenbach's consciousness. His first reaction to the sight of Tadzio is a recollection of "the noblest moment of Greek sculpture"; the boy's "expression of pure and godlike serenity" (p. 25) seems to be the perfect representation of Apollonian harmony. A little later on, Tadzio's head is that of "Eros, with the yellowish bloom of Parian marble" (p. 29). At first, Aschenbach uses the handsome boy to create a conventional aesthetic vehicle, an Apollonian conversion of and thus a defense against his own erotic impulses so deeply connected with the "lure" of "nothingness." Tadzio, "emerging from the depths of sea and sky," seems myth itself. He appears as "a primeval legend, handed down from the beginning of time, of the birth of form, of the origin of the gods" (p. 33). Aschenbach's emotional response to the boy, which he has not yet faced, inspires his philosophical and aesthetic theorizing. His speculations convey an unconscious insight into the primordial conversion of erotic impulses into religious rite and aesthetic form. He is indeed experiencing the primeval and continuous psychic processes that he reconstructs and objectifies in idealized terms. But this new defense has hidden dangers; reconstructing, however ideally, the origins of religion and art, he is soon led back to their primordial roots.

In the last stages of Aschenbach's life, he is engaged in a struggle with his own intellectual and emotional history in his compulsion to construct authentic images of his desires and terrors. This involves the processes of creation: the use of memory, displacement, projection, idealization, disguise, and finally the unconscious knowledge transformed by these processes—the recognition of the self as bound to nature in lust, cruelty, violence, and death. Ironically, Mann's great novella is the story of an unwritten mythical narrative.

As Aschenbach simultaneously constructs and enacts this

narrative, traditional myth becomes an increasingly complicated vehicle conveying the various and often devious forms
in which unconscious desires emerge into his consciousness.
A cultivated product of the best European education, he has
assimilated ancient Greek myth through its representations
in art and in literature—Homer, Plato, and other ancient
writers, idealized and romanticized by centuries of aesthetic
and scholarly interpretation. Mythical representations of external and human nature are used ironically by the narrator
as a clue to Aschenbach's past and still persistent efforts to
view his own life in idealized terms. Immediately after
Aschenbach has made his "gesture of welcome" to "what
might come," the narrator sets the scene for the ensuing
events with a description of the weather that imitates the
"morally and socially responsible epic" in language and tone:
"Now daily the naked god with cheeks aflame drove his
fire-breathing steeds through heaven's spaces . . ." (p. 40).
The parallel to this passage in Aschenbach's thoughts is one
in which he sits "gazing out dreamily over the blue of the
southern sea" or at night "among the cushions of the gondola," thinking of his summer home where "he would feel
transported to Elysium . . ." (pp. 41-42). The extended description of Elysium that follows has been identified[34] as an
adaptation of the Homeric passage in the *Odyssey* (IV, 560-69)
in which Menelaus quotes Proteus' prophecy regarding his
future immortality. But it is an adaptation of Rohde's German
translation in his *Psyche*, and its use here as Aschenbach's
temporary retreat into his past reflects Rohde's view that the
passage expresses the way in which "hope sought and found
an exit from the shadow-world which swallows up all living
energy."[35] There is nostalgia and comfort for Aschenbach in
this mythical memory, in which death seems innocuous, only
the means to immortality for the hero and his modern surro-
gate, the artist. It is within this idealized framework that he
would create his mythical conception of Tadzio.

The boy's foreign speech is "music" (p. 43); his figure
against sea and sky that of a perfect piece of marble sculpture.
Aschenbach sees behind his very existence the "discipline,"

the "precision," the "strong will" long "familiar to him" as characteristic of the "artist." As he creates an ideal image out of a handsome boy, he apprehends the very processes of his own mind, asking himself: "Was not the same force at work in himself when he strove in cold fury to liberate from the marble mass of language the slender forms of his art which he saw with the eye of his mind and would body forth to men as the mirror and image of spiritual beauty?" In the figure of Tadzio he sees or, more accurately, conceives "beauty's very essence,"[36] which he recognizes is "form as divine thought, the single and pure perfection that resides in the mind," and, in so doing, knows that its source lies in the "frenzy" of erotic desire. Unable to resist what he now recognizes as the source of his vision of pure and perfect beauty, "the aging artist bade it come." Now, his memory brings to the surface "primitive thoughts . . . which with him had remained latent." Yet, even at this stage of self-awareness, Aschenbach seeks comfort in associations that are familiar and culturally accepted; even the homoerotic has its exalted ancient prototype. If it is "Amor" who makes "visible the spirit" only through human beauty, surely Socrates wooing Phaedrus with a discourse on the "beauty-lover's way to the spirit" is hardly a base example. It is with this ideal in mind that Aschenbach makes "Tadzio's beauty" his "model" for a philosophical essay he undertakes to write on the erotic as intrinsic to the impulse toward creation. With a heightened awareness that "Eros is in the word," he is confident that he can transform his turbulent feelings into the "choicest prose, so chaste, so lofty, so poignant with feeling," that it would be generally admired. But the chaste essay of a "page and a half" does little to mitigate the drive of its source: "its origins" and "the conditions whence it sprang" (pp. 44-46).

Aschenbach extends the time of his stay in Venice indefinitely, no longer pretending to himself that he is merely on a vacation. Although he makes no more effort to write, he continually labors to give meaning and form to his "emotional intoxication" (p. 48). Still using the conventional means that have served him for so long, he tries to comprehend and thus accept his passion by associating it with the erotic principle in a mythicized external nature. Unable to sleep, he identifies his submerged sexual fantasies with ancient Greek myths about the dawn taken from Rohde's account (I, 58) of Eos "rising from the side of her spouse" to signal the sunrise. This goddess, the "ravisher of youth," surrounded by "cloudlets, . . . like attendant amoretti," transforming lust into beauty, seems to justify his own intense and painful desires. Indeed, the whole day seems to him "transmuted and gilded with mythical significance" as nature, invested with ancient gods—Poseidon, Pan, Zephyr—becomes in his mind a vehicle to stimulate and contain his erotic fantasies. He sees Tadzio as a beloved youth of myth, Hyacinthus, beautiful but "doomed." But a smile from the real Tadzio, which Aschenbach imagines as the response of Narcissus to his own reflection, arouses feelings that interrupt his romantic saga and elicit from him the "ridiculous" and "sacred" truth: "I love you" (pp. 48-52).

This admission, breaking through the disguise of Aschenbach's romanticized myth-making, reveals the motivation for such fantasies and thus brings them to an end. In his fourth week in Venice, his passion has intensified to a "mania." He can no longer create its background in the sky of Eos and the sea of Poseidon. Instead, he establishes as its symbolic framework the "unclean alleys" (p. 54), the secret terrors, the "antisocial forces which shun the light of day" (p. 65), the corruption, the odors of Venice, infected by Asiatic cholera, which has found its way from a "primeval island-jungle, among whose bamboo thickets the tiger crouches" (p. 63)— his very hallucinatory images—to this site of art and pleasure. The disease, both actual and symbolic, intensifies, as it always does in Mann's work, the union of the creative and the destructive in the artist. Now, "driven by his mania" (p. 52), Aschenbach feels himself one with the city in its "evil secret" (p. 54).

The climactic expression of Aschenbach's frenzy is his Dionysiac dream, in which he does not appear as an actual figure. Instead, it seems to him that its "theatre" is "his own soul." If the unconscious "fear and desire" that motivate this dream cannot find expression in the figure of the disciplined man of letters, for so long detached from his feelings, they nonetheless emerge through archetypal images he had encountered but to which he had never admitted an emotional response within the "cultural structure" that the dream is to leave "ravaged and destroyed." In this dream, Aschenbach's most violent feelings of lust and aggression are represented in a scene based on Rohde's account in his *Psyche* of Thracian Dionysiac rites (ii, 255-60). This work by a friend of Nietzsche's, who defended *The Birth of Tragedy* against the harsh criticism of classicists, reflects Nietzsche's influence in its admission that it is "easier for us to sympathize with" the uncontrolled sensations of the Dionysiac than with the calm and temperance of the Apollonian (ii, 255). But Rohde does not merely echo Nietzsche. He himself developed a new conception of the pre-literary origins of Greek religious practice, and the unique quality of his *Psyche* results from his insight into the psychological motivations that enter into ancient religious rite: the "monstrous phantasies" of the human imagination that seek relief in ceremonies of catharsis (ii, 296-97); the yearning for omnipotence expressed in the hallucinations, the orgiastic violence and rapture of Dionysiac frenzy.[37] Rohde's description of the Dionysiac worshipers resurrects the environment of ancient Thrace, which sanctioned the ritual expression of aggressive and erotic drives to produce a psychic state in which the initiate imagined himself as one with Dionysus.

In his dream, Aschenbach discovers how personal is the meaning of this primitive festival, which had recently become a subject of historical and cultural interest to his society. As the "long drawn u-sound" he had once thought so melodious when the boys had called out "Tadziu" becomes "a kind of howl," introducing the frenzied worshipers emerging from a mountainous wood, like that surrounding his own country house, Aschenbach recognizes an inextricable bond with a primeval realm that has existed in his unconscious mind despite all his efforts at denial. Mann's use of Rohde in this

climactic scene extends Aschenbach's psychic experience far
beyond his infatuation with Tadzio, and the experience itself
beyond his own personality. The "tension of life and mind"
is revealed in this expression of the most personal and secret
desires and conflicts through symbols recorded in the process
of scholarly investigation. The wild music with its dominant
flute, the frantic dancing, the overt sexuality of male and
female worshipers, the "sacred frenzy" that culminates in the
dismembering and consuming of an animal, which Rohde
describes and Mann echoes, are all part of history. Yet these
events on a mountain top in ancient Thrace are also symbols
of the "blind rage" and "whirling lust" beneath the elegant
surface of civilized society and its spokesman, the artist.
Aschenbach's dream is not only a confrontation with himself;
it is a recognition of the elemental forces of lust, violence, and
destruction in life itself, and their agonizing appeal both to
himself and the society that he represents. As an artist, he
has until now denied them, because inherent in them is an
attraction to the socially forbidden and an ambiguous attachment to the formless, to death itself. Mann adds to
Rohde's description another well-known feature of the
Dionysiac rites, the call to the "stranger god," the "sworn
enemy to dignity and self-control," whom Aschenbach tries
desperately to resist. The god's "obscene symbol" represents
the drive of uncontrolled erotic and aggressive impulses toward the dissolution of conscious life. Adherence to him is
surrender of all resistance not only to homoerotic desire but
to the irrational, the formless; it is a merging with the essential ambivalence of nature in worship of the productive phal-
lus and submission to the chaos of violence and death.

Although we have been told at the beginning of the dream
that Aschenbach does not see himself "as present in it,"
at the end, the "dreamer" is indeed among those who
"laughed" and "howled," who "thrust their pointed staves
into each other's flesh and licked the blood as it ran down . . . ;
the stranger god was his own. Yes, it was he who was fling-
ing himself upon the animals, who bit and tore and swal-
lowed smoking gobbets of flesh—while on the trampled moss

there now began the rites in honour of the god, an orgy of promiscuous embraces—and in his very soul he tasted the bestial degradation of his fall" (pp. 66-68). There is no contradiction in these two accounts of his role in the dream, for the participant in the Dionysiac orgy would have been unrecognizable as the man Aschenbach consciously knew as himself up to this point in his life. Now he accepts this dream image as his essential nature, which emerges in an ancient ritual from which the art of tragic drama descended. It is interesting and, I think, important to observe that Aschenbach acts out his aggressive wishes and engages in homosexual love-making only in a dream of an ancient rite that permitted the release of emotions later converted to aesthetic expression. Whatever the genesis of Mann's own homosexual inclinations, in *Death in Venice* he treats homosexuality as a primitive component of the creative impulse, an erotic perception of reality that encompasses its hidden contradictions; the homoerotic symbolizes the artist's dangerous but necessary connection to the amorphous in nature and the self.

Throughout his gradual surrender to madness, Aschenbach has continued to observe his own thoughts and conduct from a rational viewpoint. He has been actor and observer in this modern version of the familiar myth of the human being who in his pride denies Dionysus, only to be compelled by the god to participate in his rites in their most violent and self-destructive form. More gifted and more moving than Pentheus, Aschenbach enacts his destiny in a more ambiguous way, the way of the artist. Now accepting the "monstrous and perverse" (p. 69) as his only hope, like Pentheus he assumes a disguise, though his own erotic aberration dictates the alterations necessary for youthfulness rather than the female dress Pentheus assumed. But even with his bizarre make-up and his dyed hair, Aschenbach's "rouged and flabby mouth" utters fragments of sentences from Nietzsche's "archetype and progenitor" of rationality, Socrates. No longer idealized to justify his own desires, the sentences are "shaped in his disordered brain by the fantastic logic that governs our dreams" (p. 72). Aschenbach now uses Socrates as the observer and judge of the dissolution of his self, and the words to Phaedrus are a warning against such a surrender. It is Eros, says Socrates, who leads the poet to beauty, and even the most extreme detachment and preoccupation with form will ultimately return the poet to the sources of art: the "abyss" from which the creative impulse has emerged.

The last stage of Aschenbach's surrender is a peaceful one. Afflicted with cholera, he manifests none of its agonizing physical symptoms. Sitting on the beach, he feels himself beckoned by Tadzio in the role of "the pale and lovely Summoner" (p. 75), the "psychopompos,"[38] to the nothingness that is ultimate psychic dissolution, which he has desired and feared for so long. Aschenbach's death is ambiguous. It is, to be sure, the obvious result, as so many commentators have observed, of an inability to accept his instinctual impulses and thus inevitably to fall prey to their effects. But Aschenbach's story is not nearly so simple. If he is destroyed by his belated discovery of the abyss over which he and his society have established their monuments to reason, he is also curiously heroic in his compulsive quest for such knowledge. His death is the inevitable outcome of his commitment to art, which finally includes risks he had avoided: the exploration of the mind in its perception and creation of itself in everlasting erotic conflict with reality.

The mythical structure of *Death in Venice* encompasses all its ambiguities, portraying the unresolved conflict between the ecstatic and the rational, the hymnic and the moral as an archetypal drama continually reenacted in the human mind and in society itself. Mann was continually to explore the subtle but crucial determinants that separate the "glorification of instinct"[39] accompanied by contempt for the ego from the struggle to release the instinctual in the service of reason and art. Implicit in the theme and the very structure of *Dr. Faustus* is Nietzsche's "complete, we must assume, . . . deliberate, misperception of the power relationship between instinct and intellect on earth," his "corybantic overestimation" of the instinctual, and his irresponsibility in not recognizing the necessity of fostering "the weak little flame of reason, of spirit, of justice" in the modern world.[40]

Mann wrote the essay on Nietzsche in which this evaluation appears immediately after completing *Dr. Faustus*.[41] Unquestionably, Nietzsche's "frigid loneliness" and his "barbaric resplendent force"[42] are major components of Mann's "tragic hero,"[43] Adrian Leverkühn. One of the most suggestive of Mann's many references to Nietzsche in *The Story of a Novel*, his account of the creation of *Dr. Faustus*, is the direct statement: "There is the interweaving of Leverkühn's tragedy with that of Nietzsche, whose name does not appear in the entire book—advisedly, because the euphoric musician has been made so much Nietzsche's substitute that the original is no longer permitted a separate existence" (p. 32). This "interweaving" is a fundamental operation in Mann's transformation of the legendary Faustus into a symbol of twentieth-century cultural and political madness.

Adrian Leverkühn is a transmutation of the Nietzschean Dionysiac concept of "demonic intoxication"[44] into its inevitable modern expression, Faustian frigidity, pride, and mockery. Incorporating the primordial, amoral Dionysus of Nietzsche into Faustus, Mann reveals the levels of decadence and corruption to which the ideal of daemonic release can lead, the obsession to manipulate the physical and psychological processes of life through superhuman control. This transmutation of Dionysiac ecstatic surrender to the forces of creation and dissolution into daemonic violation of all boundaries—moral, aesthetic, social, and personal—creates a new conception of the Faustian. Mann's Faust is pagan, Christian, and post-Christian, embodying Dionysiac barbarism and moden skepticism regarding any moral structure—a Faust whose hell exists in relation to no opposing heaven, no perennial values, for it is the psychic incorporation of the madness of his society.

Mann's explication of the "central idea" of *Dr. Faustus* seems to indicate a resolution of his own ambivalence regarding the daemonic: "the flight from the difficulties of the cultural crisis into the pact with the devil, the craving of a proud mind, threatened by sterility, for an unblocking of inhibitions at any cost, and the parallel between pernicious euphoria ending in collapse with the nationalistic frenzy of Fascism."[45]

The final equation is unequivocal; still it is the result of a highly complicated and often ambivalent attitude toward its major components: sickness, madness, and death.

As Mann sees it, the Dionysiac in the modern world expresses itself in Romanticism, which he defines as "antiquarianism—of soul that feels very close to the chthonian, irrational, and demonic forces of life, that is to say, the true sources of life." The "priority" Romanticism "grants to the emotional, even in its arcane forms of mystic ecstasy and Dionysiac intoxication, brings it into a peculiar and psychologically highly fruitful relationship to sickness." Paradoxically, moreoever, this "revolutionary representative of the irrational forces of life against abstract reason and dull humanitarianism . . . possesses a deep affinity to death by virtue of its very surrender to the irrational and to the past."[46] These remarks, from a speech delivered at the Library of Congress during the very period when he was writing *Dr. Faustus*, indicate that, however certain Mann was that his hero "is veritably a son of hell,"[47] he never abandoned his life-long conviction of the inextricable bond between creativity and the primitive, amoral impulses of the unconscious mind. But he was also aware that such impulses can be and in the Germany following World War I were "reduced to a miserable mass level, the level of a Hitler," that "German Romanticism broke out into hysterical barbarism, into a spree and a paroxysm of arrogance and crime, which now finds its horrible end in a national catastrophe, a physical and psychic collapse without parallel."[48]

The representation of the "physical and psychic collapse" of his nation in his hero, Adrian Leverkühn, is evident, but Leverkühn's role as a gifted artist—a musician—extends his Faustian arrogance, grandiosity, and adherence to death beyond this basic similarity. In *Dr. Faustus*, as in *Death in Venice*, Mann depicts the continuous cultural and psychic bond of art with irrationality and madness. Concurring with Georg Lukács's view that *Death in Venice* is one of the "great forerunners of that trend toward signaling the danger of a barbarous underworld existing within modern German civilization as its necessary complement," Mann goes on to say that this statement reveals "prophetically the relationship between the Venetian novella and *Faustus*."[49] The connection between these two works is also evident in the figures of the artist-spokesmen who convey in madness the "barbarous underworld" of their civilization. It is this psychic manifestation, however, that finally discloses the differences that are more crucial than the similarities between the early novella and the late novel. However representative Aschenbach is, the depiction of his bizarre symptoms and the gradual breakdown of his psychic defenses creates a figure in the process of discovering his dreadful humanity. Leverkühn's madness, on the other hand, both in ecstatic creation and in infantile regression, is almost totally dehumanizing. In him, unconscious drives are diverted into devilish frigidity, arrogance, contempt, and mockery.

It is the narrator, the classicist and humanist Zeitblom, who introduces as an implicit norm the Dionysiac acknowledged and controlled within a social framework. He recalls a visit to Greece in his youth, when, looking down from the Acropolis onto the Sacred Way, he imagined the Dionysiac initiates marching, "with the name of Iacchus on their lips"; and, standing "at the place of initiation itself," he "experienced by divination the rich feeling of life which expresses itself in the initiate veneration of Olympic Greece for the deities of the depths." Moved and enlightened by this experience, Zeitblom informed his pupils that "culture is in very truth the pious and regulating, I might say propitiatory entrance of the dark and uncanny into the service of the gods" (pp. 9-10).

The rational optimist here summarizes the humanistic tradition of music and art that has become his standard. The assumptions of this tradition that the dark powers of unconscious impulse and knowledge impel creation and are themselves thus continually given new form and deeper coherence are examined throughout *Dr. Faustus*. The intrinsic psychic and spiritual values of such assumptions are tested by the grand extremes of Beethoven's last works, on the one hand, and, on the other, by Leverkühn's loveless obsession to return art to magic, to distort human emotion through the mirror of his own grandiose frigidity. As Leverkühn and Zeitblom, inheritors of the genius and knowledge of the Western humanistic tradition, increasingly become perpetrator and victim of the irrationality inherent in Germany's religious, cultural, and political history, the very nature of psychic controls is questioned, yet their necessity is implicit in the very exposure of their frailty.

In *Dr. Faustus* music is Mann's "paradigm for something more general, . . . a means to express the situation of art in general, of culture, even of man's intellect itself in our so critical era."[50] It is thus an aesthetic vehicle conveying the psychic incorporation and transformation of social values. Ever returning to its primitive origins, it is peculiarly adapted to absorb the various types of irrationality and madness at the base of civilization. In its essence, music is the Nietzschean Dionysiac art, "a repetition and a recast of the world," and the composer, in identifying himself with "primal unity, its pain and contradiction," has "surrendered his subjectivity in the Dionysian process."[51]

This Nietzschean conception of music is established early in *Dr. Faustus* in Kretschmar's lecture on Beethoven's last five piano sonatas, in which he describes the composer as going beyond even the highly individual transformation of musical convention: "Untouched, untransformed by the subjective, convention often appeared in the late works, in a baldness, one might say exhaustiveness, an abandonment of self, with an effect more majestic and awful than any reckless plunge into the personal." In these last sonatas, says Kretschmar, in which "greatness and death come together," Beethoven achieved an "objectivity" that "entered into the mythical, the collectively great and the supernatural." He then plays and explicates Beethoven's Opus 111 as a confrontation and reconciliation with the "process of dissolution." He describes "the wide gap between bass and treble" in the second movement "when the poor little motif seems to hover alone and forsaken above a giddy yawning abyss." Then, at the end of the movement, "after so much rage, persistence, obstinacy, extravagance," an "unexpected . . . mildness and goodness": a "C sharp [that] is the most moving, consolatory, pathetically reconciling thing in the world. . . . It blesses the object, the frightfully harried formulation, with overpowering humanity, lies in parting so gently on the hearer's heart in eternal farewell that the eyes run over" (pp. 52-55). The sonata confronts and exemplifies the "abyss" out of which music itself emerges with a tenderness for the majesty and vulnerability of all creation. Its self-abnegation is a surrender to its acknowledgment of mortality, the dissolution of the individual adaptation to the cosmic processes of creation and destruction, the "poor little motif . . . above a giddy yawning abyss."

In a later lecture, Kretschmar describes Beethoven's frenzy in the process of creating the *Missa Solemnis*. Unaware of time or the normal demands of life, he seems to those who observe him to have emerged from "a life-and-death struggle with all the opposing hosts of counterpoint." A "moving and terrifying" figure with "distorted" features and "dazed" eyes (p. 58), Beethoven is the prototype of the mind and soul that perceive with "overpowering humanity" the conditions of existence. He is indeed an embodiment of Dionysiac power and wisdom nourished by the very art it struggles within and finally exceeds.

But elemental forces continually reappear in forms that reflect the uniqueness not only of genius but of epochs and societies. Adrian Leverkühn is Mann's symbol of the mind irresistibly drawn to the "abyss" of personal and social history without love or reverence. As an artist, he represents the modern alienation from instinctual sources of inspiration (a word Leverkühn hates, p. 25), and a desperate effort to gain access to them, even at the cost of the emotions and values that define civilized life. The character of Leverkühn is a prophetic representation of the abuse of the "dark and the uncanny" instinctual impulses, the deliberate manipulation of such drives out of "interest," which has displaced love (p. 69). His pact with the Devil is a mythical depiction of the psychic compromises and defenses he devises in order to stimulate and control the sources of creativity within his own unconscious mind. Leverkühn deliberately evokes archaic irrationality and induces sickness and madness as avenues of extraordinary power over his own physical and mental capacities and over the society he feels he can influence by the intellectual and emotional forces thus released.

Like Aschenbach's disintegration in *Death in Venice*, Leverkühn's increasing madness is portrayed as an individual psychic transformation of a vast cultural heritage. In *Dr. Faustus*, this heritage is, of course, more extensive, but it is also different in quality.[52] Aschenbach's associations are based primarily on idealized German Hellenism, which exposes its dark side in dreams; Leverkühn's on medieval witchcraft, magic, Lutheran theology, and music evolving out of ecstatic rite into secular individualism. The town of Kaisersaschern, in which Zeitblom and Leverkühn grew up, is described as an environment hospitable to the lunatic and the visionary; it had the "stamp of old-world, underground neurosis." There, an old woman who simply looked strange was suspected of witchcraft. Zeitblom, the rationalist, suggests that the appearance of the poor woman may simply have reflected the suspicions of the townspeople, that gradually, as she identified herself with their image of her, she did indeed become strange. But for Leverkühn this "archaic" strain among people "capable of seeing something daemonic in the poverty of a little old woman," even of watching such a woman "burn" without protesting (pp. 37-38), remains a level of personal response and the ultimate source of his art. It was, says Zeitblom, Kaisersaschern that "spoke" in Leverkühn's "decision to study theology," and it was Kaisersaschern that determined the quality of his music, which, "bold," "mysterious," and "bizarre" though it might be, was yet not " 'free' music, world music," but the "music of one who never escaped" (p. 83).

Leverkühn's psychic adaptation to the primitive remnants within this "practical, rational, modern town" (p. 36) is manifested in his equation of irrationality with power, magic with control over the unknown. Even before he overtly commits himself to music, he approaches it with a "mania" for solving its problems (p. 73). Music, he says, "is almost the definition of God" (p. 78), and he is drawn to it as an abstraction of cosmic energy and mystical awareness. First, however, his "arrogance" leads him to the study of theology (p. 80), which at that time, says Zeitblom, had been infiltrated by the philosophy of "will or instinct, in short the daemonic" (p. 90). Leverkühn's studies, especially with the devilish Schleppfuss, only reinforce his inclination for the uncanny. In presenting his "daemonic conception of God" and his view of the "psychological actuality" of the Devil, Schleppfuss argues for the inseparable connection between the holy and the satanic. Expounding on witchcraft and on the evils of female sexuality, his manner is the exhortatory one of the *Malleus Maleficarum*.[53] Schleppfuss justifies medieval superstition on the basis that implicit in it is an apprehension of the subtle relationship between mind and body. His "insight into the power of mind to alter its own and accompanying physical matter" inevitably leads "to the conviction, supported by ample human experience, that mind, whether wilfully or not," by the use of magic can "alter another person's physical substance. In other words, the reality of magic, of daemonic influence and bewitchment was corroborated . . ." (pp. 99-110).

Schleppfuss's satanic arguments support Leverkühn's view of the "religious" as intrinsic "madness" and his conviction that only the Church as an organization can channel the "chaos of divine and daemonic powers" (p. 119), the province to which he commits himself when he leaves theology for music. This, the art that continually returns to the "elemental," to its own "primitive beginnings" (p. 63), becomes for Leverkühn the ultimate vehicle for the diversion of the instinctual to the daemonic. It is this psychological process—which determines Leverkühn's choice of his life's work—that is the essence of Mann's symbolic depiction of the corrupt artist. Described throughout the novel as "cold," he symbolizes instinctual forces inhibited from normal expression and diverted to omnipotent denial of their limits in extending human control over reality, which ultimately becomes a denial of reality itself. For him woman, in the role of a diseased and loving prostitute, becomes the avenue for "daemonic conception, for a deathly unchaining of chemical change in his nature" that will induce superhuman power. This "madness," as Zeitblom calls it (p. 155), is the underlying theme of his music; it is the goal of his life and of the chaotic and destructive nation that his work and his life prophetically symbolize.

In making Leverkühn the inventor of Arnold Schönberg's twelve-tone or row system, Mann emphasizes what Theodor Wiesengrund-Adorno regarded as the "dire consequences that must flow from the constructive Schönbergian approach to music." The paradoxical effect of this rigorous scheme is that "the art is cast back into a dark mythological realm."[54] When Zeitblom questions Leverkühn about his scheme, his "magic square," concerned to know whether people will "hear all that," Leverkühn replies by referring to two levels of hearing: the first, an apprehension of the means by which his order is achieved, he compares to "the order of the planets, a cosmic order and legality," and this "one would not hear." It is the province only of the god-like composer. The second level, the order that provides "unknown aesthetic satisfaction," is available to mortals (p. 192).

This episode, as well as that in which he consciously exposes himself to syphilis in his one submission to sexual passion, takes place prior to his dialogue with the Devil, both the inevitable and climactic expression of his psychological commitment to the daemonic. As a voice that speaks for the psychological compromises and risks of the artist, the Devil echoes many of Mann's utterances on the relation of art to the criminal, the sick, and the insane.[55] But Leverkühn is the absolute extreme of Mann's life-long conception of the artist as morally and socially suspect, and thus Leverkühn becomes a perversion of the artist himself. Aschenbach's immersion in sickness, his recognition of a yearning for the dissolution of the self in madness and in death connect him to humanity on its most primitive, unconscious levels of feeling and knowledge. But Leverkühn, forever alienated from his own emotions and incapable of investing feeling in any human connection, hears in the Devil's injunction that love is forbidden only a confirmation of his own dehumanized condition. He commits murder without passion or physical involvement, his madness is only the culmination of his life-long withdrawal from human relationships and concerns, and his art is the final expression of his capitulation to the barbarism of instinctual frigidity. Zeitblom describes the "finis" of Leverkühn's *Apocalypse* as a confirmation of "the theologically negative and pitiless character of the whole." He can only "think of an open abyss wherein one must hopelessly sink" (p. 360). Leverkühn's final work, *The Lamentation of Dr. Faustus*, is "the reverse" of Beethoven's "Ode to Joy"; it is "the negative, equally a work of genius, of that transition of the symphony into vocal jubilation. It is the revocation" (pp. 489-90). Leverkühn's work, like his spiritual desperation, symbolizes Germany, "self-maddened, psychologically burnt-out" (p. 482). His genius lies in his unique expression of negation and despair.

If Mann's ambivalence toward the creative impulse is not entirely resolved in the figure of Leverkühn, the bases of this ambivalence are here more sharply delineated than ever before. The drive toward creation, which is rooted in the primitive, the instinctual, the irrational constituents of individual and social development, is itself amoral. But the creator is also a product of society, which historically has institutionalized its own reflection of and conflict with instinctual demands. In the adaptation of the instinctual to communal life lies the dynamic balance at the heart of both aesthetic and social order. The artist, as "seismograph, medium of sensitivity,"[56] is the surest instrument for reflecting the uses to which society in its historical evolution puts the primordial forces underlying its systems of organization and law. As such, Leverkühn is not only a reflector but a prophet. The "dynamic archaism" of his *Apocalypse*, with its sounds of "hellish laughter" (pp. 377-79), mocking all values, including those of art, presages not only the "frenzy of Fascism" but the social and cultural narcissism of the second half of the twentieth century.

In his obsession to reach the sources of creative expression, Leverkühn is not an explorer but a manipulator; he seeks not to discover but to exploit such powers in order to negate creation itself. The paradox inherent in Leverkühn's pact with the Devil is that its terms of accession to the "barbaric" actually depict an abdication of the struggle with instinctual forces, out of which the self is forged. There is a crucial difference between the self-abnegation that Beethoven achieves in his last works—the realization that the self as part of creation inevitably recreates its void as well as its substance, its silence in sound—and the "self-alienation" (p. 505) of Leverkühn, which is a denial of the terms of human existence. His arrogant determination to manipulate his own psychic resources by "chemical changes" in his body, his allegiance to the barbaric, the hopelessness of the "fervid prayer for a soul" (p. 378) in his *Apocalypse*, and finally his regression to infantilism are prophetic representations of the current desperate quest for relief from anomie in occult powers and apocalyptic visions.

Such psychic adventurism continues to be portrayed through the myth of Dionysus. In some literary and psychological works, the Nietzschean god of primordial unity and power reappears practically unchanged. But another, much older, Dionysus also returns in Wole Soyinka's modern version of Euripides' *Bacchae*, a god whose rites of frenzy open the way to balance, self-control, and self-knowledge.

Although Norman O. Brown's apocalyptic interpretations of Freudian psychoanalytic theory already seem dated, as an expression of the anti-rationalism of the late 1950s and the 1960s they cannot be ignored. *Life Against Death*[57] and *Love's Body*[58] reflected and encouraged the then current and, to some extent, continuing, experimentation with altered states of consciousness as a potential source of individual fulfillment and social change. *Life Against Death* contains some astute social criticism, especially in its connection of instinctual repression to social pathology, but the solution Brown offers,

"Dionysian or body mysticism," which he describes as "that simple health that animals enjoy" (pp. 310-11), seems not only an ineffectual basis for reforming social and economic institutions but a simplistic approach to the Dionysiac itself. Clinging to the Nietzschean dichotomies, Brown defines Apollo as "the god of sublimation," which in his view is a negation: "the Apollonian form is form as the negation of instinct" (p. 174). Such repression in art and in society, according to Brown, merely reflects the general development in Western civilization of an Apollonian ego structure. "As long as the structure of the ego is Apollonian," he says, "Dionysian experience can only be bought at the price of ego-dissolution." The answer is by no means "a synthesis of Apollo and Dionysus," for this, according to Brown, is a "sacrifice" of "insight for peace of mind." The only avenue to full experience of one's humanity is the development of a "Dionysian ego," which, while guarding against "dissolution of consciousness," affirms "instinctual reality" (pp. 174-76).

Even in *Life Against Death*, it is hard to see how Brown distinguishes between the Dionysiac as ego-dissolution and the "Dionysian ego." The chief characteristics of the "Dionysian ego," as he defines it, are freedom from negation, from "genital organization" and sexual sublimation; it is "drunkenness" (pp. 174-76) in the sense that it accepts no limits to instinctual pleasure. Brown never makes clear how the psychic structure he designates as the "Dionysian ego" is a safeguard against "that horrible mixture of sensuality and cruelty" (Nietzsche's description, which Brown adopts, p. 175) manifested in ego dissolution. His further development of the concept of the Dionysiac in *Love's Body* reveals that the two are in fact equivalent. Hailed by reviewers in 1966 as the work of a twentieth-century prophet in the tradition of Nietzsche, *Love's Body* is actually a collection of paragraphs interpreting the Bible, St. Augustine, Freud, Róheim, Blake, Goffman, and other ancient and modern sources in visionary terms.

The unifying themes of Brown's utterances are indeed a recapitulation and extension of Nietzsche's philosophy: There is an irreconcilable division "between the *principium indi-*

viduationis and the Dionysian, or drunken, principle of union, or communion, between man and man and between man and nature" (p. 87). Thus, psychic harmony requires the "extinction of the ego, . . . to have no self, to be of no mind, . . . to be a dead man" (p. 264). Madness is a psychic goal. "Schizophrenics are suffering from the truth," and the "boundary between sanity and insanity is a false one" (pp. 159-60). In fact, the "goal" of psychoanalysis "can only be conscious magic, or conscious madness" (p. 254). By "breaking the barrier of the ego . . . natural man is transformed into superman" (pp. 196-97).

For Brown, the chief obstacle to human spiritual and bodily fulfillment, which are one, is the development of the ego, which he regards as the paramount expression of the Western tradition of "soul-body dualism."[59] In Freud's conception of the integration of ego and id, Brown sees only a threat of further repression. This is his most serious objection to Freud, whom he otherwise praises lavishly. Brown's rigid separation of the ego from the instinctual, however, reflects not Freud's dualism but his own. Brown is either unaware of or unwilling to accept Freud's view that "the ego is identical with the id, and is merely a specially differentiated part of it." Freud states explicitly: "if the ego remains bound up with the id and indistinguishable from it, then it displays its strength" (*SE*, xx, 97). Far less dualistic than Brown and other recent laudators of "non-egoic" experience, Freud recognized the inextricable connection between the perceptive and synthesizing functions of the ego and the instinctual aims and deflections from which these emerged. It is interesting to observe that as early as 1926 Freud warned against the use of his conception of the dependence of the ego on the "daemonic forces" of the id as the basis of a *"Weltanschauung."* The products of such philosophical adaptations, the "Handbooks to Life," he says, "soon grow out of date," and "even the most up-to-date of them are nothing but attempts to find a substitute for the ancient, useful and all-sufficient Church Catechism" (*SE*, xx, 95-96).

Brown's effort to expose the psychological pathology inherent in the Western tradition of rationalism culminates in a religious dedication to "creative destruction." For the "abstract idea"[60] of Christ he would substitute "Dionysian Christianity,"[61] which is ecstatic fulfillment of the human body. His program of "symbolic consciousness," the "re-sexualization of thought and speech," and "polymorphous perversity" as "a form of mystic meditation"[62] is but one of the various pseudo-systems of the sixties whose goal was to deflect instinctual aims to sensuous mysticism.

One of the dramatic versions of the Dionysus myth that appeared in the 1960s and early 1970s, *Dionysus in 69*, depicts an effort to experience this sensuous mysticism as a psychic rebirth, combining personal, religious, and political enlightenment. Directed by Richard Schechner, the Performance Group used William Arrowsmith's translation of Euripides' *Bacchae* as the basis for inducing its version of Dionysiac ecstasy on stage. Its aim was to unite actors and audience in a communal rite, in which individual desire, rage, and terror merged with protest against the war in Vietnam and other social injustices to create the "politics of ecstasy."[63]

Members of the cast invited the audience to join in their "ordeals" of ritual birth, frenzy, caress, and death in order to achieve levels of self-knowledge and a sense of communion unattainable in ordinary experience. These were intended as rites of passage "toward godhead," a state that manifested itself differently among the various members of cast and audience, but generally meant overcoming inhibitions in the ecstatic release of love and aggression. Actually, the text of *Dionysus in 69*, the performance itself, and Schechner's evaluation of the production in *Environmental Theater*[64] consistently reveal that the "polymorphous" experience, the shamanistic techniques and imitations of other rituals, the nakedness, the "turning god on," the frenzy were primarily neither communal nor political forms of expression. Breaking through what they considered to be the "obstacles" of Euripides' text, the cast used primitive rite and contemporary political and social conflict as vehicles for self-expression. The pseudo-rite of self-transcendence was reduced to narcissistic exhibition of personal grievances and grandiose fantasies.

A far more effective use of Euripides' text to restore to drama the immediacy of communal rite is the Nigerian playwright Wole Soyinka's *The Bacchae of Euripides*, first performed in London in August of 1973. Using portions of Euripides' tragedy, via the translations of Gilbert Murray and William Arrowsmith, Soyinka discloses the continuous and syncretic nature of the myth and rite of Dionysus as he identifies him with the "wilful, ecstatic being"[65] of Ogun, a Yoruba god of metal. Soyinka draws on inherent similarities between the ancient Greek Dionysus and the African Ogun which suggest that both originate in symbolic expressions of elemental strivings to adapt psychic aims to communal life. Like Dionysus, Ogun was "torn asunder" and reintegrated; a god of the hunt, of agriculture, and of song, he symbolizes, as does Dionysus, both destruction and creation. The god's complex nature and the rites performed in his honor indicate that his function in Yoruba culture in many respects parallels that of the primordial Dionysus, especially the "strengthening of the communal psyche"[66] through symbolic depiction of what Soyinka calls a "dynamic fusion" of "contradictory attributes" representing cosmic, social, and psychological conflict. In primordial Dionysiac ritual, the god's adherents enact a development from literal incorporation of human beings and animals to internalization of the god's own struggle for integration and productivity. The ritual drama celebrating Ogun depicts a "cosmic ordering" of "primordial chaos," a "resolution of the experience of birth and the disintegration of consciousness in death," and a unification of aggressive with peaceful and creative aims.[67] Most important, the rites of both gods, however frenzied, symbolically enact a connection between the regulation of psychic impulses and the development of "self-apprehension"[68] in a social context. The frenzied and "manic" elements of the rites of Ogun—the dancing on the mountain, the slaughter of a dog, which is "torn limb from limb," the indulgence in wine—are balanced by peaceful ones: the symbolism of the palm that binds the

lumps of iron ore at the tops of the poles carried by the participants, and the recessional of women who greet the revelers
at the foot of the mountain with song. In this resolution, a
"dynamic marriage unfolds of the aesthetics of ritualism and
the moralities of control, balance, sacrifice, the protagonist
spirit and the imperatives of cohesion, diffusing a spiritual
tonality that enriches the individual being and the community."[69]

Merging Ogun with Dionysus, Soyinka's version of the
Bacchae incorporates both the continuous elements and the
historical development of the myth of Dionysiac frenzy. In
the modern play, the Dionysiac rites, both peaceful and violent, convey the continuous and dynamic symbolic processes
of apprehending and integrating aggressive and libidinal
aims. But these rites also contain their own paradoxical history. Thus, Soyinka's Dionysus, appearing as the eman-
cipator of an enslaved proletariat, symbolizes the freeing of
instinctual aims deflected into servility and self-loathing by
repressive authority and the assumption of control over such
drives as a reconstitution of the ego in a new social identity.

Soyinka's most brilliant achievement in this play is his portrayal of psychic processes manifested in social and political
conflict. In the program notes to the production of the British
National Theatre, he describes Dionysus' "history" as "rich
in all the ingredients of a ravaged social psyche—displacement, suppression of identity, dissociation, dispossess-
sion, trials, and the goal of restoration." A manifestation of
"Nature in her monstrous cycle of regeneration, . . .
Dionysiac cult is both social therapy and reaffirmation of
group solidarity. It is a celebration of life, bloody and tumultuous, an extravagant rite of the human and communal
psyche."[70]

In Soyinka's version of the *Bacchae*[71] Dionysus comes to
Thebes to free the slaves of an industrialized urban society.
The god is recognized by the leader of the slaves as a revolutionary force inherent in external and human nature, "remorseless," "Unpredictable" (p. 240), destructive, and, at the
same time, a principle of regeneration. As he urges the other

slaves to accept the god's ecstatic rites, he assures them: "Nature has joined forces with us" (p. 240). The slave leader's *"control,"* says Soyinka's stage direction, *"emanates from the self-contained force of his person, a progressively deepening spiritual presence"* (p. 248), and, as the crowd becomes *"possessed"* through his influence, there is a general *"self-release"* (p. 249). In the ritual chanting and dancing of the Bacchants and the Chorus of Slaves, Dionysus is worshiped both as a principle of productivity—"the freedom of sands," "the liberation of waters," "the intuitions in the liberation of the grape" (pp. 246-47), and as a symbol of the potential freedom of human beings in harmony with nature. The basis of this freedom is self-knowledge, which includes insight into the very process of channeling instinctual drives by projecting them on the mythical deity: "Blessed, thrice blessed, the moment of recognition / Of god without as the essence within" (p. 248).

Such emotional and intellectual freedom, however, is not easily won. The vested interest of political tyranny in psychological repression is symbolized in Pentheus, who, like his ancient model, in refusing to acknowledge the god denies the emotional basis of his own humanity. Both Tiresias, "the psychic intermediary" (p. 243), and Dionysus try to break through Pentheus' rigid defenses—his insistence on "Law and order" (p. 282), which demand repression of his own and others' instinctual needs. Like Euripides' Pentheus, he interprets the emergence of the Dionysiac spirit as "Licentiousness," a judgment, Tiresias warns him, that reflects only his total dependence on the efficacy of "power." But Tiresias' counsel:

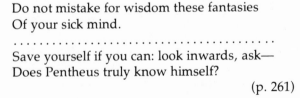

> Do not mistake for wisdom these fantasies
> Of your sick mind.
> ....
> Save yourself if you can: look inwards, ask—
> Does Pentheus truly know himself?
>
> (p. 261)

goes unheeded, as does Dionysus' explicit warning:

You do not know what life is. You do not know
What you do. You do not know the limits
Of your power. You will not be forgiven.

(p. 270)

In trying to imprison Dionysus, Pentheus becomes the victim
of his own fear and hatred, which are as ruthless turned inward as are the military and political power to which he has
diverted them. "I made the sick desires / Of his mind his goal,
and he pursued them" (p. 276), says the god, who describes
Pentheus' tormented encounter with his own fantasies.

Soyinka echoes Euripides in portraying the Bacchants as
peaceful, enjoying the fruitfulness of the earth and of their
own bodies: "That air of peace still controlled their actions"
(p. 279). Only when they are hunted by those seeking to
please Pentheus do the Bacchants "turn hunter" (p. 280),
dismembering animals and snatching children. The substitution of Pentheus for the Theban slave as the annual human
scapegoat in the final hunt depicts the release of Dionysiac
impulses in their most uncompromising political and social
terms. Intrinsic to Dionysiac power, this destructiveness is
nevertheless not its goal. Dionysus says the "secret of life is /
Balance, tolerance" (p. 277), and Tiresias, speaking for him,
describes "self-discipline" as "the greatest / Guarantee of
human will and freedom" (p. 261). In Soyinka's *Bacchae*, as in
Euripides', Dionysiac rites, both peaceful and violent, are
heuristic, exemplifying a struggle for psychic and communal
equilibrium, which must continually be renewed to promote
individual integrity and social productivity.

2. THE AESTHETICS OF MADNESS

The extremes of Gérard de Nerval's individual transformation of certain Romantic modes, like Nietzsche's, make his
work, especially his prose, anomalous within its literary and
historical period. Except for this characteristic, which seems a
peculiar modernism, the two writers are utterly different,

even in their visionary grandiosity. Despite the narcissistic isolation to which Nietzsche considers himself consigned as the last adherent of instinctual release in a repressive and decadent society, his concept of Dionysiac frenzy is a social one, a reformer's vision. But the madness that Nerval describes as his own experience has little to do with social or psychic reformation; it is an interpretation of the self within the cosmos through dreams and hallucinations. In *Aurélia*,[72] the work in which his madness is his subject, he employs the primitivism, mysticism, and exoticism characteristic of much Romantic literature to develop a metamorphic style that recreates the processes of mental pathology, particularly schizophrenia. Through this fluidity of language, structure, and tone, Nerval depicts the ever-shifting moods, images, feelings, withdrawals, and remarkable sudden insights that constitute the self as he experiences it.

In the first two paragraphs of *Aurélia* (p. 23), Nerval presents his basic material: "dreams" and the "long sickness that took place entirely within the secrets of my soul." Explaining his view of dreams as "a second life," he says that the "first moments of sleep" are an "image of death." In the "hazy numbness" which "seizes our thought" at this time, "we cannot determine the precise moment when the I, under another form, continues the work of existence." The "œuvre" that "le moi" continues in its dream life in *Aurélia* is remarkably similar to what Freud was later to describe as "the dream work," the reversals and condensations of thoughts transformed into images, the distortion of "existence" into apparent absurdities that disclose something of the "mystères" the dreamer approaches.

The hallucinations Nerval recounts are similar in the fluidity of their form and sometimes in contents to his dreams. His symptoms of madness, like his dreams, provide him with the material for a study of the human soul. He does not know, he says, why he refers to his periods of insanity as a "maladie," since he was then physically well, at times even extraordinarily energetic. Furthermore, he seemed, during these periods, "to know everything, to comprehend everything; my imagination supplied me infinite delight," and he wonders whether, "in recovering what men call reason," he has not "to regret having lost" such satisfactions (p. 23). Nerval's account of his madness records his depression and terror as well as times of manic joy, but he makes no distinction between these moods as avenues of discovery, and they are often alternating responses to the continual metamorphoses of his symbolizations.

The soul that Nerval professes to study in *Aurélia* is, of course, his own, but he suggests that his is a paradigm of the self released in dreams and in the hallucinations that he describes as "the overflowing of dream into real life" (p. 28). These states constitute a *"Vita nuova"* (p. 24) and, like Dante, who is one of his models (p. 23), Nerval centers his quest upon an ideal woman who symbolizes the merging of sexual desire, religious purity, and mystical yearnings. But Dante's visions of Beatrice in the *Vita nuova*, his fantasies of his death and hers, his feelings of being confused and possessed by his imaginings, serve Nerval only as allusive extensions in time and space of his own emotional fixations. Actually, the differences between Nerval and this "model" are more important than the similarities. Most crucial is Nerval's almost total divergence from Dante's method of representation, which he explicates (*Vita nuova* xxv) in distinguishing between the nature of affective experience and its reification through the rhetorical devices of metaphor or simile. For Nerval the visions centered around his idealized love are substantial; his method of fusing probable events with fantastic ones, the ancient past with the present and the future, is designed to convey the reality of dreams and hallucinations as superseding the generally accepted limits of time and space.

The question of whether Nerval wrote from memory of his own hallucinatory experience, the accounts of others, his own imaginary reconstructions combined with literary associations, or, as is probable, all three, is actually irrelevant to his method of conveying his accommodation to a continually shifting conception of existence. This he does by depicting fragmentation as a process of self-creation and discovery, which are one in *Aurélia*. Nerval uses his panic, his projections of his desires on beneficent forces and his anger on hostile ones, his paranoia, the splitting of his ego, his grandiosity, and other schizophrenic symptoms as means of communicating his perception and assimilation of experience.

In one hallucination in which "everything changed its form around me," the spirit who had been instructing him is transformed into a youth whom he now teaches. Frightened by his assumption of a dominant role and by his own recurrent Faustian "obscure and dangerous" questioning, the narrator immediately transforms himself into a wanderer in a more placid environment, "a populous, unknown city," in which he discovers a primitive race from the primordial past continuing to maintain its integrity and influence under modern urban conditions. He participates in this merging of past and present by feeling his feet "sinking into successive layers of buildings of different epochs" and by first observing and then being welcomed by and responding affectionately to the "primitive, heavenly family" the archaic race has now become. But these forms soon melt away, leaving only grief and confusion. Having concluded his account of this "vision," Nerval comments, without transition, on the "cataleptic state in which [he] had been for several days" and disparages the "scientific" explanation for it that he was given (pp. 34-37). The sinking feet, the ideal harmonious family, the merging time and shifting forms, the melting faces, the tears shed at "the memory of a lost paradise" are all the "moi" who has withdrawn from a reality that cannot fulfill its cravings or assuage its guilt, an explanation more "logical" than the "scientific" one he rejects.

Another hallucination recreates the world from its beginnings, the narrator struggling with monsters in the "chaos of nature." Even his own body is "as strange as theirs." Within this monstrous combat with nature there appears "a singular harmony" that "reverberates through our solitude," and suddenly the "confused cries, the roaring and hissing" of the primitive creatures assumes "this divine melody." There follow "infinite variations" and "metamorphoses" in the cosmos and in the earth and its inhabitants as they respond to this celestial influence. The miracle, of course, has been performed by a "radiant goddess" (pp. 42-43), one of the many versions of the image of the all-loving mother, the goal in the fragmentation of madness and, paradoxically, the potential source of integration. This image incorporates all the metamorphoses of mood and tone, of scene and episode of which the dreams and hallucinations are composed. No sooner does it appear than its other aspect—the hostile and denying—emerges, producing blood and groaning, years of "captivity" (pp. 44-45), and infinite recurrences of the monstrous in varied metamorphoses of the self. But in the second part of *Aurélia*, this "goddess" appears to the narrator in a dream vision and explains her role: "I am the same as Mary, the same as your mother, the same one whom in every form you have loved. In each of your trials, I have laid aside one of the masks by which I hide my features and soon you will see me as I am" (p. 69).

This moment of illumination occurs in a paradisaical atmosphere, which denies the mundane reality of the insight, and the narrator emerges from the dream with the delusion that he is Napoleon, inspired to accomplish "great things." Incorporating the real world into his delusional system, he believes that everyone in the galleries of the Palais-Royal is staring at him. Although he makes no overt connection, this delusion seems related to those he next alludes to—his "persistent idea that there were no more dead" and that he "had committed a sin" to be discovered by "consulting his memory" which was "that of Napoleon." His delusions grow more grandiose as, installed in an asylum, he imagines that he has the power of a god (pp. 69-70).

From this point on, the narrator almost consciously decides to use his delusions to reestablish a more stable identity. In another asylum, observing the "insane," he understands that "everthing had been an illusion for [him] up to then." Nevertheless, he submits to a "series of trials" which he feels he owes to the goddess Isis (p. 70). These are delusions centered on his own "role" in reestablishing "universal harmony" by Cabbalistic arts and other occult powers (p. 72). The most dreaded of his projections, the "magnetic rays emanating from [himself] or others," can serve as means not only of domination but of communication with all of the created universe (p. 73). He emerges from a hallucination of decapitation and dismemberment—which he himself recognizes as symbols of fragmentation (p. 77)—to offer friendship to another patient with whom he feels "united" by "a certain magnetism" (p. 78).

Near the end of *Aurélia*, the narrator asks himself if it is possible to "dominate his sensations instead of submitting to them, . . . to master this fascinating and terrible chimera, to impose order on these spirits of the night which play with our reason." His answer lies in discovering the meaning of his dreams and in the "link between the external and the internal worlds." He is now convinced of his own immortality and of the "coexistence of all the people [he] has loved" (p. 84). Through Nerval's very method of narration, in which a few factual details serve to link dream, hallucination, and delusion, he creates "le moi" he seeks in every image, every idealized figure, every fantastic episode, and every metamorphosis that represents what Freud calls (*SE* xv, 183) "unconscious mental acts." The timelessness of the unconscious becomes for the narrator of *Aurélia* evidence of his own immortality and the continuous existence of those he loves. Through condensation, displacement, and reversal, he fuses elements of his fragmented identity, investing conflicting feelings in symbols of eternal unification, a fragile defense against the "void," the image of "nothingness" (p. 74) that he fears may be the definition of his own soul.

In Lautréamont's *Les Chants de Maldoror*,[73] which appeared in 1868-69, a little more than a decade after *Aurélia*, nothingness is the goal of the stylistic caricature of the symptoms of madness. Although *Maldoror* is entirely concerned with the bizarre, sadistic desires of its narrator, they seem to belong to no person. It is not that the self is fragile or shattered; it is non-existent. According to Leo Bersani, "every aspect of [Lautréamont's] work contributes to the dispersion or the crumbling of fixed identities." The "adventures of an imaginary Maldoror" are "told by a narrator elusively floating among various physical and moral identities."[74] Actually, the notion of "identities" seems imposed by the critic. Reading *Maldoror*, one experiences no sense of fragmentation or "crumbling"; the process is eliminated, and only highly contrived products are displayed. In *Aurélia* the suspense produced by the metamorphic style results from its implicit threat of extinction, but in *Maldoror* the suspense is elicited only by the bizarre ingenuity of the narrator's metamorphic externalizations of his obsession with rebellion as cruelty, destruction, and death.

The metamorphoses that constitute the narrative method of *Maldoror*, though ostensibly imitating the delusions and hallucinations of madness, do not actually convey the quality of unconscious experience. It is true, as Albert Camus says, that *Maldoror* expresses Lautréamont's conviction that the "reign of mankind must . . . be brought back to the level of the reign of the instinct. . . . It is no longer a question of recognizing appearances, by making a determined and conscious effort, but of no longer existing at all on the conscious level."[75] But Lautréamont's series of spectacular metamorphoses defeats this purpose. The narrator's sexual prowess and cruelty, his dreams of entering the body of a hog, his copulation with a shark, his transformation into a swan, and his various other manifestations and feats are a panorama of the marvelous, the evil, and the disgusting, eliciting only wonder at the imagination that conceived them. What Camus says about the "burning ardor" of Maldoror's dedication to crime, "It costs nothing" (p. 84), is true in another sense about the disintegration of structure in *Maldoror*, which conveys neither the psychic intensity of instinctual desire nor the complexity of its fulfillment in sexuality or violence. Actually, the metamorphoses, the puns, the irony, the mockery of *Maldoror* succeed only in their highly contrived, conscious efforts to shock. Maldoror's commitment to annihilation is a marvel of ingenuity, a grand, oversimplified inversion of the Romantic yearning to merge with the universe.

This, at least in part, explains the appeal of Lautréamont to the surrealists, to whom he seemed a model of rebellion against the conscious mind, inhibiting individual fulfillment by perpetuating the tyrannical hypocrisy of established social order. The implications of the surrealist movement's determination to free the unconscious mind are broad and sometimes contradictory, but in at least one important respect—its commitment to the creative power of the instinctual and the irrational—it can be said to have had a crucial effect on twentieth-century European, English, and American literature, even on works that seem unrelated to its central purposes.

Everyone acquainted with modern literature is familiar with André Breton's definition of surrealism in his first manifesto (1924) as "Psychic automatism in its pure state, by which one proposes to express—verbally, by means of the written word, or in any other manner—the actual functioning of thought."[76] This suspension of consciousness is to be achieved mainly by the inducement and exploration of dreams and hallucinations and by automatic writing in which "images appear like the only guideposts of the mind" (p. 37). In these processes the distinction between the liberation of the unconscious and madness disappears. Breton is "willing to admit that" the mad "are, to some degree, victims of their imagination, in that it induces them not to pay attention to certain rules . . . ," but this is merely a social inconvenience. The mad have the advantage of "comfort and consolation from their imagination," and they are fundamentally a source of knowledge of the workings of the mind: "I could spend my whole life prying loose the secrets of the insane" (p. 5).

The surrealists were not concerned with the broad range of symptoms manifested in psychosis; for the most part, it was the hallucinations, the images of "the actual functioning of thought," that interested them as the most extreme and daring products of the irrational. In this respect, as in their involvement in social and political issues, the surrealists' principle of the irrational contains an implicit contradiction, the demand, in Camus' words, "to extract reason from unreason and to systematize the irrational." Surrealism, he goes on to say, "after Rimbaud, wanted to find constructive rules in insanity and destruction."[77] No matter how extreme Breton's position became in his various manifestoes, he never actually deviated from certain principles contained in the first. As he continued to elaborate on the advantages of "psychic automatism," he also continued to indicate those to be derived from the unification of conscious and unconscious processes as he described this in the first manifesto: "I believe in the future resolution of these two states, dream and reality, which are seemingly so contradictory, into a kind of absolute reality, a *surreality*, if one may so speak" (p. 14).

In the second manifesto, he deplores the fact that "more systematic and sustained efforts, such as Surrealism has consistently called for—have not been made in the sphere of automatic writing . . . and in the description of dreams." His chief criticism of the practitioners of automatic writing is of their failure at "self-observation," their lack of *"awareness"* (pp. 157-61). Such conscious processes are intrinsic to the surrealist aesthetic and social rebellion against rationalism.

The concern of the surrealists with what Breton calls "the problem of social action" (p. 151) is inextricably connected with their aesthetic position. This goes beyond the early commitment of most of the surrealists to Marxism and Breton's and others' break with the Communist Party in 1933. More consistent and more lasting than their adherence to revolutionary violence and their sporadic nihilism is their belief that "psychic automatism" could restore "naturalness and truth" not only to art but to society (p. 231), that it was indeed essential for human emancipation. Breton's outrage in 1935 that "the sign survives the thing signified" is directed at political and moral stagnation (p. 216). In 1953, recapitulating the major aesthetic principles of surrealism and its goal of bringing "language back to true life," he returns to this subject: "rather than go back from the thing signified to the sign that lives after it (which, moreover, would prove to be impossible), it is better to go back in one leap to the birth of that which signifies" (p. 299).

In the poetry of Breton, Louis Aragon, Paul Eluard, Robert

Desnos, and other surrealists, this principle is realized in a variety of ways, but chiefly in the creation of images that unite diverse and even contradictory levels and areas of experience. Discussing the poetry of Paul Eluard, Mary Ann Caws says that "there is no gap between the visual and the mental for him; his poetic theories are all based on this simplicity of sight and thought and on this union or reunion of disparate or disordered elements: 'J'établis des rapports. . . .' Such relationships (rapports) as he establishes apply to the human as well as to the object world: by linking the elements of one, he links those of the other. The search for a 'fil conducteur' is common to all the surrealists."[78]

The image in its immediacy and freshness unites unconscious instinct with social need in a new order that accommodates the dynamic processes of the mind of the poet and reader. The continual metamorphoses of images in surrealist poetry transmit the mind's capacity for infinite transformations, and images are connected not by conventional emotional and intellectual associations but by the process of generation itself. Caws points out that Eluard's " 'Sans âge' can be read either as a poem about surrealism or about Communist fraternity, or about the fraternity of poets, or better still as an example of the similarity between all three" (p. 146). In opening themselves to the revelations of the unconscious, in merging with the non-human natural world, and even in rejecting so-called rationality, which they regarded as mere rigidity, the surrealist poets did not aim at the dissolution of the self, but rather at the continual rebirth of consciousness on all possible levels. There is, as Caws and others have pointed out, a fundamental optimism in the aesthetics of surrealism. However mad and shocking the products of psychic automatism may be, in the image they unite the poet with his fellow human beings in a revolutionary consciousness at once aesthetic and social, continually rediscovering and recreating the world.

The only member of the early surrealists whose work has become a literary vogue in recent years and has drawn a great deal of critical attention is Antonin Artaud, who was expelled from the movement in 1926. Artaud himself regarded the question of whether the surrealists "drove [him] out or whether [he] walked out on their grotesque parody" as irrelevant,[79] but his objections to the movement, which he states in *In Total Darkness, or the Surrealist Bluff*, are important in considering his role as a contemporary cultural model. The decision of Breton and his followers to join the Communist Party seemed to Artaud a betrayal of the fundamental principles of surrealism, since they were now committed "to seek in the realm of facts and of immediate matter the culmination of an action that could normally develop only within the inmost confines of the brain" (p. 139). Artaud, as always, no matter what the issue, returns to its base in his own psychic need: "What does all the Revolution in the world mean to me if I know that I will remain in endless pain and misery in the charnel house of myself?" Yet he does not stop there. His own position is exemplary: the "complete Revolution" permits every man to "refuse to consider anything beyond his own deepest sensibility, beyond his inmost self . . ." (p. 140). Artaud's apolitical revolutionary stance is intrinsic to his anti-aesthetic, anti-literary reifications of his unconscious mind as simultaneously the source of and the barrier to creation. In the manifestoes, letters, essays, poems, plays, film scripts, and performances that constitute his work, it is his own mind, chiefly in a psychotic state, that is his material, but it is his mind as a paramount example of the physiology and psychology of what he calls "elementary consciousness" (p. 91). The second difference he cites in his break with the surrealists is "that they love life as much as I despise it" (p. 141). Theirs is a pleasure in existence that he finds antithetical to "true magic" which demands asceticism, a rejection of the body. Paradoxically, in his obsessive search for the physiological origins of consciousness, the body he despises is his chief preoccupation and the basis of his reformation of language.

Artaud admits that surrealism did offer him "a new kind of magic." This lay in "that whole intense liberation of the unconscious," through dream and imagination, which effects "profound transformations in the scale of appearances, in the value of signification and the symbolism of the created" (p. 142). But, in valuing "the treasures of the invisible unconscious" (p. 143), Artaud differs profoundly from the surrealists. This difference, it seems to me, is the very basis of the lifelong conflict with language that determines his antiliterary theory of creation.

For the surrealists, the infinitely metamorphic image was the product of the unconscious mind and the vehicle for liberating its creative activity, but for Artaud, the products of the unconscious in dreams and hallucinations were only the beginning. In his view, the surrealists' contribution was to bring literature "closer to the essential truth of the brain" (p. 143), and it is this essential truth, beyond image, beyond symbol, and beyond words themselves that he seeks. Artaud's parting words to the surrealists in *In Total Darkness* are: "I, of course, have in my favor psychological and physiological circumstances which are desperately abnormal and of which they would never know how to avail themselves" (p. 145). His lifelong dedication was to this abnormality, his curse and his gift, which he was determined to probe to its physiological roots.

Even before his break with the surrealists, Artaud had written of his compulsion to reach beyond what Freud calls the "psychical representatives," the "ideas" or symbolizations by which the instincts make themselves known, to their wordless, nameless physiological substrata. In *The Nerve Meter*, which appeared in 1925, he attributes his "malformation of thought" to "Malformation, disorganization of a certain number of those vitreous corpuscles of which you make such unconsidered use. A use which you do not know, at which you have never been present." The "terms" in which he chooses to think have the "literal sense" of "true terminations, borders"; his actual thought is "ELSEWHERE" (p. 83). *Fragments of a Diary from Hell*, also published in 1925, is more explicit in its expression of his obsessive need to reach the somatic processes which enter into thinking and feeling and to confront the painful connection between the physiological and the psychic. In this work he describes his symptoms—"I feel the ground under my thought crumble"—and concludes that "this erosion which attacks the very foundations of my thought, in its most urgent communications with intelligence and with the instinctiveness of the mind" damages not the mind itself, although it experiences the effects in "bristling with barbs," but "the neurological pathways of thought" (p. 94). His psychic anguish is intensified by his sense of the hopelessness of his ever discovering its exact locus: "No precise information can ever be given by this soul that is choking; for the torment that is killing it, flaying it fiber by fiber, is occurring below the level of thought, below the level that language can reach . . ." (p. 95).

Artaud's psychic quest for this level took many forms as he returned to it again and again in all his written work, but its goal was always to fill "the void," the absence of self, as if his discovery of the physical mechanisms of existence could finally produce the integrated being he could never experience as himself. No writer has portrayed more exactly the anguish of depersonalization, of having no sense of somatic and psychic identity. Artaud's work communicates his alternations between agonizing resignation to this condition and efforts to establish palpable defenses against it, of which his writing itself is the chief example.

In *Fragments of a Diary from Hell*, recording his psychopathic symptoms, Artaud says: "my unconscious governs me completely" (p. 92). With extraordinary insight, in this and later writings, he describes his thought disorders and their relation to the sense of inner "emptiness" that tormented him. In this connection, two letters written to his doctor, George Soulié de Morant, in February of 1932 are extremely important. Both were written at a time when he felt himself in a condition of "relative improvement," but Artaud was convinced even then that his "disease" had only "partly disappeared" (p. 287). In the first letter, he tells how, when observing his own "emptiness" and trying "to produce a thought, the drama begins, the intellectual drama in which I am perpetually defeated" (p. 289). Yet he will not relinquish his efforts to grasp its meaning: "Yes, it is the notion of this private intellectual vacuum which I should like to *illuminate* once and for all. It seems to me the dominant characteristic of my condition" (p. 290).

The second letter is more detailed in its delineation of the "fissure" between "every idea or image arising in the unconscious" and the "unspoken word" it "constitutes." These fissures, moreover, which do not allow for the development of thought, Artaud is convinced, prevent him from "being validly and lastingly aware of who I am, or what I think." He describes his inability to retain "archetypical images corresponding to [his] personal sensations and representations," which prevents self-awareness and causes his failure to make appropriate responses, his "immense and constant anxiety," and most of all the "terrible sensation of emptiness" (pp. 291-95).

Ironically, language—which he hated because it seemed to taunt him, ever eluding what he diagnosed as the verbally inexpressible, somatic sources of his psychic pain—was his chief vehicle for obsessively portraying this condition. Concrete, violent language was his principal means of conveying the rage and frustration of instinctual diffusion and repression. Language, as concrete object, as incantation, became a substitute for "personal sensations and representations" in his creation of a conception of physical reality endurable without an image of self. His own being, which eluded every "idea" or "image," could be experienced only in the word as concrete object, inseparable from any representation, deprived of the threat of instinctually and emotionally charged abstraction.

In the poems of his last years, he explicitly repudiates the "self," the "I," that had for so long eluded him, interpreting his experience of emptiness as a form of concrete verbal spirituality with which he hopes to remake existence. To the end of his life he sought illumination in the concreteness of the organic. Writing to Wladimir Porché about the decision to cancel the radio broadcast of his play *To Have Done with the Judgment of God* (later performed for select audiences), he says:

I wanted a fresh work, one that would make contact
   with certain organic points of life,
a work
in which one feels one's whole nervous system
illuminated as if by a miner's cap-lamp
with vibrations,
consonances
which invite

      man
      TO EMERGE
      WITH
      his body
to follow in the sky this new, unusual, and radiant
   Epiphany.

                           (p. 579)

The concrete body finally achieves immortality, inconceivable
for an abstract soul. But this is only a temporary vision of
consolation. In the play itself "consciousness" is "nothingness." There is only "the internal nothingness / of my self"
and the "only one thing / which is something" is

      the presence
      of my bodily
      suffering. . . .

                       (pp. 563-66)

Like Nerval, Artaud adapted some of the classic symptoms
of schizophrenia—concrete thinking and language, paranoia,
grandiosity, "phantoms of the non-self" (p. 530), magical and
daemonic forces—to express his unique transformation of
experience, in his case, to create an aesthetics of madness,
which combines exploration of and speculation on its
symptoms and causes, the "collapse of language" (p. 189)
and its restitution as idiosyncratic concrete object, and the
breakdown of form to reflect the unstructured, fragmented
consciousness. Susan Sontag has shown how Artaud's conception of theater mirrors his own "consciousness . . . without boundaries and fixed position," his agony over language,

and his various obsessions. Her discussion of his theater as a "projected image . . . of the dangerous, 'inhuman' inner life that possessed him" is entirely convincing, but her suggestion that it "is also a homeopathic technique for treating that mangled, passionate inner life"[80] misrepresents the psychic condition that Artaud depicts so accurately. The "intellectual drama" Artaud describes as emerging out of his conflict between the production of thought and his "emptiness," which he transformed into a theory of drama, is anything but passionate. In fact, essential to Artaud's aesthetics of madness is its substitution of violence, obscenity, the erotization of thought, bodily functions, and words for the passions of the self. "In matters of feeling," he says, "I can't even find anything that would correspond to feelings" (p. 195).

Artaud's most direct effect has been on the modern theater, especially on the theater of the sixties. *The Theater and its Double* (1938), a collection of his essays, manifestoes, and various other works on the theater, and his own example, influenced such companies as the Living Theater, the Theater of Cruelty, La Mama, and the Performance Group in adapting techniques that are by now standard in avant-garde production. Technically, the most obvious and most important elements of his theory are the freeing of the theater from "subjugation" to the text and the rediscovery of "a kind of unique language halfway between gesture and thought," the aim of both being to restore the "magical" origins of art, "like renewed exorcisms"; in short, "to call into question not only the objective and descriptive external world but the internal world." The spectator is provided with the material of dreams, "in which his taste for crime, his erotic obsessions, his savagery, his fantasies, his utopian sense of life and things, even his cannibalism, pour out on a level that is not counterfeit and illusory but internal." Masks, distortion of speech through intonation, rituals, the human body "elevated to the dignity of signs," gestures, and "frenzied pounding out of rhythms and sounds" all contribute to "the concrete language of the theater" (pp. 242-47).

All these aims and their more or less effective execution

are by now familiar to American and European audiences. Equally familiar is the adaptation to dramatic, literary, and non-literary uses of Artaud's role as anarchic revolutionary. His writings on drama contain many statements, generally supported only by the evidence of personal reaction, condemning the whole of modern Western society and defining his own "revolutionary" stance. In *Manifesto for a Theater that Failed*, written in 1927, he says that "the Revolution most urgently needed consists of a kind of regression into time. Let us return to the mentality or even simply to the way of life of the Middle Ages. . . ." This regressive fantasy seems innocuous enough, but, as always in Artaud's writing, it is somehow connected with violence: "If anything should be blown up," he concludes, "it is the foundations of most of the habits of modern thinking, European or otherwise" (p. 162). In *The Theater and its Double*, he is more direct: "Well, I say that the present state of society is unjust and should be destroyed. If it is the business of the theater to be concerned about this, it is even more the business of the machine gun" (p. 235).

In reaction against contemporary dramatic portrayals of psychological conflict, Artaud's objection is to "human" concerns in general, which "stink unbelievably of man, transitory and physical man, I will even go so far as to say *carrion man*" (p. 235). The human, the individual consciousness, "disgust[s]" him; social preoccupations bore him. Only a theater of spiritual transcendence can point the way to reformation of a sick, mad world. Artaud's conception of revolution is, as he himself makes clear, regression to an aesthetic concept of the "sacred," in which human psychological, social, and economic concerns are absorbed and prohibited individual expression. Indifferent to individual human life, in fact, disgusted by its very manifestations, he is engaged only by the revolution that can serve his own psychic need to fill the "emptiness" that makes the very idea of autonomous existence unbearable.

Whereas adaptations of Artaud's techniques of shock, stylization, and externalization have led to exciting innovations in contemporary theater, imitations of his role of anarchic prophet, enacted in such productions as *Dionysus in 69*, amount to a call to revolution for the sake of the director's or actors' or audience's psychic conflicts. Madness, or frenzy, is interpreted as social action and given a spurious theoretical significance as a political weapon. In the Living Theater's *Mysteries*, the presence of Artaud was behind Julian Beck as self-righteous guru who, with the rest of the company, acted as judge of the audience's readiness for revolutionary consciousness and initiator into Eastern mysticism combined with political dissent through the shouting of slogans. Apart from the theater, Artaud seems less an influence than a cultural manifestation, a forerunner of the current involvement with Eastern mysticism, magic, drugs, and madness. In literature, along with Nerval, he presages the confessional mode of adapting the symptoms of madness to the techniques of creation, nothingness as its subject: "you create yourself by flowing to your death, to your new state of death" (p. 122).

In America, madness as a theme and a point of view determining the techniques of poetry reached its height in the 1950s and 1960s and has waned only recently. Poets as vastly different from each other as Allen Ginsberg, Theodore Roethke, John Berryman, and Sylvia Plath all use their own experience of the shifting images and moods of dreams and hallucinations. Their particular adaptations of this material, which disclose an extremely broad range of experience, response, and symbolic transformation, are continually felt in the highly individual voices of these poets and their personae. The contents of such hallucinations, having evaded the boundaries of the ego, often seem to emerge through the presence of a persona both familiar and strange to the poet, to whom he or she seems to be listening. This hallucinatory material, however personal, reflects contemporary cultural attitudes toward the unconscious mind. The discoveries of psychoanalysis, which were revolutionary to the surrealists, are assumptions to these poets, whatever reservations they may have about their own experience of psychiatric treatment. Ginsberg is obsessed with the disillusionment of post-war America and its values of material success based on a cold-war economy and paranoiac suppression of dissent, which infect his dissociated, prophetic persona. Roethke ignores contemporary America and struggles only with the conflicts of his personal history. All of them, however, react against the anonymous, genteel persona characteristic of the poetry of the 1950s by calling on the processes of psychic dissolution to release their most extreme instinctual cravings, their anger, and their visions, as the vehicles of their talent.

In Ginsberg's poetry, madness is a destructive product of the corrupt values and heartlessness of American society, but it is also a defense against these evils and a means to combat them by confronting that society with its own soul. Most important, it is a way to self-realization in prophetic utterance. Many people who have not even read Ginsberg's work are familiar with the first line of "Howl":[81] "I saw the best minds of my generation destroyed by madness, starving hysterical naked." In this poem, hallucinations induced by alcohol and drugs serve two ends: an escape-route from the poverty, ugliness, and repression of their environment for those "who bared their brains to Heaven under the El," and a challenge to the conformists; the "scholars of war," who betrayed the texts they taught; and the managers of Los Alamos and Wall Street.

The language and rhythms of "Howl" transmit the heightened consciousness induced by drugs, the obsessive accumulation of evidence, as if every detail of the remembered experience were intensified to an almost unbearable degree. Undifferentiated rage, sorrow, ecstasy, accusation, hate, shock, and tenderness are combined without transition in the apparently ceaseless flow of incident and association and in the violent concreteness of language, the obsessive repetition, the lines that imitate the breathlessness of a voice that cannot stop pouring out its message. But in "Howl" madness is not only the voice of poetry; it is also a reduction to silence: the rebels are given "the concrete void of insulin metrasol electricity hydrotherapy psychotherapy occupational therapy pingpong & amnesia," and they rest "briefly in catatonia." Years later, they return "to the visible madman doom of the wards of the madtowns of the East." The description of life in "Pilgrim State's Rockland's and Greystone's foetid halls" creates the mind endlessly adapting whatever remains of its desires to the confines of the internalized asylum: "bickering with the echoes of the soul, rocking and rolling in the midnight solitude-bench dolmen-realms of love, dream of life a nightmare, bodies turned to stone as heavy as the moon."

The next association is "mother," the mad Naomi of "Kaddish,"[82] the poem in which Ginsberg most fully realizes the thematic and stylistic possibilities of madness. In "Kaddish" he refers briefly to a period when he was a patient at the Psychiatric Institute of Columbia-Presbyterian Medical Center in 1949 only to indicate that it is not his subject: "I was in bughouse that year 8 months—my own visions unmentioned in this here Lament—" (p. 25). Yet "Kaddish" unites the most realistic and sordid details of his mother's schizophrenic breakdowns with his own visionary impulse to creation, a commitment to the processes of psychic dissolution as an initiation into the ancient art of prophecy. Naomi, the mad mother, is also the

> . . . glorious muse that bore me from the womb, gave suck first mystic life & taught me talk and music, from whose pained head I first took Vision—
> Tortured and beaten in the skull—What mad hallucinations of the damned that drive me out of my own skull to seek Eternity till I find Peace for Thee, O Poetry—and for all humankind call on the Origin
>
> (p. 29).

The whole of "Kaddish" is a series of transformations—Communism and McCarthyism into paranoid hallucinations, the mother's obsessions and terrors into the son's consciousness of his destiny, Naomi's mad eyes into the "great Eye" of the Lord, the prayer for the dead into an exaltation of individual consciousness merging with the universal.

"Kaddish," as John Tytell points out, reveals the psychic effects of the drugs Ginsberg took throughout the brief, in-

tense period when he composed most of it: "The racing,
breathless pace of the poem reflects its manner of composition—the stimulation of morphine mixed with meta-
amphetamine (then new to Ginsberg, and a conflicting
combination as well since morphine slows time while amphetamine speeds it up) as Ginsberg sat at his desk from six
in the morning and wrote until ten the following night, leaving the poem only for coffee, the bathroom, and several doses
of Dexedrine."[83] Drugs, no doubt, intensified Ginsberg's
feelings and the rush of associations that creates the breathless tone of "Kaddish," but the poem also conveys other
states of consciousness in which Ginsberg came to poetic
terms with the memories of a lifetime. He wrote part IV in
1958 in Paris[84] and obviously had been living with the poem
for a long time.

Addressing his mother at the beginning of the poem, he
reveals two important sources of its rhythms and moods, and
even, however submerged, its contents: he has been "reading the Kaddish aloud" and "listening to Ray Charles blues
shout blind on the phonograph." The Hebrew Kaddish is re-
cited in memory of the dead, but it does not refer to death. It
is a prayer in praise of God, in which mortality is linked to
His transcendent power. Chanted in a communal setting of
congregation and mourners, it deals not with the grief of the
individual mourner but the attachment of each life to the life
of Israel and the eternal existence of God. This essential quality of the Kaddish appears most clearly in Ginsberg's poem in
the Hymmnn that concludes II, but it exists throughout it.
However intimate and bizarre his personal revelations, there
is no exhibitionistic leer in them but rather the compulsion to
make a public offering. In "Kaddish," the house in Newark,
the horrors of Naomi's paranoia, the details of her physical
and mental disintegration, and Ginsberg's own homosexual
and incestuous desires are the materials of life offered up in a
prayer for transcendence of the self and death. The rhythms
of Ray Charles, the union of blues, gospel songs, and jazz,
are transmuted by Ginsberg into a rhythmic intensity of both
broken phrases and lines accumulating power in their length.

Imitating Charles, Ginsberg imposes a contemporary and highly individual sensibility on the rhythmic associations of an oral religious and cultural tradition. The most mundane details of "Kaddish" take on the tones of chanting.

In "Kaddish," Ginsberg, like an ancient prophet, uses the violent and painful memories and disordered associations of the past to transmit a social vision. Identifying his own mantic possession with his mother's "learning to be mad" (p. 8), he re-experiences her life and his as one, and both as part of the political and social history of an era, which, even in its shoddiness and its horror, is given a strange dignity transformed in the anguished, dissociated consciousness of mother and son, as the "great Eye" of the Lord "stares on All" (p. 36).

Ginsberg learned from the surrealists, to whom he pays tribute, that the expansion of consciousness through drugs, dreams, and hallucinations is essential for instigating social reform. In "At Apollinaire's Grave,"[85] he feels the poet's presence ("his madness is only around the corner") in Paris "the day the U.S. President appeared in France for the grand conference of heads of state." The surrealists are an "inspiration" for his own explorations of consciousness in poetry:

> I've eaten the blue carrots you sent out of the grave and
>   Van Gogh's ear and maniac peyote of Artaud
> and will walk down the streets of New York in the black
>   cloak of French poetry
> improvising our conversation in Paris at Père Lachaise
> and the future poem that takes its inspiration from the light
>   bleeding into your grave . . .

and his use of his discoveries as a political weapon:

> Artaud alone made accusation
>   against America,
> Before me. . . .[86]

Some of Ginsberg's poems written under the influence of drugs seem mere recordings of their effects, the "experiments" of "Aether."[87] In these poems there are momentary exaltations observed by an ironic rational consciousness:

....I stood on the balcony
  waiting for an explosion
of Total Consciousness of the All—
being Ginsberg sniffing ether in Lima.

("Aether")

Ginsberg has referred to his use of drugs as "pious investigations,"[88] and there is no doubt that he used them as a means
of exploring his own mind for the material and manner of
prophecy. As he has turned from drugs to the use of the man-
tra to incorporate the mood and style of yoga meditation into
poetry, he has turned from identification with madness to a
striving for oneness with the processes of life, which include
death. Even this change in emphasis came to him in a
prophetic dream. In his *Indian Journals*,[89] he tells of his disillusionment with drugs after showing an Indian poet his
"Aether": "I realized how much of my life I'd put into this
sort of exploration of mind thru drugs, & how sad & futile I
felt now that I had gotten to the point with hallucinogens
where I no longer liked what I felt & was too disturbed &
frightened to continue" (p. 44). Twelve days later in a dream
recorded in a poem, he says:

> I feel companion
> to all of us now before death
> waiting inside Life: One big
> place we are here.

(p. 46)

The poem ends with resignation to death and separation, but
the theme recurs in such poems as "Death on all Fronts" and
"Friday the Thirteenth"[90] expanded, as is common in
Ginsberg's work, to include his involvement with his society,
the world, and the universe. For him, actual insanity, the
simulation of its processes through drugs, meditation, and
chanting are all intrinsic to the techniques of an art inseparable from the development of a new social consciousness. In
this respect, he is unique among the recent American poets
who have adapted the psychic processes of madness to depict
the mind in the act of creation.

Ginsberg, in his outrage, often internalizes America, *Time* magazine, and various institutions of society as presences haunting his mind, his bed, and his streets. "It occurs to me that I am America,"[91] he says, erasing any separation between himself and the obsessively loved and hated nation. This breakdown of boundaries between the self and the external world also determines the language, moods, and tones of Roethke's poetry, but it is the world of external nature with which he merges, in a union that seems to exclude any but personal concerns. There is an obsessive, repetitive quality in Roethke's absorption in his terrors of the "abyss" and his efforts to merge with a principle of harmony by defining the searching, creating self beyond its rational manifestations. But his identification of his own psychic underworld with the life beneath and of the soil—its roots, insects, plants, and animals—extends his focus to the mysterious processes of all organic life, of which the mind is part.

In Roethke's poetry,[92] the speaker transmits the "Forms of his secret life" ("The Exorcism") through the instinctual patterns of animals, birds, and insects, and the inevitable flowering and decay of the earth's products, at once vivid in their realistic detail and dream-like in their implications. But to describe Roethke's "world" as that "of a schizophrenic who returns us to where we have always been," as John Vernon does, seems to me a distortion of both Roethke's poetry and schizophrenia. Equating schizophrenia with an idealized primitivism and with childhood, Vernon interprets Roethke's work as "the perfect illustration of the schizophrenia that unites madness and sanity."[93] Actually, Roethke's struggles with his own psychic conflicts and the resolutions he arrives at are more complicated than the Laingian generalities that Vernon imposes on the body of his work.

In his poetry of the late 1950s and 1960s, Roethke, through his very dreams and fantasies of merging with natural life, conveys his inevitable separateness within the laws and manifestions of the physical universe. His ever-present awareness, "I live near the abyss," is confirmed by the stones that have his "own skin" and the "beast with fangs" within "his own house" ("The Pure Fury"), the self that is ever alone despite its continual search for connection. The momentary awakening of a sense of "pure being" ("The Exorcism") is challenged as

> In a dark wood I saw—
> I saw my several selves
> Come running from the leaves,
> Lewd, tiny, careless lives
> That scuttled under stones,
> Or broke, but would not go.

In this poem, he gives an entire stanza to the explicit statement: "I was myself, alone."

The purely instinctual existence of the creatures that enact his psychic needs only confirms this aloneness in the section "They Sing, They Sing" of the poem "The Dying Man." Here he has "the lark's word for it, who sings alone"; the "fury of the slug beneath the stone" is the frustration of any hope of merging with an eternal principle of harmony in the physical universe. In the last stanza, the resolution of the conflict includes yet defies the poet's identification of the self with natural creation:

> Nor can imagination do it all
> In this last place of light: he dares to live
> Who stops being a bird, yet beats his wings
> Against the immense immeasureable emptiness of things.

This, of course, is not Roethke's final resolution. The terror of and yearning for dissolution of the self within and by creation are described in poem after poem and resolved, only partly and temporarily, in a mystical concept of eternal order. "The Abyss" begins with a series of questions and answers in the rhythms of a nursery rhyme, which convey fragmentation, the loss of any fixed concept of external reality characteristic of a terrifying dream or hallucination. There remains only the sense of nothingness everywhere. When the "world," reality, invades the speaker again, he must escape the "terrible hunger for objects" that threatens to overwhelm him by identifying himself with a "furred caterpillar" which he calls "My symbol!" It is both a refuge and a reduction to the elemental, an approach to dying. He lives with death, which appears like "a sly surly attendant" in an asylum, observing his renewed efforts at escape in merging with the "mole," the "otter," and finally, "like the bird, with the bright air." In this poem, as in other late ones, it is ultimately the "Lord God" who relieves his despair, but fusion with God, as with nature, is in Roethke's poetry a tentative definition rather than a lasting experience of wholeness, a defense against the dissolution of the self that remained to the end a perennial threat and his most insistent goal.

As this chapter has indicated, the "abyss" of the self as the material and formative process of creation is the most personal yet the most characteristic motif of modern literature. Taking this "dangerous path," as Roethke calls it in "The Abyss," the "vague, the arid / Neither in nor out of this life," has meant for some recent poets what it did for Mann's Aschenbach and Leverkühn, following the lure of psychic dissolution to its inevitable goal in suicide. Madness in the poetry of John Berryman and Sylvia Plath is a series of "partial suicides,"[94] fantasies and memories of attempts at self-destruction that enact the persona's most intense experiences of being and creating.

Guilt, madness, death, and suicide are recurring motifs of Berryman's *Dream Songs*. Yet his insistence that his persona of *The Dream Songs* is "not the poet, not me"[95] only confirms the sense these poems convey that such intimate experience is being filtered through a consciousness detached from its emotional immediacy. The major persona, Henry, externalizes dreams; he is an intermediary who converts them into the conscious acts and responses of daily existence. The language and tone of most of *The Dream Songs* is reportorial and self-instructive, evoking not dreams but notations in a diary. In Song 327, Berryman says that "a dream is a panorama / of the whole mental life," an accurate definition not of actual dreams but of his own series of sensational, pathetic, and comic episodes, a fragmented panorama, like Lautréamont's, that discloses little about the mental or emotional processes that conceived it.

The suicides of friends and fellow poets are occasions to be noted for their sorrow; they elicit a conventional response and an explicit, pathetic self-identification. Mourning the death of Randall Jarrell (90), the speaker instructs himself: "Let Randall rest, whom your self-torturing / cannot restore one instant's good to, rest. . . ." Even as he tells of the suicide of Delmore Schwartz, he consciously prevents himself from suppressing its implications for him.

> I give in. I must not leave   the scene of this same death
> as most of me strains to.
> There are all the problems to be sorted out. . . .

The Song (156) ends with the speaker's feeling that he "nearly would follow him below." The suicide of Sylvia Plath evokes a similar, though less personal, reaction, except at the end, where Henry wonders why, after all the deaths and suicides of fellow poets, he "alone breasts the wronging tide" (172). Thoughts of his own madness and possible suicide are chiefly factual and often witty. "Madness & booze, madness & booze" (225), Henry sings as he wonders which one produced the other. Considering suicide (345), he contemplates the "blood & the disgrace" and the effect on the "survivors," and instructs himself in avoiding the meaning of his own mental anguish: "Sit still, / maybe the goblins will go away, leaving you free. . . ."

The Dream Songs, Love and Fame, Delusions, etc., and the novel *Recovery* all express more or less explicitly Berryman's conviction that his compulsive need for love and alcohol, its destructive effects on him, the fragmentation of his sense of self and of reality, and his depressions, guilts, and fantasies of suicide are intrinsic to his writing. In the descent into hell sequence (78-91) of *The Dream Songs*, Berryman goes so far as to imagine the ultimate fragmentation of the self in death:

> I am—I should be held together by—
> But I am breaking up. . . .

Henry, who has "held together" his fragmented thoughts, has "now come to a full stop" (85). But this death is merely a respite, a preparation to return to the world, like "Lazarus with a plan / to get his own back" (91). The fantasy of being among the "violent dead," where he can "pick their awful brains" (88) is an ironic quest for release from guilt and conflict and for ultimate fellowship in art and in death, which are inseparable in his consciousness. The "I" of *The Dream Songs* "clasps" Hölderlin and Kleist "to Henry's bosom: / a suicide & a madman, / to teach him lessons who was so far neither" (310). His poetry emerges out of his perpetual hunger and "need need need." This need for "women, cigarettes, liquor," which destroys his equilibrium and makes him go "to pieces," is inherent in the process of creation:

> The pieces sat up & wrote. They did not heed
> their piecedom but kept very quietly on
> among the chaos.
>
> (311)

Berryman is even more explicit about his cravings for love and alcohol, his hallucinations, breakdowns, attempts at recovery in psychiatric hospitals, and his return to religion as a source of strength in *Love and Fame, Delusions, etc.*, and his unfinished novel, *Recovery*. Although the "I" of the two volumes of poetry and Severance, the persona of the novel, seem to omit no personal detail in their eagerness to reveal their "whole mental life," Berryman never finds the vehicle he obviously seeks for expressing the connection between his personal anguish and the act of creation. However fragmented the associations, however rapidly and abruptly the moods change, however exact the details about his "Reflexions on suicide," and frequent the references to his father, mother, and wife, and to his own determination to "labour and dream,"[96] the language almost always evades the psychic and emotional source of its subject. Berryman is an exact reporter of what he knows, but his eyes, as he himself says, are "bleary as an envelope cried-over / after the letter's lost." The most he can do is to "chip away at the mystery."[97]

The autobiographical episodes, self-analysis, group therapy, and psychiatrists' reports of *Recovery* leave its narrator essentially unknowing and unknown. What is most vivid to him and the reader is the inexplicable "irresistible descent, for the person incomprehensibly . . . determined," the compulsion to destroy the self he is so painfully reconstructing, to return to "every abyss"[98] he has dreaded and longed for, to its despair, hallucinations, and terrors. Among the prayers to and praises of God and the resignations to existence of *Delusions, etc.* the wish remains "for some soft & solid & sudden way out / as quiet as hemlock in that Attic prose. . . ."[99] Berryman's personae are all one in their self-conscious exemplification of the artist as irretrievably drawn to the abyss of the self, which is its ultimate destruction, but his work describes rather than illuminates this compulsion, which takes precedence over any other commitment—to religion, love, and finally art.

The modern poet whose language and imagery most precisely construct the "psychical representatives" of the drive to creation in conflict with its opposition, the impulse toward self-annihilation, is Sylvia Plath. Like Nietzsche and Mann, she returns to the primordial language of these impulses, dream and myth. Plath's adaptations of traditional mythical figures—gods, goddesses, Hades, the Furies, maenads—is readily apparent. A recent book by Judith Kroll,[100] entirely devoted to this subject, attempts to demonstrate that Robert Graves's White Goddess served as the model for Plath's own mythical conception of herself, which became her means of resolving and finally transcending unbearable tension. Whereas Kroll's study of Plath's readings in Graves, anthropology, Jung, Zen Buddhism, and other works does elucidate many allusions and images of her poetry, the central thesis of *Chapters in a Mythology* seems to me questionable. Among the many meanings Plath invested in myth, no doubt one was a conquest of the limitations of mortality, but the brilliance of Plath's mythical imagery lies not in its resolutions but in its representation of the physical and psychological nature of irresolvable conflict. Death symbolically becomes the only state in which opposing demands can coexist, and the need for resolution no longer makes its claims on body and mind. Kroll is eager to prove that, though autobiographical material is the basis of Plath's poetry, "mythic rebirth" and finally "ecstatic apprehension of a larger identity" in religious mysticism express her "need to transcend personal history" (p. 210). Actually, mythical conceptions of rebirth and transcendence are among Plath's most authentic autobiographical symbols. It is useless to argue about where her poetry is autobiographical and where it ceases to be so. Her most moving poems are about herself; at the same time, her language releases a more general possibility of psychic life: the intense, agonizing, bizarre manifestations of conflicting drives unmediated by the unifying ego.

By now the central human figures mythicized in Plath's poetry are so well known as to require little discussion: the father of German descent who died when she was nine, the mother who remained alone to support and educate her and her brother and whose struggle for survival seemed indistinguishable from a fierce ambition, which the daughter internalized as love, and the "I" who from childhood sought and found "a sign of election and specialness" to prove that she was "not forever to be cast out." A childhood sign was a wooden monkey, a "totem, . . . a Sacred Baboon" washed up by the sea;[101] later signs were the language of her poetry, inspired by "Disquieting Muses,"[102] the nightmare and hallucinatory figures who testify to her omnipotence and her nothingness, to her role of goddess deprived of selfhood.

The central myth of death as release and rebirth is constructed out of warring drives and emotions that transmit the poet's persona as diffuse, elusive, trapped, and raging in the mythical world that is her own creation. In "Getting There,"[103] the image of the realm of Hades is explicit, waiting at the end of a nightmare for her arrival. But first there are the child's questions in the insistent ritualistic rhythms common in her poetry:

> How far is it?
> How far is it now?

Such innocent questions plunge the speaker into a nightmare train-ride to war, death camps, hunger, and wounds. She is the victim of the wheels, which are

> The terrible brains
> Of Krupp, black muzzles
> Revolving, the sound
> Punching out Absence! like cannon.

The wheels of the train "eat"; they are "like gods," with "will— / Inexorable" and "pride." The train has "teeth / Ready to roll, like a devil's." The self in this poem is lost:

> I am a letter in this slot—
> I fly to a name, two eyes.

It exists only in the repeated question: "How far is it?" until, emerging from hate and terror, from the train "Insane for the destination," it arrives to

> Step to you from the black car of Lethe,
> Pure as a baby.

Reality mythicized as gods and devils is set in opposition to the mythical realm of the dead. The horrors of World War II are transformed into a private nightmare world, the "wheels" of her mind driving the persona to the "place . . . Untouched and untouchable," where she sheds the meanings of the past even as she returns to her very beginnings.

In "Lady Lazarus," the "call" comes explicitly from the god of death, who is addressed by many names: he is "Herr Doktor," "Herr Enemy," "Herr God," "Herr Lucifer." He is the Nazi father of "Daddy," the despised and adored tyrant, lover, deserter, deity, and devil, all of whom she symbolically controls by incorporating their power. As she creates them and death, she creates herself:

> Dying
> Is an art, like everything else.
> I do it exceptionally well.

She rises from the dead, renewed but unchanged, to "eat men like air," assuming the role of her enemy who is also the bestower of her divine power, thus leaving the conflict between love and hate, yearning and rage forever unresolved.

Throughout Plath's poetry, the violent images piled on one another—myths, realistic details of bodily parts, waste, gore, odors, emerging in the rhythms of nursery rhymes or in abrupt one-word lines, like the rapidly shifting action of dreams; the disclosures of nothingness through mundane articles of daily life which substitute for identity; the portrayals of the "I," crippled, accused, assaulted, wounded, bleeding, killing itself again and again—seem forced into consciousness by the violence and chaos of unconscious fear and hate uncontrolled by any order except that of the words themselves. Whatever remnants of the self still exist are continually shattered in its verbal representations:

> And I
> Am the arrow,
>
> The dew that flies
> Suicidal, at one with the drive
> Into the red
>
> Eye, the cauldron of morning.
>
> ("Ariel")

The cultic glorification of Sylvia Plath as a poet whose art in its daring finally required her death distorts her achievement. There is no evidence to support such a conclusion and much biographical data to refute it. She is obviously not the only writer who has portrayed the unconscious, irrational determinants of her subjects, language, and imagery, and her scope is far narrower than Mann's or Ginsberg's or that of many others for whom psychic dissolution has been a source and subject of art. What finally distinguishes Sylvia Plath from the many other poets who in recent years have used similar mental and emotional experience as their subject and symbolic framework is her discovery of a unique language to create what would seem inexpressible—the self as nothingness, emptiness, impelled to explore in "Words dry and riderless" ("Words") its own psychic incorporation of the failure of love and the violence of history.

VI

Conclusion

Certain motifs that occur in the literature of madness from the fifth century B.C. to the present—the identification of the mad with animals by society and by the mad themselves, the hunt as a symbol of their persecution, the concept of reason or insight in madness, the incorporation of an accusing or sustaining deity—are originally symbolic portrayals of adaptive psychic mechanisms in the development of the self in its relation to communal life. These ritual expressions of the struggle for psychic integration within a social framework are used, in literature from the Middle Ages to the end of the eighteenth century, as symbols of individual regression for survival and efforts to reconstitute a self notwithstanding prevailing limitations on its role and function. In imaginative writing from the late Romantic period to the present, the increasing sense of aloneness in an indifferent universe and an amoral society is symbolically transformed into assaults on the very notion of an autonomous self. The traditional motifs of ancient ritual madness recur in new forms, conveying instinctual aims converted to social alienation: personal gratification in regressive fantasies, the renunciation of psychic integration for illusions of omnipotence, the expansion of consciousness in dissociation and hallucinations as an avenue to individual and communal rebirth.

The literary works discussed throughout this book indicate that the conception of madness as a revelation of mind or an expansion of consciousness, sometimes regarded as peculiarly modern, actually has a long history. Dionysiac and mantic frenzy and the externalized Erinyes as represented in ancient Greek drama reinforce the evidence of myth, ritual, and philosophy that the exploration and channeling of unconscious processes were intrinsic to the very foundation of certain religious and social institutions. Moreover, the literary products of the various periods and cultures considered in this study are only a small portion of the evidence of continuous interest in the psychic experience revealed in madness and its relation to general mental functioning.

What primarily distinguishes the modern approach to the mind through the non-rational primary processes from earlier ones is not only the cultural adaptations of psychoanalytic discoveries, but, beginning with Nietzsche, the growing belief that, since God is dead, the individual consciousness supersedes all authority. This consciousness, restricted for millennia by its rational masks and lies, can be freed, it is assumed, only by a return to its eternal roots in the primordial processes manifested in madness. Implicit in Nietzsche's conception of the Dionysiac is a restoration of its original social function of producing a new apprehension of reality, but this is to be achieved not through the projection of instinctual impulses on a deity but rather through the recognition of deity within; the human being, unfettered, is himself the superman, the god. In this respect, Nietzsche is the progenitor of the religious character of many modern proposals of the value of non-egoic experience. But this is a religion without its original function of social cohesion. Inherent in its very genesis is the failure of any societal avenue—political, cultural, as well as religious—to engage individual action and response. The commitment to non-egoic transcendence of hitherto known reality is based on the belief that only an individual rebirth into undifferentiated mystic apprehension can restore the mind alienated from the products of rational consciousness.

Particular developments of this idea in much contemporary imaginative literature and literary criticism can be traced to the influence of R. D. Laing's view of schizophrenia as a split between the true but hidden self and the false outer being whose chief functioning processes are determined by the need to adjust to the demands of society and the family as its offshoot. The "inner" or "true" self "is occupied in maintaining its identity and freedom by being transcendent, unembodied, and thus never to be grasped, pinpointed, trapped, possessed."[1] In Laing's view, in the most extreme forms of psychosis, even the " 'true' self" is rejected and becomes "a mere vanishing point." Yet, believing as he does that "it is perhaps never true to say that the 'self' has been utterly lost, or destroyed,"[2] Laing conceives of madness as a struggle for liberation from false attitudes and values, an encounter with primary feelings and impulses which constitutes a possibility for a rebirth of the "true" self.

The history of the literature of madness makes it abundantly clear that the idea that madness can produce extraordinary insight is not a revolutionary one. It is perhaps as old as human beings' interest in the mind and is reflected in the self-revelations of the mad protagonists of ancient myth and in Plato's remarkable descriptions of prophetic and inspired madness. Furthermore, scientific investigations long before Laing recognized in delusions and other forms of mental aberration distorted yet signficant communications of deeply suppressed human impulses. What characterizes Laing's particular approach to the human mind is not his understanding that authentic aspects of the self can be conveyed in madness, but his conception of the "true" self that emerges in such regression and of the "falseness" he considers the inevitable result of psychic differentiation between conscious and unconscious processes—in essence, his devaluation of the function of the ego in the realization of human potentiality.

A central idea in Laing's *The Politics of Experience* is that human beings, having lost their *"selves,"* have "developed the illusion that we are autonomous *egos.*"[3] He contrasts the *"transcendental experiences"* which are "the original wellspring of all religions" with what he calls the *"egoic"* approach to reality of most people, the experience of "the world and themselves in terms of a consistent identity, a me-here over against a you-there, within a framework of certain ground structures of space and time shared with other members of their society." To Laing, "egoic" experience, which, like Norman Brown, he vastly oversimplifies, is essentially a form of "socially accepted madness"; on the other hand, a state of "ego-loss," generally regarded as psychotic, may be for the person involved "veritable manna from heaven" (pp. 137-38). "True sanity," he says, "entails in one way or another the dissolution of the normal ego, that false self competently adjusted to our alienated social reality; the emergence of the 'inner' archetypal mediators of divine power, and through this death a rebirth, and the eventual re-establishment of a new kind of ego-functioning, the ego now being the servant of the divine, no longer its betrayer" (pp. 144-45).

Laing's rigid division of mental and social experience into two sharply separated levels—"true" irrationality and "false" rationality—is a mythical construct, which discloses his own vision of a reality inhabited by "demons, spirits," and other supernatural presences.[4] This visionary retreat can be achieved by yielding to irrational terrors, conflicts, rages, and hallucinations, all of which communicate a rejection of the demands of a sterile and corrupt society. Laing denies any possibility of authentic joy or productivity for the conscious mind; in his work it appears as one-dimensional, deprived of its complex function as mediator between the inner realm of instinct, dream, and fantasy and the limitations, compromises, and challenges of the world outside.

The literature of madness refutes Laing's gross divisions. Its depictions of the diffusion of drives and loss of ego are extremely varied, but it more often portrays despair, chaos, pain, and emptiness than it does transcendental oneness. These, moreover, do not merely reflect social assumptions about insanity, for such feelings are described in many works that counter generally accepted attitudes toward madness. The "divine" that Laing regards as betrayed by the ego often appears in representations of madness as malevolent, terrorizing and subjugating the mind that creates this image out of its own guilt and hunger. But divinity also emerges in madness as reason itself, restoring a conviction of selfhood. The restitution of the ego, a dominant theme of the literature of madness, involves a recognition, however oblique, of instinctual diffusion and narcissistic demands. It is a confrontation not with the divine, but with the human in society and the self in all its grandiose projections and painful limitations. Lear in madness recreates his own character by infusing the legendary figure symbolizing instinctual indulgence and omnipotence with reason, which explores his psychic incorporation of the values and gratifications of the oppressive, hypocritical society he has represented for so long, and which acknowledges his aloneness in an indifferent universe.

Laing's is merely one version of a contemporary yearning to restore some form of ritual madness in the hope of producing a god to replace all the others who failed. But common as such manifestations are, in current religious movements and in literature, they are fundamentally expressions not of social engagement but of narcissistic alienation. Norman Brown's Dionysus is his own attendant deity. The gods who haunt the poetry of Sylvia Plath and Anne Sexton are personal projections. Even Allen Ginsberg, whose vision of expanded consciousness as a social instrument was so fundamental to his poetry in the 1950s and 1960s, in his recent work mocks his own conception of his omniscient prophetic role. Summarizing his involvement in religious mysticism, his political activity, his experiments with drugs, and his aspirations to sainthood, he reduces them all to a "solitary" expression of himself:

Solitary in worlds full of insects & singing birds all solitary—who had no subject but himself in many disguises. . . .[5]

This disclaimer does not negate the deep connection of Ginsberg's past and present work with his participation in the social and political concerns of his time. It is a commentary on the peculiarly narcissistic quality of responses to social problems and even of commitment to social change in the second half of the twentieth century.

Many of the recent novels[6] in which madness is a mode of release and discovery depict the protagonist's struggle with society as fundamentally centered on the self. The hero of

Doris Lessing's *Briefing for a Descent into Hell*,[7] a professor of classics, is emotionally detached from his wife, his mistress, his friends, and his profession. In a state of shock, he is admitted to a hospital, where in hallucinations and dreams he is a sailor, drifting through the South Seas. His companions are absorbed into a Crystal, a kind of "shining disc," the essence of light, "vibration," and sound (pp. 16-17), and, alone, he makes his way to a primitive land to await the return of the Crystal for him. When he too is finally absorbed, he is redeemed into a "fusion" with people he had known in the past and a sense of "wholeness" in the universe. His madness has become a "new mode of feeling" (pp. 96-97). In this state he revaluates the society he has left in the light of "Necessity," symbolized by the moon, countering the "tiny human mind" that "looks for reasons and answers" (p. 108). He sees the earth through the perspective of the universe. Mankind, viewed in this way is a

> crust of microbes, . . . mad moonmad, lunatic. To celestial eyes, seen like a broth of microbes under a microscope, always at war and destruction, this scum of microbes thinks, it can see itself, it begins slowly to sense itself as one, a function, a note in the harmony, and this *is* its point and function, and where the scummy film transcends itself, here and here only, and never where these mad microbes say I, I, I, I, I, for saying I, I, I, I, is their madness. . . .
>
> (p. 109)

Professor Watkins' dreams expose the narcissistic and destructive values of late twentieth-century society, but his response to these—withdrawal and a lonely, religious vision of primal unity—reveals him as its fairly typical product. In the end, he submits to psychiatric adjustment and returns to the attitudes and preoccupations of his former life. He has partaken of cosmic revolution only in dreams and hallucinations about a reversal of time to prehistory, before human beings defined their separateness from earth, sky, and planets.

In *Surfacing*,[8] Margaret Atwood's heroine also returns to a primitive realm in a state of dissociation, but her landscape is the earth. Retreating from the mechanical shoddiness of contemporary urban life to her childhood home in the Canadian wilderness, she gradually enters a hallucinatory primitive stage of existence. Like many of the mad characters throughout literature, she regresses to identification with animals for self-preservation; she waits for her "fur" to grow, leaves her "dung, droppings on the ground" and kicks "earth over. All animals with dens do that." She sleeps "in relays like a cat" (pp. 208-209) and fears the "hunt," the violence of her pursuers—"the police . . . or sightseers, curious tourists" (p. 214). Identifying herself with the natural world of earth, trees, and animals, she experiences a religious vision of rebirth into a new knowledge of her past, which is one with the earth's. Unlike Lessing's professor, the heroine of *Surfacing* returns to the present with an awareness that the gods who symbolize instinctual regression "give only one kind of truth, one hand." She "can't afford" their continual presence. She concludes: "No total salvation, resurrection, Our father, Our mother, I pray, Reach down for me, but it won't work: they dwindle, grow, become what they were, human. Something I never gave them credit for; but their totalitarian innocence was my own." Her reexperience of her personal past and its relation to the primeval past of the human race has taught her that she need not be a "victim," and she assumes responsibility for her action in her "own time" (pp. 221-23). The "I" of *Surfacing* is alone in her exorcism of the violence and emotional sterility of her "time" through her mythic reunion with the primeval and in her acknowledgment of its essential but limited effect on her existence as she resumes "the usual way" of loving, losing, and renouncing (p. 221). For all its archetypal symbolism, *Surfacing* is the account of an individual's exploration of her own psychic internalizations, the irreducible relationship between the archaic and the contemporary, with which she makes a kind of peace.

In contemporary literature, madness as a symbol of alienation from the goals and values of mechanized society is often a withdrawal for personal gratification through mystical illumination, in which visions of social amelioration are a substitute for political engagement. In this respect, the theme discloses, as it always has, the mind of the protagonist or persona incorporating the limitations and defenses of its society at the same time that it exposes their effects. Viewed through the lens of the long history of madness as a theme of literature, the present vogue of the madhouse as a temple of consciousness represents a common but by no means an inevitable psychic defense. Explorations of madness throughout literature portray a great variety of psychic oppositions to environmental demands. Among these, the narcissistic withdrawal from social and intrapsychic struggles is but one detour of the human mind in its internalization of family, society, and history.

Notes

CHAPTER I

1. *Wild Men in the Middle Ages: A Study in Art, Sentiment, and Demonology* (Cambridge: Harvard University Press, 1952), p. 3. See also *The Wild Man Within: An Image in Western Thought from the Renaissance to Romanticism*, ed. Edward Dudley and Maximillian Novak (Pittsburgh: University of Pittsburgh Press, 1972). For further discussion of the wild man myth, see below, chapter II, footnote 28.

2. Cf. Ernst Kris, who describes "the psychotic condition" as one "in which the ego is overwhelmed by the primary process," *Psychoanalytic Explorations in Art* (1952; rpt. New York: Schocken Books, 1964), p. 60.

3. *The History of Psychiatry: An Evaluation of Psychiatric Thought and Practice from Prehistoric Times to the Present* (New York: Harper and Row, 1966), p. 7.

4. *Ibid.*, p. 32.

5. See Plato, *Phaedrus* 265A, where he makes a clear distinction between the two kinds of madness: one resulting from "human sickness," the other from the liberating influence of the gods. In *Theaetetus* 158D, he refers to "madness and other sicknesses." In the *Republic* 573A-C, the despot at his worst is depicted as mad, similar to the drunkard, the sensualist, or the choleric. For the conception of madness as sickness in Greek drama, see below, chapter II.

6. Marshall Edelson, *The Idea of a Mental Illness* (New Haven: Yale University Press, 1971), p. 36.

7. Gregory Bateson, *Steps to an Ecology of Mind* (New York: Ballantine Books, 1973), p. 205.

8. *Ibid.*, p. 261.

9. "Lettres Aux Médecins-Chefs des Asiles de Fous," *Oeuvres Complètes*, Supplément au Tome I (Paris: Gallimard, 1970), p. 186.

10. Edelson, *The Idea of a Mental Illness*, p. 48.

11. See, for example, Ainsworth O'Brien-Moore, *Madness in Ancient Literature* (Weimar: R. Wagner Sohn, 1924); Josef Mattes, *Der Wahnsinn im griechischen Mythos und in der Dichtung bis zum Drama des fünften Jahrhunderts* (Heidelberg: Carl Winter Universitätsverlag, 1970); Bennett Simon, *Mind and Madness in Ancient Greece: The Classical Roots of Modern Psychiatry* (Ithaca: Cornell University Press, 1978); Penelope Doob, *Nebuchad-*

nezzar's Children: Conventions of Madness in Middle English Literature (New
Haven: Yale University Press, 1974); Robert Reed, *Bedlam on the Jacobean
Stage*, 2nd. ed. (Cambridge: Harvard University Press, 1968); Max Byrd,
Visits to Bedlam: Madness and Literature in the Eighteenth Century (Colum-
bia: University of South Carolina Press, 1974); Michael V. DePorte,
Nightmares and Hobbyhorses: Swift, Sterne, and Augustan Ideas of Madness
(San Marino: The Huntington Library, 1974); John Vernon, *The Garden
and the Map: Schizophrenia in Twentieth-Century Literature and Culture*
(Urbana: University of Illinois Press, 1973); and Gian-Paolo Biasin, *Liter-
ary Diseases: Theme and Metaphor in the Italian Novel* (Austin: University of
Texas Press, 1975). Most of these and briefer considerations of literary
madness will be mentioned below in discussions of particular works.

12. "On This Adaptation," Program Notes by Wole Soyinka for his adaptation, *The Bacchae of Euripides*, performed at the National Theatre, London, August 1973.

13. *The Standard Edition of the Complete Psychological Works of Sigmund Freud*,
trans. from the German under the general editorship of James Strachey
in collaboration with Anna Freud (London: Hogarth Press, 1966-74),
XX, 65. References to Freud's work are to this edition, hereafter referred
to in the text and notes as *SE*.

14. In summarizing some of Lacan's major ideas, I refer to his *Ecrits* (Paris:
Seuil, 1966). Equally influential in recent structuralist criticism is Jacques
Derrida's approach to language, especially his conception of the structural relationship of emotional disturbance to literature. Derrida's formulations are, in fact, based on what he regards as an intrinsic connection between disease and literature. See especially *L'écriture et la
différence* (Paris: Seuil, 1967). See also Sergio Piro, *Il linguaggio schizo-
frenico* (Milan: Feltrinelli, 1967).

15. "Desire and the Interpretation of Desire in Hamlet," trans. from the
French by James Hulbert, *Yale French Studies* 55-56, pp. 11-52.

16. (New Haven: Yale University Press, 1975).

17. *SE* xxiii, 172. See also iii, 281; iv, xxiii; xix, 151; xxii, 15-16, 221, 244-45.

18. Dreamers and madmen are equated in Plato's *Theaetetus* 158B. In Aristotle's *On Dreams* (a work to which Freud refers near the beginning of
his *Interpretation of Dreams, SE* iv, 2-3), dreams are said to be produced
by the same faculty as that which causes deception in illness (458B).
They are thus like the products of delirium. Among those who point out
the similarity between dreams and the delusions and hallucinations of
madness are Bartholomaeus Anglicus in *Batman upon Bartholome, his
booke De proprietatibus rerum* (London: Thomas East, 1582); Robert Burton
in *The Anatomy of Melancholy* (1621); Thomas Tryon, in his *A Discourse of
the Causes, Natures, and Cure of Phrensie, Madness, or Distraction*, added to

his *A Treatise of Dreams and Visions* . . . , 2nd ed. (London: T. Sowle, 1695); Jacques Jacob Moreau in his *Du Hachisch et de l'aliénation mentale* (Paris: Librarie de Fortin, Masson et cie, 1845); and C. G. Jung in *The Psychology of Dementia Praecox* (Princeton: Princeton/Bollingen Paperback Edition, 1974).

19. Kris, p. 254.

20. My approach to this concept is based chiefly on the definitions of Freud and of Paul Federn in *Ego Psychology and the Psychoses* (London: Imago Publishing Co., 1953), and on Ernst Kris's description of "the organizational functions of the ego . . . , its capacity of self-regulation and of regression and . . . its capacity of control over the primary process" (p. 28).

21. *The Idea of a Mental Illness*, p. 35.

22. *Psychoanalytic Theory, Therapy, and the Self* (New York: Basic Books, 1971). See also Eric Fromm, *The Anatomy of Human Destructiveness* (1973; rpt. New York: Fawcett Crest Books, 1975). For an excellent discusson of the usefulness of the theory of instinctual drives, misunderstandings of this theory, and other matters related to its application to human motivation, see *The Collected Papers of David Rapaport*, ed. Merton M. Gill (New York: Basic Books, 1967), pp. 853-906. It is not possible or useful here to discuss the many other commentaries—whether adaptations, distortions, objections, or justifications—on this theory by contemporary psychoanalysts, anthropologists, sociobiologists, and psychobiologists. In developing my own position, however, which is based primarily but not entirely on the evidence of myth and literature, my refutations of what I regard as distortions and invalid objections will inevitably emerge.

23. *The Maturational Processes and the Facilitating Environment* (New York: International Universities Press, 1965), p. 45.

24. *Collected Papers*, pp. 878-86.

25. *Aspects of Internalization* (New York: International Universities Press, 1968), pp. 44-45. Jerome Bruner approaches the problem of "aim" from another, but equally interesting point of view: "The perceptual processing of the organism that yields inferences of intent seems not to be all that illusory as an account of what is going on in the nervous system. Not only is there good reason to believe that human behaviour is in fact organized into acts carried out 'for the sake' of achieving certain ends, but also the receptive human nervous system is ready to perceive behaviour as so structured, indeed, perhaps *too* ready." ("Psychology and the Image of Man," Herbert Spencer Lecture, given in Oxford on October 29, 1976, published in *TLS*, December 17, 1976, pp. 1589-91).

26. *A New Language for Psychoanalysis* (New Haven: Yale University Press, 1976) and *Language and Insight* (New Haven: Yale University Press, 1978). For other references and objections to the antimetapsychological school, see Joel Kovel, "Things and Words: Metapsychology and the Historical Point of View," *Psychoanalysis and Contemporary Thought* I, 1 (1978), 21-88. It was Kovel's article that brought to my attention Ricoeur's remarks on the problem of language.

27. *Freud and Philosophy: An Essay on Interpretation*, trans. from the French by Denis Savage (New Haven: Yale University Press, 1970), pp. 393-95.

28. *New York Times Magazine*, July 4, 1976, p. 109.

29. *Collected Papers*, p. 862.

30. *The Lives of a Cell* (New York: Viking, 1974), p. 147.

31. *Ibid.*, p. 60.

32. See Lillian Feder, *Ancient Myth in Modern Poetry* (Princeton: Princeton University Press, 1971), chapter II, "Freud and Jung on Myth."

33. "Some Biomythology," *The Lives of a Cell*, pp. 141-48.

34. *Reality Lost and Regained, Autobiography of a Schizophrenic Girl*, with analytic interpretation by Marguerite Sechehaye, trans. from the French by Grace Rubin-Rabson (1951; rpt. New American Library, 1970), p. 63.

35. *Ego Psychology and the Psychoses*, p. 188. For a different and very convincing point of view, see D. W. Winnicott's brilliant paper, "The Fear of Breakdown," in which he says: "It is wrong to think of psychotic illness as a breakdown, it is a defence organization relative to a primitive agony. . . ." *The International Review of Psycho-analysis*, I, parts 1-2 (1974), 104.

36. *Symbolic Realization*, trans. from the French by Barbrö Würsten and Helmut Würsten (New York: International Universities Press, 1951), pp. 133-34.

37. *Psychoanalytic Explorations in Art*, pp. 114-17. See also p. 100 for references to "verbal attempts at restitution."

38. Solomon H. Snyder, *Madness and the Brain* (New York: McGraw-Hill, 1974), p. 4.

39. *Mind: An Essay on Human Feeling* (Baltimore: The Johns Hopkins Press, 1967), I, 64-65.

40. *Children of the Mire: Modern Poetry from Romanticism to the Avant-Garde* (Cambridge, Mass.: Harvard University Press, 1974), p. v. One is reminded also of Wallace Stevens' comment: "There is more than the romantic in the statement that the true work of art, whatever it may be, is not the work of the individual artist. It is time and it is place, as these

perfect themselves." *The Necessary Angel: Essays on Reality and the Imagination* (New York: Vintage Books, 1942), pp. 139-40.

41. *Childhood and Society*, 2nd. ed. (New York: Norton, 1963), p. 36.

42. This is Erikson's phrase. I have found his *Childhood and Society* especially valuable for general background on the effects of social forces on individual development. Jules Henry's *Pathways to Madness* (1965; rpt. New York: Vintage Books, 1973), although not as far-reaching in its implications, deals more extensively with the effects of family life on individual mental illness.

43. *Madness in Society: Chapters in the Historical Sociology of Mental Illness* (New York: Harper and Row, 1969).

44. *Madness and Civilization: A History of Insanity in the Age of Reason*, trans. from the French by Richard Howard (1961; rpt. New York: New American Library, 1967).

45. *History of Psychiatry*, p. 53.

46. See Alexander and Selesnick, *History of Psychiatry*, pp. 112-13, 117-20; Gregory Zilboorg in collaboration with George W. Henry, *A History of Medical Psychology* (New York: Norton, 1941), pp. 315-29; and George Rosen, *Madness in Society*, pp. 275-76.

47. Philippe Pinel, *A Treatise on Insanity*, trans. from the French by D. D. Davis, M.D. (Sheffield: W. Todd, 1806), p. 3, originally published as *Traité médico-philosophique sur l'aliénation mentale, ou la manie* (Paris, 1801).

CHAPTER II

1. Pp. xx-xxi.

2. *Pathways to Madness*, p. xx.

3. *Mind* i, 99-100.

4. Theodore Lidz, *The Origins and Treatment of Schizophrenic Disorders* (New York: Basic Books, 1973), p. 4.

5. Euripides, *Bacchae*, edited with Introduction and Commentary by E. R. Dodds, 2nd ed. (Oxford: Clarendon Press, 1960), p. xi. Like most readers of and commentators on Euripides' *Bacchae*, I am deeply indebted to Dodds, despite my disagreements with him on major issues of interpretation. In quoting or summarizing Dodds's views on the *Bacchae* and in quoting from the play, I refer to this edition. Unless otherwise noted, all translations from the *Bacchae* and other Greek plays discussed in this chapter are my own.

6. See Lewis Richard Farnell, *The Cults of the Greek States* (Oxford: Clarendon Press, 1909), v, 156, 164-69; and Plutarch, *Themistocles* 13. For the

dispute over the dating of the myth of Dionysus' dismemberment, see Dodds, *The Greeks and the Irrational* (1951; rpt. Boston: Beacon Press, 1957), pp. 155-56. The evidence Dodds presents that this myth is not "a Hellenistic invention" but much older, and his suggestion that it is connected with the "ancient Dionysiac ritual of *Sparagmos* and *Omophagia*," seem to me entirely convincing.

7. Dodds, pp. xx-xxi.

8. See, for example, Erwin Rohde, *Psyche: The Cult of Souls and Belief in Immortality among the Greeks*, trans. from the German by W. B. Hillis, 8th ed. (New York: Harper Torchbooks, 1966); Farnell, *The Cults of the Greek States* v; W.K.C. Guthrie, *The Greeks and Their Gods* (Boston: Beacon Press, 1955); Henri Jeanmaire, *Dionysos: Histoire du Culte de Bacchus* (Paris: Payot, 1951); and Dodds's Introduction.

9. *The Greeks and Their Gods*, pp. 153-57.

10. See, for example, Mircea Eliade, *Traité d'Histoire des Religions* (Paris: Payot, 1949), chapter viii; and Jeanmaire.

11. Jean Bayet, *Croyances et Rites dans la Rome Antique* (Paris: Payot, 1971), pp. 245-47.

12. See especially *Biology and Knowledge* (Edinburgh: Edinburgh University Press, 1972).

13. *Aspects of Internalization*, p. 9. I have omitted his italics.

14. Of course, these words occur in other tragedies, especially in Aeschylus, but, to my knowledge, they are not repeated elsewhere to the extent that they are in the *Bacchae*. It is, moreover, in connection with madness that the repeated use of terms related to thinking and especially "soundness of mind" is so striking. σώφρων and other forms of the word are also important in relation to the conception of madness in Sophocles' *Ajax* (see below). For an extremely illuminating discussion of the terms φρήν and φρονεῖν, see Richard B. Onians, *The Origins of European Thought about the body, the mind, the soul, the world, time and fate* (Cambridge: Cambridge University Press, 1951), p. 13 ff. One of Onians' comments on φρονεῖν indicates that the word develops even in historical times as it reflects the greater differentiation of mental processes expressed in literature: "In later Greek φρονεῖν has primarily an intellectual sense, 'to think, have understanding', but in Homer it is more comprehensive, covering undifferentiated psychic activity, the action of the φρένες involving 'emotion' and 'conation' also. . ." (p. 14).

15. *Ibid.*, p. 21.

16. See Freud's "The Antithetical Meaning of Primal Words," *SE* xi.

17. See Dodds, p. xxv and note 2 on that page.

18. Cf. Sophocles' version of the Lycurgus story in *Antigone*, l. 954 ff.

19. *Aeschylus* II, *Agamemnon, Libation-Bearers, Eumenides, Fragments*, with an English trans. by Herbert Weir Smyth, appendix ed. Hugh Lloyd-Jones (Loeb Classical Library, Cambridge, Mass.: Harvard University Press, 1963), pp. 399-401. Aeschylus' play *Xantria*, which is not extant, dealt with the *sparagmos* of Pentheus. For a discussion of the role of Lyssa as the instigator of madness in this play, see O'Brien-Moore, pp. 80-81.

20. Gilbert Norwood interprets this line to suggest "the overthrow of" Lycurgus' "palace by the might of the god" (*Greek Tragedy* [Boston: J. W. Luce, 1920], p. 117). See also O'Brien-Moore, p. 133, note 1.

21. For a version in which Orpheus was devoured, see Farnell v, 105-106.

22. Plutarch, *Moralia, The Greek Questions*, 299E, F.

23. *The Library*, III, v, 2; II, ii, 2.

24. See, for example, Hesiod, *The Catalogues of Women and Eoiae*, 18; Nonnus, *Dionysica* IX, 37 ff.; XLVIII, 917-24.

25. Nonnus, VI, 169-205.

26. *Ibid.*, IX, 25-54.

27. P. 248.

28. See Weston La Barre, *The Ghost Dance, Origins of Religion* (1970; rpt. London: Allen and Unwin, 1972), especially p. 436, for a discussion of animals and birds identified with Neolithic and Bronze Age Greek gods and heroes as "relicts of an earlier shamanistic age of hunters." The wild man myth, which is analogous in certain respects to Dionysus myths, seems to be associated with similar rites. Although "wildness," as it appears in the savage conduct of the wild man in the many versions of his myth, and madness are by no means the same, traits of the Dionysiac reveler and the band pursuing or led by the wild man do have common features. Hayden White points out that one of "the main components of the Wild Man myth as it comes down from the Bible into medieval thought" is that "Cursedness, or wildness, is identified with the wandering life of the hunter (as against the stable life of the shepherd and farmer) . . ." (*The Wild Man Within*, p. 16). Many features of the wild man rites are similar to those of the Dionysiac: dancing, the identification of the wild man with the bear, and his role "either as the leader of or at least as a participant in the activities of the Wild Horde" (see Bernheimer, pp. 50-84). In the hunts that are also an important part of the rituals connected with the wild man himself, he is the hunted rather than the pursuer. But as leader of or participant in the Hunt of the Wild Horde, he is involved in frenzied violence and destructiveness similar to those of the Dionysiac band. Bernheimer points out that the wild man has a "dual nature . . . as a harbinger of fertility and as an

embodiment of the returning dead," which is reflected "in the ambiguity of the rituals accorded to him" (p. 56). Bernheimer suggests, moreover, that it is in the latter role of "demon of death" that he "may be hidden behind the Germanic leaders of the Wild Horde" (p. 80). Like Dionysus, the wild man in his bizarre rites enacts the principles of death and of fertility and renewal. There can be little doubt that in the pursuit and capture of the wild man the control of destructive forces in human beings and in the universe is symbolically enacted but, like Dionysiac frenzy, the wild man's savagery and violence continually reappear in various and oblique forms.

29. The proto-Dionysus can certainly be regarded as a shaman. "That Greek religion began in shamanism is an idea entertained by Hellenists for almost half a century now" (La Barre, p. 440). La Barre cites the many authorities who hold this view (p. 440), which seems incontestable, as does his conclusion that in general there "were shamans before there were gods" (p. 161). I have, however, avoided the use of this word and prefer to use the term proto-Dionysus or similar terms because my view of both the development and nature of god-prototypes differs in important respects from earlier ones. In attempting to reconstruct the symbolic representations of evolving controls over instinctual impulses through the use of a prototypical god-figure, it seems best to avoid the connotations that have accumulated around the shaman throughout history. Also, though I do not object to La Barre's definition of the "first god" as "the *mana* power or will man thinks he sees in nature, the *anima* or soul he is sure comes and goes in the bodies of men and of animals" (p. 182), it seems to me that his description of the mental processes involved in the creation of this concept is sometimes anachronistic. His reconstruction of both the shaman's and other early human beings' mental functioning in terms that would be suited to present-day psychosis clouds the issue. In the remnants of early man's mythical constructs, one observes evidence not of mental aberration but of evolving mental processes. Some psychotic symptoms do shed light on and indeed can themselves be regarded as regressions to archaic traits that persist in ontogenetic development. Evidence that this is so, however, can more effectively be obtained by tracing the development of unconscious and conscious processes through the narrative structure and symbols of extant myth than by applying anachronistic labels. A different point of view from La Barre's is to be found in Carleton S. Coon's *The Hunting People* (Boston: Little, Brown, 1971). "In the anthropological literature, shamans have often been categorized as natural neurotics who would have been social misfits in a society like our own—the craziest hunters of all. Actually, they were exceptionally intelligent and well-disciplined men, as able to hunt as nonshamans are" (p. 390). Mircea Eliade, who defines shamanism in more particular terms than does La Barre, would exclude Dionysus from "the healers, divin-

ers, or ecstatics who might be connected with shamanism" (*Shamanism: Archaic Techniques of Ecstasy*, trans. from the French by Willard Trask [Princeton: Princeton University Press, 1972], p. 388). For his discussion of the relationship between shamanism and psychopathology, see pp. 23-32.

30. Grahame Clark and Stuart Piggott, *Prehistoric Societies* (1965; rpt. Harmondsworth, Middlesex: Penguin Books, 1970), p. 148.

31. *Ibid.*, p. 149. See also J. Z. Young, *An Introduction to the Study of Man* (Oxford, Clarendon Press, 1971), who discusses the evidence of "a further advance in symbolic thought and presumably language" in Mesolithic designs executed on stone (pp. 511-12), and Pedro Laín Entralgo, *The Therapy of the Word in Classical Antiquity*, trans. from the Spanish by L. J. Rather and John M. Sharp (New Haven: Yale University Press, 1970), who considers the value of the "therapeutic charm" in societies in which "agriculture and animal husbandry have won social importance" (pp. 25-26).

32. Much of the material summarized here is taken from Morton I. Teicher's *Windigo Psychosis: A Study of a Relationship between Belief and Behavior among the Indians of Northeastern Canada*, Proceedings of the 1960 Annual Spring Meeting of the American Ethnological Society, ed. Verne F. Ray (Seattle: University of Washington Press, 1960). For variants of the name "Windigo," see Teicher, p. 2.

33. Teicher, p. 13.

34. *Ibid.*, p. 6.

35. John M. Cooper, "The Cree Witiko Psychosis," *Every Man His Way: Readings in Cultural Anthropology*, ed. Alan Dundes (Englewood Cliffs, N.J.: Prentice Hall, 1968), p. 290.

36. Teicher, p. 57.

37. *Ibid.*, pp. 37-38.

38. Cooper, pp. 290, 292. Teicher takes essentially the same approach.

39. Cooper, p. 290.

40. P. 113.

41. Dodds, p. 83.

42. La Barre, p. 83; see also Coon, p. 217.

43. "The choral odes of the *Bacchae* of Euripides," *Yale Classical Studies* 22 (Cambridge: Cambridge University Press, 1972), p. 147. See also René Girard, *Violence and the Sacred*, trans. from the French by Patrick Gregory (Baltimore: The Johns Hopkins Press, 1977). Girard also deals with the question of control, but from a viewpoint entirely different from Arthur's or my own. He regards the violent action of Euripides' *Bacchae* as

one example of a prevailing function of violence in its intrinsic connection with the sacred. The myth, he argues, merely repeats an original "spontaneous outburst," an unpremeditated "assassination" in which the victim was used "to polarize all the fears, anxieties, and hostilities of the crowd" (p. 131). Although it is generally accepted that ritual is one means of channeling and thus controlling aggression, Girard's refusal to accept what he calls "psychic motivations" and his simplistic conception of the "spontaneous" origins of rite weaken his argument. In this respect, incidentally, there is at least one important difference between his original French version and the recent English translation. In *La Violence et Le Sacré* (Paris: Bernard Grasset, 1972), p. 188, Girard says, "Pour comprendre le rite, il faut le rapporter à autre chose qu'à des motivations psychiques conscientes ou inconscientes," which is translated (p. 132) as "We cannot hope to understand the rite merely by attributing it to psychic motivations, either conscious or unconscious." Obviously, the word "merely," which does not appear in the French, changes the meaning significantly. The translated statement seems totally acceptable, but Girard's development of his thesis makes it clear that the original French version is what he actually means.

44. See Arthur, Appendix B: "τὸ σοφόν," pp. 176-79; also R. P. Winnington-Ingram, "Euripides, *Bacchae* 877-881=897-901," *BICS*, no. 13 (1966), 34-37; and D. J. Conacher, "A Note on *sophos, to sophon, sophia, to phronein, and nomos* in the *Bacchae*," *Euripidean Drama: Myth, Theme, and Structure* (Toronto: University of Toronto Press, 1967), pp. 73-77.

45. Conacher, p. 57; Dodds, p. xl.

46. The evidence that this narrative originates in ritual rather than history is overwhelming; see Dodds, p. xxvi. An attempt to separate the so-called historical from the ritual aspects, such as Conacher makes (p. 56), is unconvincing and seems merely arbitrary.

47. For commentary on the rationalist positions of Tiresias, see Dodds, p. 91 and Conacher, pp. 62-63.

48. *The Bacchae of Euripides*, a translation and commentary by Geoffrey S. Kirk (Englewood Cliffs, N.J.: Prentice Hall, 1970), p. 25.

49. *Ibid.*, p. 46.

50. The translation of the second sentence is by Harry L. Levy, whose justification for this version of a disputed passage is totally convincing. See his "Euripides' *Bacchae* 326 f.: Another Interpretation," *Hermes* (100 Band, Heft 3, 1972), pp. 487-89.

51. P. 59.

52. See Dodds, pp. 122-23, and Arthur, p. 154.

53. Dodds, p. 130.

54. See, for example, R. P. Winnington-Ingram, *Euripides and Dionysus* (Cambridge: Cambridge University Press, 1948), pp. 106-108 and Kirk, pp. 13-15.

55. As is the entire passage, from l. 997 to l. 1010. See Dodds, p. 202 ff.

56. Guthrie, pp. 178-79.

57. George Thomson, *Aeschylus and Athens* (New York: International Publishers, 1950), p. 36.

58. *Cults of the Greek States* v, 437-44.

59. Oxford text of Aeschylus, ed. G. Murray, 2nd ed. (Clarendon Press, 1955).

60. There is an especially interesting reference in the *Odyssey* (xv, 233-34), in which the Erinys is said to bring *ate*, a word used frequently in connection with the Erinyes in the *Oresteia*.

61. O'Brien-Moore, p. 75.

62. *On Aristotle and Greek Tragedy* (New York: Oxford University Press, 1962), p. 84.

63. τοῖσ δ'αὖ μα]ταίοισ [σώφρονασ φύω]φ[ρένας.] *Unknown Play* (II b), 282, l. 19, *Aeschylus* ii, appendix, p. 579.

64. *The Justice of Zeus* (Berkeley: University of California Press, 1971). This idea is developed throughout the book; see especially p. 161.

65. Susanne Langer, *Mind* ii, 283.

66. In the essay "Nyakyusa Ritual and Symbolism" Monica Wilson describes "dance as a form of mourning." She quotes a member of the Nyakyusa tribe as follows: "We dance because there is war in our hearts—a passion of grief and fear exasperates us." Another says, "A kinsman when he dances assuages his passionate grief; he goes into the house to weep and then comes out and dances the war dance; his passionate grief is made tolerable in the dance; it bound his heart and the dance assuages it" (*Myth and Cosmos*, ed. John Middleton [Garden City, N.Y.: Natural History Press, 1967], p. 153).

67. The most extensive and useful recent discussion of the "hunting net, the yoke, the shackle, and the fetter" as "a major system of kindred imagery" in the *Oresteia* can be found in Anne Lebeck, *The Oresteia, A Study in Language and Structure* (Washington, D.C.: Center for Hellenic Studies, 1971).

68. E. R. Dodds, *The Greeks and the Irrational*, p. 42; and John Jones, p. 272.

69. *The Greeks and the Irrational*, pp. 69-70.

70. *Madness in Society*, pp. 55-62. For an excellent discussion of the question of the psychopathology of the prophet and references to the extensive literature on this subject, see the entire section, "Prophecy, Ecstasy and Madness," pp. 42-62.

71. See also Plato's *Phaedrus* 244.

72. *Greek Oracles* (London: Hutchinson University Library, 1967), pp. 79-80. See also Dodds, *The Greeks and the Irrational*, pp. 72-74.

73. Parke, p. 80.

74. Oxford text of Euripides, ed. G. Murray (Clarendon Press, 1913).

75. O'Brien-Moore, p. 85.

76. *Ibid.*, pp. 130-32.

77. Oxford text of Sophocles, ed. A. C. Pearson (Clarendon Press, 1967).

78. Lewis Farnell, *Greek Hero Cults and Ideas of Immortality* (Oxford: Clarendon Press, 1921), pp. 306-308.

79. "There is no assertion that Ajax was mad until the *Little Iliad*" (O'Brien-Moore, p. 69, note).

80. "The Ajax of Sophocles," *Sophocles: A Collection of Critical Essays*, ed. Thomas Woodward (Englewood Cliffs, N.J.: Prentice Hall, 1966), pp. 56-57.

81. *Ibid.*, p. 34.

82. Cedric Whitman, *Sophocles: A Study of Heroic Humanism* (Cambridge, Mass.: Harvard University Press, 1951), p. 70.

83. "Experience has confirmed Freud's statement that each suicide is multiply determined by the interaction of several motives. Suicide is by no means a homogeneous or unitary piece of human behavior. On the contrary, suicide comprises a variety of behaviors with many important aspects—historical, legal, social, and philosophical, as well as medical and psychological" (Robert E. Litman, "Sigmund Freud on Suicide," *Essays in Self-Destruction*, ed. Edwin S. Shneidman [New York: Science House, 1967], p. 338). See also Lawrence S. Kubie, "Multiple Determinants of Suicide" in the same volume.

84. The problem of whether Ajax is here trying to conceal his intention to commit suicide, which has occupied many commentators, is best solved by Knox, who says that in the first thirty-nine lines of this speech Ajax attempts neither to conceal nor to reveal his intentions: "He is talking to himself" (pp. 41-42).

85. *Ibid.*, p. 57.

CHAPTER III

1. All quotations from *King Lear* are from *The Arden Edition of the Works of William Shakespeare, King Lear*, ed. Kenneth Muir (Cambridge, Mass.: Harvard University Press, 8th ed., reprinted with further corrections, 1959).

2. *Ego Psychology and the Psychoses*, p. 124.

3. Zilboorg and Henry, pp. 119-26; Alexander and Selesnick, pp. 61-66; Judith Neaman, *Suggestion of the Devil, The Origins of Madness* (New York: Anchor Books, 1975), pp. 8-26.

4. In *Medicine in Medieval England* (London: Oldbourne History of Science Library, 1967), C. H. Talbot makes a salutary comment on recent claims for the "modernity" of Bartholomaeus' approach to madness: "In the fourth and fifth chapters he deals with frenzy and mental disturbance, chapters which, when published some years ago, attracted a great deal of attention. It was not considered possible that anyone in the Middle Ages should have gained so firm a grasp of this complex subject: and yet no surprise should have been expressed at all, since most of the material was taken from Constantine [the African], who himself had borrowed it from late classical and Byzantine writers" (p. 87).

5. *Three prose versions of the Secreta Secretorum*, ed. Robert Steele, EETS, es 74 (London: Kegan Paul, Trench, Trübner, 1898).

6. Neaman, p. 55.

7. This subject has been treated at length by Penelope Doob in her study of madness in medieval literature referred to above. The chief limitations of Doob's book result from her effort to classify enormously varied expressions of madness within the narrow categories she derives from the biblical story of Nebuchadnezzar, and her apparent lack of interest in the emotional experience depicted in much of the literature of madness she investigates. Her approach is chiefly descriptive, and in this respect serves a useful purpose in pointing out many examples of the treatment of madness in late medieval literature and indicating the major directions this theme takes within the confines of a religious context and point of view.

8. Doob, p. 54.

9. *Ibid.*, p. 12.

10. *Ibid.*, p. 228.

11. See Doob, pp. 226-30; Eva M. Thornley, "The English Penitential Lyric and Hoccleve's Autobiographical Poetry," *NM* 68 (1967), 295-321; and Jerome Mitchell, *Thomas Hoccleve: A Study in Early Fifteenth-Century Poetic* (Urbana: University of Illinois Press, 1968), chapter I.

12. *Hoccleve's Works III: The Regement of Princes and 14 Minor Poems*, ed. F. J. Furnivall, EETS, es 72 (London: Kegan Paul, Trench, Trübner, 1897).

13. All quotations from the *Complaint* and *Dialogus cum Amico* are from *Hoccleve's Works: The Minor Poems*, ed. F. J. Furnivall and I. Gollancz, revised by Jerome Mitchell and A. I. Doyle, EETS, es 61 and 73 (New York: Oxford University Press, 1970).

14. "Hoccleve's *Complaint* and Isidore of Seville," *Speculum* 45 (1970), 564-74.

15. The words "morbus" ("morbum mentium"), "aegritudo," and others denoting disease, and the concept of "tuae curationis," "Si operam medicantis expectas" occur throughout the *Consolatio Philosophiae*. Quotations from Boethius are from *The Theological Tractates and The Consolation of Philosophy*, Loeb Classical Library (Cambridge, Mass.: Harvard University Press, 1968).

16. See Doob, especially p. 229.

17. *Ibid.*, p. 231.

18. *A History of Medical Psychiatry*, p. 144.

19. *Malleus Maleficarum*, trans. Montague Summers (1928; rpt. New York: Benjamin Blom, 1970), pp. 100-101.

20. See especially pp. 225-31.

21. *Malleus Maleficarum*, p. 101.

22. Rossell Hope Robbins, *Encyclopaedia of Witchcraft and Demonology* (New York: Crown, 1959), p. 162.

23. *Ibid.*, p. 337.

24. *The Elizabethan Malady: A Study of Melancholia in English Literature from 1580 to 1642* (East Lansing: Michigan State University Press, 1951). See also Bridget Gellert Lyons, *Voices of Melancholy: Studies in literary treatments of melancholy in Renaissance England* (New York: Barnes and Noble, 1971).

25. Geoffrey Bullough, *Mirror of Minds: Changing Psychological Beliefs in English Poetry* (Toronto: University of Toronto Press, 1962), p. 49.

26. See Robert Reed, *Bedlam on the Jacobean Stage*, especially chapters 3 and 4.

27. Quotations from Lavater are from a "line-by-line reprint of R. H.'s [Robert Harrison's] English translation" of *De spectris. . .* , ed. J. Dover Wilson and May Yardley, printed for the Shakespeare Association (Oxford: Oxford University Press, 1929).

28. *De Praestigiis Daemonum et Incantationibus ac ueneficijs*, Libri V (Basil: per Ioannem Oporinum, 1564). For an excellent discussion of contemporary

reactions to Weyer's contributions, especially of the church's disapproval and of Jean Bodin's efforts to discredit him, see Zilboorg and Henry, pp. 233-44.

29. Christopher Baxter, "Johann Weyer's *De Praestigiis Daemonum*: Unsystematic psychopathology," *The Damned Art: Essays in the Literature of Witchcraft*, ed. Sydney Anglo (London: Routledge & Kegan Paul, 1977), pp. 53-75; also Baxter's essay, "Jean Bodin's *De la Démonomanie des Sorciers*: The logic of persecution," pp. 76-105, and Sydney Anglo, "Reginald Scot's *Discoverie of Witchcraft*: Scepticism and Sadduceeism," pp. 106-39, in the same volume.

30. "Johann Weyer's *De Praestigiis Daemonum*: Unsystematic psychopathology," p. 71.

31. *Ibid.*, pp. 53-54.

32. See, for example, Andrew Boorde, *The breviary of healthe, the seconde boke of the brevyary of health, named the extravagantes* (London: Powell, 1552), and Philip Barrough, *The method of phisicke, conteyning the causes, signes, and cures of inward diseases in mans body* . . . (London: Thomas Vautrollier, 1583).

33. *The Discoverie of Witchcraft, Wherein the lewde dealing of witches is notablie detected* . . . (London: Brome, 1584).

34. "Reginald Scot's *Discoverie of Witchcraft*: Scepticism and Sadduceeism."

35. T. Bright, *A Treatise of Melancholie*, reproduced from the 1586 edition printed by Thomas Vautrollier (New York: Facsimile Text Soc., Columbia University Press, 1940), Introduction, p. xiii.

36. *A Treatise of Melancholie* . . . (London: Thomas Vautrollier, 1586), p. 1.

37. *Ibid.*, unpaged "Epistle Dedicatorie."

38. *Ibid.*

39. As Paul Jorgensen points out: "it was not unnatural that what was preeminently, even at times reluctantly, an age of discovery should, as the growing number of psychological works testify, find a challenging area for exploration within man himself (*Lear's Self-Discovery* [Berkeley and Los Angeles: University of California Press, 1967], p. 33). In studying various Renaissance treatises on self-knowledge, Jorgensen finds (in Bright and in Pierre Charron's *On Wisdome*, for example) occasional psychological insights startling in their modernity.

40. For a discussion of the contrasting medieval and Renaissance "worldviews" in *King Lear*, see Bernard McElroy, *Shakespeare's Mature Tragedies* (Princeton: Princeton University Press, 1973), especially pp. 9-12; 146-49. See also, Don Cameron Allen, *Doubt's Boundless Sea: Skepticism and Faith in the Renaissance* (Baltimore: The Johns Hopkins Press, 1964).

41. For a discussion of Shakespeare's legendary and literary sources in *King Lear*, see *Narrative and Dramatic Sources of Shakespeare* vii, ed. Geoffrey Bullough (New York: Columbia University Press, 1973), 269-308.

42. Robert Heilman, *This Great Stage: Image and Structure in King Lear* (Baton Rouge: Louisiana State University Press, 1948), p. 198.

43. Introduction, *King Lear*, p. lx. The various interpretations of Lear's madness as a psychic corrective for his intellectual or moral blindness generally oversimplify the mind revealed in his ravings and hallucinations. Approaches of this type are extremely common. The two cited immediately below exemplify rather extended discussions of 1) a fairly typical moral emphasis, and 2) an intellectual one. In "The Storm Within: The Madness of King Lear," *Shakespeare Quarterly* 13, 2 (Spring 1962), 137-54, Josephine Waters Bennett modifies her own somewhat narrow view of Lear's madness as an "analysis of the overthrow of reason by forces within—and they are evil forces" (p. 148) by later indicating that "the storm within Lear's mind goes beyond good and evil, beyond the narrow world of preceptoral morality, to the imponderable realities of cause and effect, of man's ignorance, his weakness, his blindness. . . ." Still her emphasis is essentially on Lear's "pride and willfulness" (p. 153), which she regards as the causes of his insanity. These faults, in her view, are finally overcome by "the disciplining of this willful man by all the conditions of life, . . . so that he may learn his own limitations and the true values of life" (p. 152). In *Lear's Self-Discovery*, Paul Jorgensen introduces his "study of Lear's self-discovery, its intellectual meaning and its dramatic expression," by frankly admitting that the "subject of the present study is a cliché." Although Jorgensen does fulfill his promise to introduce fresh material, his major theme is a familiar one: Lear is forced "over the brink of madness," at least in part, by "the learning process" (p. 83). In fact, in Jorgensen's opinion, "Lear is assuredly the best example of madman as thinker in all literature" (p. 80), and the chief point of his chapter "The Emergence of Lear as Thinker" is that Lear achieves a "new flexibility and inquisitiveness of mind in madness" (p. 81). There are many variations on these rather typical approaches. For example, Terence Hawkes describes Lear's development from "an initial acceptance of the way of life and the values of reason" to "a rejection of these in favour of the way of life and the values of intuition" (*Shakespeare and the Reason: A Study of the Tragedies and the Problem Plays* [London: Routledge and Kegan Paul, 1961]). For sensible objections to such interpretations of Lear's madness, see Marvin Rosenberg, *The Masks of King Lear* (Berkeley and Los Angeles: University of California Press, 1972). Rosenberg convincingly demonstrates that it "is doubtful that Shakespeare meant Lear's madness to carry a positive value, to be instructive, regenerative, as is sometimes argued" (p. 208).

44. The phrase is Federn's, p. 191.

45. There has been much disagreement on the precise moment at which Lear becomes mad, a point which, as my discussion of the text will indicate, I consider irrelevant. See, for example, Bennett, pp. 137-40 and Rosenberg, pp. 214-15.

46. The barbarous Scythian,
Or he that makes his generation messes
To gorge his appetite, shall to my bosom
Be as well neighbour'd, pitied, and reliev'd,
As thou my sometime daughter.

(I, i, 116-20)

47. Quoted by Muir, note 122, p. 11.

48. Bernard McElroy deals at some length with the ways in which Lear identifies his own "constant will with the will of nature" and his assumption that "nature endorses his actions" (see especially pp. 169-70). His further discussion of the "collapse of the subjective world" of Lear, "the destruction of all Lear's assumptions about himself, those around him, and the cosmos," and the "almost palpable sense of dissolution in *King Lear*" is extremely perceptive, but his consideration of Lear's psychic dissolution mainly illustrates what seems a fairly obvious point: "To Shakespeare mental disintegration seemed to suggest the perfect dramatic emblem for the destruction of the personal world . . . " (pp. 145-205).

49. See Rosenberg, p. 139.

50. Kenneth Muir has indicated that "for Edgar's feigned lunacy Shakespeare drew on *A Declaration of Egregious Popish Impostures* in which Harsnett analysed the confessions of bogus demoniacs" ("Madness in *King Lear*," *Shakespeare Survey* 13 [1960], 39). See also his article on Shakespeare's use of Harsnett in *RES* (1951), pp. 11-21, and the Arden ed. of *King Lear*, pp. 253-56.

51. Jorgensen, pp. 38-39.

52. *The Masks of King Lear*, p. 166.

53. For a different interpretation, see Rosenberg, p. 192, who says that "Lear touches here an image that the subconscious in the character design has been tracking since his first rages and will follow further—a compelled hunt, in terror and fury, for the source of life."

54. Rosenberg, p. 193.

55. See Freud's discussion of "dreams . . . endeavouring to master the stimulus retrospectively, by developing the anxiety whose omission was the cause of the traumatic neurosis" in *Beyond the Pleasure Principle*, *SE* xviii, 32.

56. Muir's note, Arden ed. of *King Lear*, p. 120.

57. Rosenberg, p. 213.

58. Hayden White, "The Forms of Wildness: Archaeology of an Idea," *The Wild Man Within*, p. 21.

59. Rosenberg, p. 213. Although Rosenberg's analysis of Lear's psychological experience is often perceptive and valuable, he sometimes oversimplifies Lear's extremely subtle and complicated inner drama. One could hardly disagree with Rosenberg's interpretation of Lear's regression as often childish or infantile, but it seems to me that the label "king-child" (pp. 178, 195, 267) oversimplifies to the point of distortion conduct that expresses many levels of development and experience at once. Furthermore, it is shocking to find so scholarly and sophisticated a critic echoing the popular distortion of the key psychoanalytic term "ego." Thus, Rosenberg writes of Lear's "immense storm-defying ego" (p. 195); and expresses the notion that Lear responds to "necessity," an experience that enlarges his perception, by "breaking at last out of the cage of his ego" (p. 204). Such abuse of technical language obscures the central conflict within Lear, which can be understood only in relation to the breakdown and restitution of that aspect of Lear's self which the precise meaning of the term ego designates. See above p. 135.

60. I am indebted to Paul Federn's discussion of the "regression of the ego to earlier developmental states" in psychosis (pp. 190-91).

61. Rosenberg (pp. 267-68) prefers the Folio version: "They cannot touch me for crying," but there is not sufficient justification for substituting this for the more commonly accepted reading, "coining."

62. Note to line 83, p. 174.

63. For various sixteenth- and seventeenth-century definitions of the term "coin," see Eric Partridge, *Shakespeare's Bawdry* (New York: Dutton, 1969), p. 81.

64. See Muir's notes to lines 3 and 4, p. 164.

65. *Ibid.*, note to line 94, p. 175.

66. Harley Granville-Barker, *Prefaces to Shakespeare*, ed. M. St. Clare Byrne (Princeton: Princeton University Press, 1963), II, 36.

CHAPTER IV

1. "A Satyr against Mankind," *The Complete Poems of John Wilmot, Earl of Rochester*, ed. David M. Vieth (New Haven: Yale University Press, 1968).

2. *The Anatomy of Melancholy*, 1621; ed. The Rev. A. R. Shilleto, 3 vols. (London: George Bell, 1926-27), "Democritus to the Reader."

3. Thomas Willis, *Two Discourses concerning the Soul of Brutes* . . . , Englished by S. Pordage (London, 1683), p. 208.

4. See Zilboorg and Henry, pp. 263-64; Michael De Porte, *Nightmares and Hobbyhorses*, p. 6.

5. Willis, p. 206.

6. Zilboorg and Henry, p. 263. See also D. B. Klein, *A History of Scientific Psychology, its Origins and Philosophical Backgrounds* (New York: Basic Books, 1970), p. 322.

7. *A History of Medical Psychology*, p. 264.

8. *The Passions of the Minde in General*, cor. and enlarged ed. (London: A. Helme, 1620).

9. *Tutela Sanitatis sive Vita Protracta. The Protection of long Life and Detection of its brevity, from diaetetic Causes and common Customs* . . . (London: Thompson and Basset, 1664).

10. See Aristotle, *On the Soul*, 413a-414a; *Nicomachean Ethics*, 1102a-1103a.

11. For an excellent summary of this theory and its adaptation in the Renaissance, see Babb, especially chapter I; see also Ruth Leila Anderson, *Elizabethan Psychology and Shakespeare*, 1927 (rpt. New York: Russell and Russell, 1966).

12. In his chapter, "Abnormal Psychology in England 1660-1760," De Porte summarizes the major ideas of Willis, William Battie, Thomas Tryon, and other well-known commentators on madness. In discussing the common eighteenth-century association of excessive imagination with madness, De Porte points out that Hobbes and Locke, from their different positions, were important in intensifying suspicion of individuality and idiosyncrasy: "Followers of Hobbes might worry most about the factiousness of the masses, those of Locke about the misused prerogatives of the sovereign, but the political theory of the age, whether absolutist or republican, addresses itself strongly to the problem of controlling anarchic individualism" (p. 47). De Porte's summary of eighteenth-century theories of madness is useful. Even more so is Richard Hunter and Ida Macalpine, *Three Hundred Years of Psychiatry 1535-1860* (London: Oxford University Press, 1963) in which selections from major theories are introduced with brief but excellent commentaries.

13. *Leviathan, The English Works of Thomas Hobbes*, ed. Sir William Molesworth (London: John Bohn, 1966), III, 57-58.

14. *A Treatise of Dreams & Visions wherein The Causes, Nature, and Uses, of Nocturnal Representations and the Communications both of Good and Evil Angels, as also departed Souls, to Mankinde, Are Theosophically Unfolded* . . . , to

which is added *A Discourse of the Causes, Natures and Cure of Phrensie, Madness or Distraction.*

15. See Hunter and Macalpine, p. 233, and De Porte, p. 110.

16. See above, pp. 288-89, note 18.

17. *Lucida Intervalla: Containing divers Miscellaneous Poems, Written at Finsbury and Bethlem* (London, 1679).

18. See, for example, Hildebrand Jacob, "Bedlam," *The Works of Hildebrand Jacob* (London: W. Lewis, 1735); Thomas Fitzgerald, "Bedlam," *Poems on several occasions* (London: Watts, 1733); and Myles Cooper, "The Pleasures of Madness," *Poems on Several Occasions* (Oxford: W. Jackson, 1761).

19. A contemporary reference to *crocus metallorum* makes Carkesse's disgust all the more understandable. Théodore Turquet De Mayerne's *A treatise of the gout. Written originally in the French tongue . . . Whereunto is added, advice about hypochondriacal-fits by the same author . . . Englished for the general benefit, by Thomas Sherley, M.D.* (London: Newman, 1676) recommends it as follows: "Let Vomitives lead the Van, as well for to cleanse effectually the first Region of its Ballast, as to remove those things which will be a hinderance to the efficacy of Specificks, from which only is to be expected the Victory over Melancholly: Amongst which, I know none of greater force, and less danger, than the infusion of *Crocus metallorum* in Canary Wine." The author goes on to insist: "You must Vomit three or four several times, . . . after which, you must proceed to Purgation. . . ." After all of this it may be necessary to undergo further vomiting and purges, to be followed by the use of "Steel Medicines" (Hunter and Macalpine, pp. 149-50). Such bizarre treatments of mental disorder continued to be justified on various bases. Forced vomiting as a method of restraint through depletion was employed in psychiatric wards in North America at least until the middle of the twentieth century.

20. *A Treatise of the Spleen and Vapours: or, Hypocondriacal and Hysterical Affections . . .* (London: J. Pemberton, 1725).

21. *The London Spy: The Vanities and Vices of the Town Exposed to View,* ed. Arthur L. Hayward (London: Cassell, 1927), p. 54.

22. *Nightmares and Hobbyhorses;* see also John R. Clark, *Form and Frenzy in Swift's Tale of a Tub* (Ithaca: Cornell University Press, 1970).

23. Clark, p. 155.

24. Thomas Hobbes, "The Questions Concerning Liberty, Necessity, and Chance. . . ," *English Works* v, 186.

25. *A Tale of a Tub, to which is added The Battle of the Books and the Mechanical Operation of the Spirit,* ed. A. C. Guthkelch and D. Nichol Smith (Oxford: Clarendon Press, 1920).

26. "Swift's *Tale of a Tub* Compared with Earlier Satires of the Puritans," *PMLA* 47 (1932), 171-78; "Swift and Some Earlier Satirists of Puritan Enthusiasm," *PMLA* 48 (1933), 1141-53; "The Satiric Background of the Attack on the Puritans in Swift's *Tale of a Tub*," *PMLA* 50 (1935), 210-23.

27. *Swift and Anglican Rationalism: The Religious Background of A Tale of a Tub* (Chicago: University of Chicago Press, 1961).

28. De Porte, pp. 38-39.

29. Unless otherwise noted, all quotations from Pope will be taken from *The Poems of Alexander Pope*, Twickenham ed., general ed. John Butt (London: Methuen, 1938-61), i-vi.

30. See, for example, Patricia Meyer Spacks, *An Argument of Images: The Poetry of Alexander Pope* (Cambridge, Mass.: Harvard University Press, 1971); David B. Morris, "The Kinship of Madness in Pope's *Dunciad*," *PQ* 51 (October 1972), 813-31; and Max Byrd, *Visits to Bedlam*.

31. *A New System of the Spleen, Vapours, and Hypochondriack Melancholy . . .* (London: A. Bettesworth, W. Innys, and C. Rivington, 1729).

32. Note to line 43 ff. in Twickenham ed.

33. Byrd, p. 31.

34. *A Treatise of the Spleen and Vapours*, pp. 96-99.

35. *The Prose Works of Alexander Pope*, ed. Norman Ault (Oxford: Basil Blackwell, 1936), i, 153-68.

36. See Lillian Feder, "*Sermo* or Satire: Pope's Definition of His Art," *Studies in Criticism and Aesthetics, 1660-1800*, Essays in Honor of Samuel H. Monk (Minneapolis: University of Minnesota Press, 1967), pp. 140-55.

37. "Reason and the Grotesque: Pope's *Dunciad*," *Critical Quarterly* 7 (1965), 152.

38. *Minor Poets of the Eighteenth Century*, ed. Hugh I'Anson Fausset, Everyman's Library (New York: Dutton, 1930), pp. 101-105.

39. *Ibid.*, pp. 209-29.

40. For an annotated list of such studies, see Lodwick Hartley, *William Cowper: The Continuing Revaluation, An Essay and a Bibliography of Cowperian Studies from 1895 to 1960* (Chapel Hill: University of North Carolina Press, 1960). See also Morris Golden, *In Search of Stability: The Poetry of William Cowper* (New Haven: College and University Press, 1960).

41. *Memoir of the Early Life of William Cowper, Esq., Written by Himself and Never Before Published*, from 2nd London Edition (New York: Taylor and Gould, 1835).

42. It is generally assumed that Cowper also feared the threat by the sponsor of a competitor for the post that he would make known to the Lords a physical (probably genital) deformity of Cowper's. Cowper does not refer to this in his *Memoir*, but it is possible that his horror of public exposure results, at least in part, from the emotional consequences of such a defect. See Thomas Wright, *The Life of William Cowper*, 2nd ed. (London: Farncombe, 1921), p. 42.

43. "The Prisoner and His Crimes: Summary Comments on a Longer Study of the Mind of William Cowper," *Literature and Psychology* vi (May 1956), 55.

44. All quotations from Cowper's poetry are taken from William Cowper, *Poetical Works*, ed. H. S. Milford, 4th ed. with corrections and additions by Norma Russell (London: Oxford University Press, 1971).

45. *The Correspondence of William Cowper*, ed. Thomas Wright (1904; rpt. St. Clair Shores, Mich.: Scholarly Press, n.d.), i, 132.

46. "Cowper's Love of Subhuman Nature: A Psychoanalytic Approach," *PQ* 46 (January 1967), 43-45.

47. Letter to the Rev. William Unwin, May 8, 1780, *Correspondence* i, 188.

48. Gregory, "Cowper's Love of Subhuman Nature," p. 56.

49. See Maurice J. Quinlan, *William Cowper: A Critical Life* (1953; rpt. Westport, Conn.: Greenwood Press, 1970), pp. 194-99 and Golden, pp. 64-69.

50. *Correspondence* i, 358.

51. *Ibid.*, iv, 505.

52. *Ibid.*, iv, 498. See also Cowper's letter of September 26, 1795 to Lady Hesketh, in which he says: "My heart's desire . . . has always been frustrated in everything that it settled on, and by means that have made my disappointments inevitable" (*Correspondence* IV, 495), and other letters of the last years of his life in which he repeatedly writes of the profound despair that hardly masks his great anger at his suffering.

53. *Ibid.*, iv, 505.

54. Christopher Smart, *Jubilate Agno*, re-edited from the original manuscript with an introduction and notes by W. H. Bond (New York: Greenwood Press, 1969), p. 11. All quotations from Bond's introduction and from Smart's *Jubilate Agno* are from this edition.

55. See Christopher Devlin, *Poor Kit Smart* (Carbondale: Southern Illinois University Press, 1961), p. 95; and Arthur Sherbo, *Christopher Smart, Scholar of the University* (East Lansing: Michigan State University Press, 1967), pp. 122-28.

56. "The Apocalypse of Christopher Smart," *Studies in the Eighteenth Century*, ed. R. F. Brissenden (Toronto: University of Toronto Press, 1968), pp. 269-84.

57. Hope's outline of Smart's system in relation to these sources clarifies not only the theological background of *Jubilate Agno* but specific passages in the poem.

58. Bond edition, note 2, p. 106.

CHAPTER V

1. (Boston: Little, Brown and Co., 1976).

2. Friedrich Nietzsche, *Twilight of the Idols*, trans. from the German by Walter Kaufmann, *The Portable Nietzsche* (Harmondsworth, Middlesex, England: Penguin Books, 1977), p. 560.

3. "Nietzsche and the Tradition of the Dionysian," trans. from the German by Timothy F. Sellner, *Studies in Nietzsche and the Classical Tradition*, ed. James C. O'Flaherty, Timothy F. Sellner, and Robert M. Helm (Chapel Hill: University of North Carolina Press, 1976), pp. 165-89.

4. *Twilight of the Idols*, p. 483.

5. "Schopenhauer," *Essays by Thomas Mann*, trans. from the German by H. T. Lowe-Porter (New York: Vintage Books, 1958), p. 299.

6. Friedrich Nietzsche, *The Birth of Tragedy and the Case of Wagner*, trans. from the German by Walter Kaufmann (New York: Vintage Books, 1967), p. 37, and similar phrases passim.

7. "Nietzsche's Philosophy in the Light of Contemporary Events," *Nietzsche: A Collection of Critical Essays*, ed. Robert C. Solomon (Garden City, N.Y.: Anchor Books, 1973), p. 359.

8. "Attempt at a Self Criticism," preface added by Nietzsche to the 1886 edition of *The Birth of Tragedy*, edition cited above, p. 26.

9. Trans. from the German by Walter Kaufmann, *The Portable Nietzsche*.

10. *Ecce Homo*, in *On the Genealogy of Morals and Ecce Homo*, trans. from the German by Walter Kaufmann (New York: Vintage Books, 1969), p. 304.

11. *Ibid.*, pp. 306-309.

12. Trans. from the German by Walter Kaufmann (New York: Random House, 1967), p. 536.

13. Trans. from the German by R. J. Hollingdale (Harmondsworth, Middlesex, England: Penguin Books, 1973), p. 200.

14. P. 563. Just a few pages before this statement, Nietzsche declares: "I have given mankind the most profound book it possesses, my *Zarathustra*" (p. 556).

15. Gilles Deleuze, "Nomad Thought," trans. from the French by David B. Allison, *The New Nietzsche: Contemporary Styles of Interpretation*, ed. David B. Allison (New York: Dell, 1977), p. 146. See also in the same volume, Deleuze's essay, "Active and Reactive," pp. 80-106, and Jean Granier, "Nietzsche's Conception of Chaos," pp. 135-41.

16. *Beyond Good and Evil*, p. 98.

17. Deleuze, "Nomad Thought," p. 143.

18. *Twilight of the Idols*, p. 519.

19. *Death in Venice and Seven Other Stories*, trans. from the German by H. T. Lowe-Porter (New York: Vintage Books, 1954). All quotations from *Death in Venice* are from this edition.

20. *Letters of Thomas Mann 1889-1955*, Selected and trans. from the German by Richard and Clara Winston (New York: Vintage Books, 1975), p. 96.

21. "Schopenhauer," *Essays by Thomas Mann*, p. 297.

22. See, for example, Franz H. Mautner, "Die griechischen Anklänge in Thomas Manns 'Tod in Venedig'," *Monatshefte* 44 (1952), 20-26; André von Gronicka, "Myth Plus Psychology: A Stylistic Analysis of *Death in Venice*," (1956); rpt. *Thomas Mann: A Collection of Critical Essays*, ed. Henry Hatfield (Englewood Cliffs, N.J.: Prentice-Hall, 1964), pp. 46-61; Herbert Lehnert, "Thomas Mann's Early Interest in Myth and Erwin Rohde's *Psyche*," *PMLA* 79 (June 1964), 297-304; Burton Pike, "Thomas Mann and the Problematic Self," *Publications of the English Goethe Society* 37 (1967), 120-41; Hans W. Nicklas, *Thomas Manns Novelle Der Tod in Venedig* (Marburg: N. G. Elwert, 1968).

23. Thomas Mann, "Freud and the Future," *Essays by Thomas Mann*, p. 316.

24. Thomas Mann, *Briefe*, ed. Erika Mann (Frankfurt am Main: S. Fischer, 1962-65), I, 162-63. When German texts are used, unless otherwise indicated, the translation is my own.

25. *Letters of Thomas Mann*, p. 96.

26. *Ibid.*, p. 72.

27. The phrase is from Katia Mann's *Unwritten Memories*, ed. Elisabeth Plessen, trans. from the German by Hunter and Hildegarde Hannum (New York: Knopf, 1975), p. 63. Thomas Mann's most explicit statement regarding the autobiographical nature of *Death in Venice* occurs in *Lebensabriss* (1930), *Gesammelte Werke* XI (Frankfurt am Main: S. Fischer, 1960), p. 124, where he says that "in 'Death in Venice' nothing is invented." He then goes on to list practically every character, including

Tadzio, various episodes in the journey and in Venice, the cholera, and adds: "everything was there." See also *Letters of Thomas Mann*, p. 95.

28. *Betrachtungen Eines Unpolitischen* (1918), *Gesammelte Werke* xii, 573.

29. *Die Forderung des Tages* (Berlin: S. Fischer, 1930), p. 175.

30. *Letters of Thomas Mann*, p. 73.

31. *Ibid*., pp. 93-96. In *Lebensabriss*, Mann says that Aschenbach's story proved to have a will of its own, expressing meanings beyond those that he had consciously intended (*Gesammelte Werke* xi, 123).

32. *Letters of Thomas Mann*, p. 72.

33. "*Death in Venice* by Thomas Mann: A Story about the Disintegration of Artistic Sublimation," *Psychoanalysis and Literature*, ed. Hendrik M. Ruitenbeek (New York: Dutton, 1964), pp. 282-302.

34. See Franz H. Mautner, André von Gronicka, p. 60, and Herbert Lehnert, pp. 299-300.

35. i, 55-56.

36. In the German, Tadzio is referred to as "das Schöne," *Gesammelte Werke* viii, 490.

37. For a fine evaluation of Rohde's contribution, see W.K.C. Guthrie's introduction to the edition of *Psyche* cited above.

38. In a letter to Karl Kerényi (February 18, 1941), Mann says: "I could not help being pleased to note that the psychopompos is characterized as essentially a child divinity: I thought of Tadzio in *Death in Venice*." *Mythology and Humanism: The Correspondence of Thomas Mann and Karl Kerényi*, trans. from the German by Alexander Gelley (Ithaca: Cornell University Press, 1975), p. 101.

39. "Schopenhauer," *Essays by Thomas Mann*, p. 301.

40. Thomas Mann, "Nietzsche's Philosophy in the Light of Contemporary Events," p. 368.

41. Thomas Mann, *The Story of a Novel: the Genesis of Dr. Faustus*, trans. from the German by Richard and Clara Winston (New York: Knopf, 1961), p. 232.

42. Thomas Mann, "Nietzsche's Philosophy in the Light of Contemporary Events," p. 359.

43. Thoman Mann, *Dr. Faustus, the Life of the German Composer Adrian Leverkühn as Told by a Friend*, trans. from the German by H. T. Lowe-Porter (New York: Knopf, 1948), "Author's Note."

44. *The Story of a Novel*, p. 17.

45. *Ibid*., p. 30.

46. "Germany and the Germans," an address by Thomas Mann, Fellow of the Library of Congress, presented in the Coolidge Auditorium, May 29, 1945, typescript, pp. 9-10.

47. *Mythology and Humanism*, p. 123.

48. "Germany and the Germans," p. 10.

49. *The Story of a Novel*, p. 142.

50. *Ibid.*, pp. 41-42.

51. Nietzsche, *The Birth of Tragedy*, p. 49.

52. Mann's "montage" technique has been widely discussed. The most comprehensive explication of his sources is Gunilla Bergsten's *Thomas Mann's Doctor Faustus: The Sources and Structure of the Novel*, trans. from the German by Krishna Winston (Chicago: University of Chicago Press, 1969). Although I cannot entirely agree with Bergsten's analysis of Mann's theme, especially her interpretation of the conclusion of the novel, like many readers of *Dr. Faustus* I am grateful for her comprehensive study of Mann's adaptations of historical, literary, musical, and biographical materials. See also Erich Kahler, "The Devil Secularized: Thomas Mann's Faust" (1949; rpt.), *Thomas Mann: A Collection of Critical Essays*, pp. 109-122; and Patrick Carnegy, *Faust as Musician: A Study of Thomas Mann's Novel Doctor Faustus* (London: Chatto and Windus, 1973).

53. Mann mentions his reading of the *Malleus Maleficarum* in connection with the writing of *Dr. Faustus, The Story of a Novel*, pp. 26-27.

54. *Ibid.*, p. 45.

55. See, for example, Mann's Preface to *The Short Novels of Dostoevsky* (New York: Dial, 1945), written during the time he was at work on *Dr. Faustus*.

56. *The Story of a Novel*, p. 143.

57. (New York: Random House, 1959).

58. (New York: Vintage Books, 1966).

59. *Life Against Death*, p. 158.

60. *Love's Body*, p. 222.

61. *Ibid.*, p. 196.

62. *Ibid.*, p. 250.

63. The Performance Group, *Dionysus in 69*, ed. Richard Schechner (New York: Farrar, Straus, and Giroux, 1970). The quotations from and about the play are from this edition, the pages of which are not numbered.

64. (New York: Hawthorn Books, 1973).

65. Wole Soyinka, "On this Adaptation."

66. Wole Soyinka, *Myth, Literature and the African World* (Cambridge: Cambridge University Press, 1976), pp. 27-30.

67. *Ibid.*, pp. 28-31.

68. This term and concept is extremely important to Soyinka. See especially *Myth, Literature and the African World*, pp. ix-xii.

69. *Ibid.*, pp. 31-32; 158-59.

70. "On this Adaptation."

71. Wole Soyinka, *The Bacchae of Euripides, Collected Plays* I (New York: Oxford University Press, 1973). All quotations from the play are from this edition.

72. Ed. Pierre-Georges Castex (Paris: Société D'Edition D'Enseignement Supérieur, 1971). Translations from *Aurélia* are my own.

73. *Lautréamont's Maldoror*, trans. from the French by Alexis Lykiard (New York: Thomas Y. Crowell, 1970). As is well known, the Comte de Lautréamont was actually Isidore-Lucien Ducasse. Since "the identity presumably 'behind' *Les Chants de Maldoror*—that of Isidore Ducasse—gets lost in its derivations" (Bersani, p. 193), most commentators follow Ducasse in using his literary pseudonym.

74. *A Future for Astyanax*, pp. 196-97.

75. *The Rebel, An Essay on Man in Revolt*, trans. from the French by Anthony Bower (New York: Vintage Books, 1956), p. 85.

76. *Manifestoes of Surrealism*, trans. from the French by Richard Seaver and Helen R. Lane (Ann Arbor: University of Michigan Press, 1969), p. 26.

77. *The Rebel*, p. 81.

78. *The Poetry of Dada and Surrealism* (Princeton: Princeton University Press, 1970), p. 138.

79. *Antonin Artaud, Selected Writings*, ed. Susan Sontag, trans. from the French by Helen Weaver (New York: Farrar, Straus, and Giroux, 1976), p. 139. All subsequent quotations from Artaud are from this edition.

80. "Introduction," *ibid.*, p. xxxvi.

81. *Howl and Other Poems by Allen Ginsberg* (San Francisco: City Lights Books, 1956).

82. *Kaddish and Other Poems, 1958-1960* (San Francisco: City Lights Books, 1961).

83. *Naked Angels: The Lives and Literature of the Beat Generation* (New York: McGraw-Hill, 1976), p. 235.

84. Allen Ginsberg, *Journals: Early Fifties, Early Sixties*, ed. Gordon Ball (New York: Grove Press, 1977), p. xx.

85. *Kaddish and Other Poems*.

86. *Journals*, p. 195.

87. *Reality Sandwiches, 1953-60* (San Francisco: City Lights Books, 1963).

88. Jane Kramer, *Allen Ginsberg in America* (New York: Random House, 1969), p. 21.

89. *Indian Journals, March 1962-May 1963* (San Francisco: Dave Haselwood Books, City Lights Books, 1970).

90. *The Fall of America: poems of these states, 1965-1971* (San Francisco: City Lights Books, 1972).

91. "America," *Howl and Other Poems*.

92. *The Collected Poems of Theodore Roethke* (Garden City, New York: Doubleday, Anchor Books, 1975). All quotations from Roethke's poetry are from this edition.

93. *The Garden and the Map*, pp. 158-60. Another book that deals with the treatment of the fragmented self in recent American poetry, but with a different point of view, is Karl Malkoff's *Escape from the Self* (New York: Columbia University Press, 1977).

94. Otto Fenichel, *The Psychoanalytic Theory of Neurosis* (New York: Norton, 1945), p. 401.

95. (New York: Farrar, Straus, and Giroux, 1969), author's prefatory comment. References in the text are to the numbers of the Songs.

96. The quotations are from "Of Suicide," *Love and Fame* (New York: Farrar, Straus, and Giroux, 1970), but these subjects recur throughout Berryman's poetry.

97. "Dante's Tomb," *Love and Fame*.

98. *Recovery (A Novel)* (New York: Dell, 1974), pp. 123-24.

99. "No," *Delusions, etc.* (New York: Farrar, Straus, and Giroux, 1972).

100. *Chapters in a Mythology: The Poetry of Sylvia Plath* (New York: Harper and Row, 1976).

101. Sylvia Plath, "Ocean 1212-W," *The Art of Sylvia Plath: A Symposium*, ed. Charles Newman (Bloomington: Indiana University Press, 1971), p. 270.

102. *The Colossus and Other Poems* (1957; rpt. New York: Vintage Books, 1968).

103. This and the other poems by Plath referred to from this point on are in *Ariel* (New York: Harper and Row, 1966).

CHAPTER VI

1. *The Divided Self* (1959; rpt. Harmondsworth, Middlesex, England: Penguin Books, 1971), pp. 94-95.

2. *Ibid.*, pp. 168-71.

3. (1967; rpt. New York: Ballantine Books, 1973), p. 73.

4. *Ibid.*, p. 26.

5. "Ego Confession," *Mind Breaths: Poems 1972-1977* (San Francisco: City Lights Books, 1977).

6. For an excellent discussion of madness as a prevalent theme of German fiction of the 1950s and 1960s, see Theodore Ziolkowski's chapter "The View from the Madhouse" in his *Dimensions of the Modern Novel* (Princeton: Princeton University Press, 1969).

7. (New York: Bantam, 1972).

8. (New York: Popular Library, 1972).

Index

abandonment, 131, 138, 144, 195, 198, 201; fear of, 132, 179, 182; by God, 190-91
"Active and Reactive," 310n
Aeschylus, 36, 45-46, 76-84, 87-89, 292n, 293n, 297n
  works cited: Lycurgus-trilogy, 45-46; Oresteia, 35-36, 76-88, 136, 297n. See also conscience; Erinyes; justice, in Oresteia; madness, and guilt; Orestes; psychic adaptation
Agamemnon, 78-79, 88, 96
Agave, 10, 46, 70, 74-75
aggression, 105, 110, 143, 174, 183-84, 221; in Bacchae, 55-56, 66-67, 68, 70-72, 74, 75; in Bacchae of Euripides, The, 245; in Complaint, 105; in Dionysos in 69, 243; in dreams, 84, 227, 229; as instinctual, 17-18, 19, 20-22, 24-25, 43, 48-49, 51, 53, 128-29, 185, 188; in Oresteia, 79, 83-84
Ajax, 10, 90-97, 114, 298n
"Ajax of Sophocles, The," 298n
Alexander, Franz and Selesnick, 5-6, 29, 291n, 299n
alienation, 33, 101, 125, 170; in Cowper, 180, 182, 186, 187; defense against, 174; and grandiosity, 5, 235; and narcissism, 283, 285; from the self, 14, 239, 240, 282; from society, 90-95, 98, 134, 279, 280, 285; suicidal, 8
Allen, Dr. Thomas, 156
Allen, Don Cameron, 301n
Allen Ginsberg in America, 314n
Anatomy of Human Destructiveness, 289n
Ancient Myth in Modern Poetry, 290n
Anderson, Ruth Leila, 305n

anger, as defense, 121-24, 127, 132, 158, 159-60; of God, 185, 186; release of, 127, 140, 144, 180, 186, 265; repressed, 182, 194; and suffering, 162, 308n; symbolic expression of, 11, 26, 92, 128, 132, 183-84
Anglo, Sidney, 117, 301n
animals, 93, 118, 201, 241; association with, 56, 69; in delusion, 91-92; dismemberment of, 47, 70, 228, 244, 247; dreams of, 253; as food, 51; identification with, 41, 49-50, 60, 97, 101, 117, 125, 134, 162, 186-88, 197-98, 202, 279, 285, 293n; images, 70, 72, 81, 87, 109, 112, 116, 125, 133-34, 160-61, 201, 270. See also bull, hunt
Aphrodite, 65-66
"Apocalypse of Christopher Smart, The," 309n
Apollo, 46, 79, 80, 81, 84, 87, 89, 156, 157, 159-60, 190, 208, 241. See also Nietzsche; Apollonian-Dionysiac conflict in
Apollodorus, 45, 46
Aragon, Louis, 254
Argument of Images, An: The Poetry of Alexander Pope, 307n
Aristotle, 105, 113, 149-50, 151, 288n, 305n
  works cited: De Anima, 150, 305n; On Dreams, 288n; Nicomachean Ethics, 151, 305n
Arrowsmith, William, 243, 244
Artaud, Antonin, 7, 256-64, 268
  works cited: Antonin Artaud, Selected Writings, 313n; Fragments of a Diary from Hell, 258-59; In Total Darkness or the Surrealist Bluff, 257, 258; "Lettres Aux Médecins-Chefs des

Library of Congress Cataloging in Publication Data

Feder, Lillian.
    Madness in literature.

    1. Mental illness in literature.   I.   Title.
PN56.M45F37   809'.933353   79-3206
ISBN 0-691-06427-X